Sacerdos In Aeternum

Prayers and Blessings for Priests

Second Edition

Edited by Denis Robinson, O.S.B.

ISBN Number 978-0-87029-436-5
Library of Congress Catalog Number 2009941380
Published by Abbey Press
1 Hill Drive
St. Meinrad, IN 47577
Printed in the United States of America

Table of Contents

Prayers for Vocations and Seminarians

Prayers for Ordinations and Daily Prayers

Prayers and Blessings for the Sacraments of the Church

Death of a Priest and General Prayers

Stations of the Cross for Priests

Selected Prayers to the Saints

Introduction
by Fr. Denis Robinson, O.S.B.
That in All Things God May Be Glorified

Ideals

As priests, all of us live with ideals; it is part of being a human person. It is an essential part of being a priest. We have a vision in our minds of what we think the life of the priest should be like, what we want to achieve, what we desire our ministry and our lives as priests to be. Sometimes these ideals are quite realistic, at other times they are not. Life, however, would be almost meaningless if we had no vision, no goals, and no ideals for living.

Priestly life, whether it is lived in the context of a parish or some other work of the Gospel, is no different. As priests, we look to the Gospel to set the tone and pace for our daily living. Christ establishes the parameters of our lives by showing us his Way. The Way of Christ is very concrete. That is to say, it is not merely a set of good ideas or values. The sacramental nature of our lives is realized in that place where the spiritual and the corporeal meet. The identity of the priest is one that necessarily touches on every aspect of our living, including the material. Likewise, Christian priesthood is manifested not only in the overtly "religious" components of our lives, but even in the mundane and the everyday.

Priests are first and foremost disciples of Jesus. As disciples of Jesus, we take seriously our task of being completely immersed in the Christian identity, of turning our entire lives increasingly over to God.

In our contemporary setting, a great deal of social and cultural confusion still prevails. We are confused about how we are to live our lives, and various and varying "ways of life" vie for our attention. In a complex and ever-changing social and cultural order, being a Christian or even a priest can sometimes be relegated to an "aspect" of living. Christian and priestly identity can become one of a number of identities that any individual might live. Priesthood becomes a part of our lives, but not the governing principle of our lives. As priests, however, we cannot accept this kind of "spiritual brokenness"; rather, in our lives we insist that the life of the priest, the Christian life, the way of discipleship, must completely govern our individual identities.

The identity of priest and disciple governs all the aspects of our lives; it determines how we act in both great and small ways. In other words, I must be a priest first. Any other "identities" I may have must conform to this. In order to make this a reality, our faith proposes that we fix our gaze on Christ alone, and in doing so, order every aspect of our lives, even the most minute, toward this goal. How do the gospels and the wisdom of our Catholic tradition conceive this?

That in All Things God May Be Glorified (1 Peter 4:11)

The famed injunction from the First Letter of St. Peter, in many ways, guides the ethos of priestly spirituality. The life of the priest is the persistent attempt to find God in the most mundane activities and the most commonplace things. Dedicating each day to this relentless pursuit of the Divine One gives priests their particular charism.

Priests have ways of realizing this ideal. We have the practices of the priesthood, the customs of dioceses and religious communities, and the mandates of our ordinations, by which our priesthood is *realized* in a purposeful way. We have particular customs, traditions, and ways of doing things that are less formalized. There is a spirit in the priestly life, a degree of formality or informality, and a seriousness by which every action of the day is intent on the pursuit by which God may be glorified in all things.

Most priests have a schedule that governs each aspect of the day. They have patterns of work and behavior and rituals (both formal and informal) that give life and structure to their pursuit. They have particular ways of dressing and living arrangements that give witness to the importance of this central goal. In other words, the life of the priest has a *material culture* that supports and testifies to its values. This material culture is an outward sign of a central value. If in all things God must be glorified, this applies to "all things," to everything the priest encounters. Certainly God must be glorified in praise and worship, in the liturgy of the hours, Eucharist, and private prayer; but equally, God must be glorified in the more commonplace aspects of life. The way we dress, the way we work, the way we eat, the design of our buildings, the décor of our living quarters, the way we go about our day: all of these things are equally ways of glorifying God.

If God is to be glorified in *all* things, it is essential that we not reduce the status of some things in our lives as not manifesting this ideal. In other words, if we only think that God should be glorified in prayer but not necessarily in dishwashing, we run the risk of assuming that God is not involved in the more commonplace aspects of our existence, that God is not totally present to us. We likewise risk pigeonholing our priesthood in "religious" actions and relegating other aspects of our lives to the "secular" or the non-religious. If God is to be glorified in all things, then there is a Christian way to wash dishes, a Christian way to serve the meal, to facilitate work, to guide meetings, to study, to engage in neighborhood life, and even to recreate. God is involved in all things, and the relentless task of finding God in all things underlies the spirituality of the priest.

This is a very significant ideal for priests. It means that our surroundings are not incidental to the way we live. Priests have a very particular goal. How is it possible to live the life of the priest fully, in every way?

I think one of the problems of priests is that of "commonplace" identity. Of course, this is a question for most people in our culture today. The disciple asks: "How can I be Christian in the world?" For many, this has entailed a hyper-spiritualization of the priestly way of life. We think that priestly identity is something engendered by what we do in church. This identity orders our inner life. Of course, the ordering of the inner life is essential, but it is not authentically priestly or Catholic if that internal ordering does not manifest itself in external practices. Theologically, we can speak of a full priestly life as an expression of the sacramental principle: the reality of God is not only an internal reality, but is equally and significantly manifested in external signs and actions.

Maintenance of a particular way of life that has no material culture can be challenging to the point of frustration. Sociologists tell us that human beings need material culture and community to support our value systems. However, in our time, religious culture seems to have been systematically divesting itself of supposedly outmoded practices and identifying factors. Catholics were formerly very recognizable in terms of their practices and cultural identity. They lived a certain way. They did certain things. Many of these practices were customs that may have since become outdated (e.g., certain devotional practices, head coverings, etc). The question is, have they been replaced with newer and sounder practices and customs? If the sociologists are right and people need cultural identifiers to give life to their particular identities, and if they do not find these identifiers in the religious culture, they may seek another cultural expression that has more of these particularities.

This book aims at helping priests to shape this ideal of glorifying God in all things by offering prayers, blessings, and other devotions that order the daily life of the priest. It offers today's priest the opportunity of deepening his priestly life through the value of continual prayer, and the glorification of God in all aspects of his priestly life.

Many of the prayers are new; many are drawn from tried and true sources of our Catholic tradition. The reflections of great leaders in our faith such as Cardinal John Henry Newman, Pope John Paul II, and Pope Benedict XVI bring together the new and the old.

It is my hope that this book offers priests the opportunity to draw upon this great tradition and to employ the blessings and prayers given here to sanctify their lives and the lives of those whom they serve.

For 150 years Saint Meinrad has prepared priests for service to an ever-changing, yet always ancient Church. This book gratefully honors that ideal.

—Father Denis Robinson, O.S.B.
President-Rector
Saint Meinrad Seminary
and School of Theology

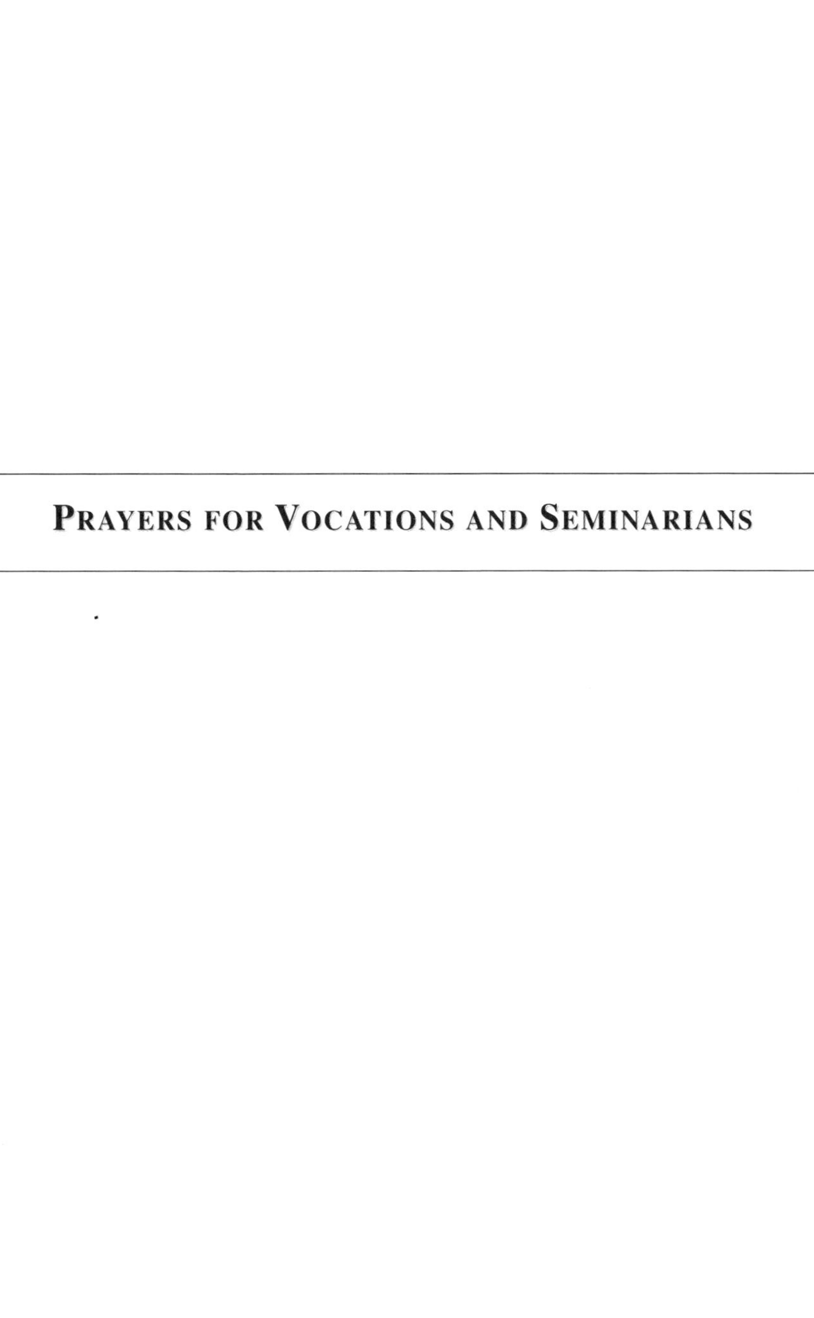

Prayers for Vocations and Seminarians

Prayer to Saint Joseph to Know One's Vocation

O Great Saint Joseph, you were completely obedient to the guidance of the Holy Spirit. Obtain for me the grace to know the state of life that God in his providence has chosen for me. Since my happiness on earth, and perhaps even my final happiness in heaven, depends on this choice, let me not be deceived in making it.

Obtain for me the light to know God's will, to carry it out faithfully, and to choose the vocation which will lead me to a happy eternity.

Prayer to Know One's Vocation

Lord Jesus, up until now you have been quietly preparing me to be your disciple. Now the time of preparation is ending. I seem to hear you say to me as once to Peter: "Will you also go away?" You were saddened then by friends who failed you. But Peter did not fail. "Lord," he said, "to whom shall we go? You have the words of eternal life."

I stand with Peter. Through prayer and counsel, show me, Lord, where it is in your vineyard that you want me to serve. Then give me strength to be faithful.

Mary, Mother and Model, help me to respond in generous love to the call of your divine Son.

Prayer for Vocations

Jesus, High Priest and Redeemer forever, we beg you to call young men and women to your service as priests and religious. May they be inspired by the lives of dedicated priests, brothers, and sisters. Give to parents the grace of generosity and trust toward you and their children so that their sons and daughters may be helped to choose their vocations in life with wisdom and freedom.

Lord, you told us that *the harvest indeed is great but the laborers are few. Pray, therefore, the Lord of the harvest to send laborers into his harvest.* We ask that we may know and follow the vocation to which you have called us. We pray particularly for those called to serve as priests, brothers, and sisters; those whom you have called, those you are calling now, and those you will call in the future. May they be open and responsive to the call of serving your people. We ask this through Christ, our Lord. Amen.

⁂

We praise you for your goodness. We thank you for your gifts, O Lord. We ask you to strengthen us to live in love and service to others after the example of your son, Jesus Christ. Help us to see our vocations as a journey toward you. You have called us, not to set us apart, but to bring us together with others who need our love. Make us faithful signs of your presence in our midst. We ask you through Christ, our Lord. Amen.

⁂

Lord our God, you established the Church as a sign of your continuing presence in the world. We ask you to raise up faithful ministers to your Church in the priesthood and religious life, so that the message of faith, justice, and love contained in the gospel may be brought into the hearts of all people. We ask this through Christ, our Lord. Amen.

—Archbishop John R. Quinn

⁂

O Lord, in this season of joy we want to share the gift of your love. We especially ask you to give us that faith, love, and spirit of joyful sacrifice which will inspire us to offer our youth to your service and cause us to rejoice in their call.

—Archbishop Daniel M. Buechlein, O.S.B.

⁂

Breath of God, the Church's source of life, strengthen those in sacred orders and religious vows and all who witness their baptismal promises through public ministry. Complete the ministry of Christ in the Church, that we may be your sacrament in the world and a source of joy for all men and women.

—Archbishop Wilton D. Gregory

Prayer for Vocations

Loving God, help us to follow the example of the Blessed Virgin Mary in willingly giving of ourselves in service to your Church. Stir up the grace of religious vocation in the hearts of many within our community and send your Spirit to guide and strengthen them in answering your call.

Prayer for Vocations

Creator of the Universe, God of the Nations,
your people are longing to hear your word.
Send laborers into your harvest—
women and men on fire with your love:

Dedicated single people—
who incarnate your presence
in their daily lives,
whose availability enables them
to respond to a diversity of needs.

Married couples—
whose relationships serve as a sign
of your fidelity to your people,
whose love overflows
to their children and neighbors.

Ordained ministers—
who gather the prayers and longing
of your people,
who serve as a channel of your presence
through the sacraments.

Religious sisters, brothers, and priests—
whose life in community foreshadows
our eternal unity in Christ,
whose service brings your life to the world.

May each of us respond with courage and generosity
to our particular vocations, and may the Church recognize
the Spirit's call to men and women of good will,
trusting in your abundance to answer all our needs.

Amen.

Prayer for Vocations

O God, you have called us to salvation and have sent your Son to establish the Church for this purpose, and you have provided the sacred ministers. The harvest is ever ready but the laborers are scarce. Inspire our youth to follow Jesus by serving your people. Amen.

Spanish Prayers for Vocations

Oración por las Vocacíones

Te damos gracias, Dios nuestro, por
tu llamada del Bautismo
a ser tu pueblo

Te respondemos otra vez con nuestro "Sí".

Danos fidelidad para tu causa
y en para nuestra vocación.

Renueva con un espíritu de
entusiasmo a todos los que
se dedican al servicio de
tu pueblo.

Da a nuestros jóvenes el deseo
de dedicarse a este servicio
en la vida religiosa, en el
sacerdocio, como diáconos
o ministros laicos.

Llena sus corazones con tu
Espíritu de Sabiduría para
que proclamen tu evangelio,
y den testimonio de tu presencia
entre nosotros.
Amén.

Amadísimo y generoso Dios,
eres Tú quien nos llamas
por nuestro nombre y
nos pides que te sigamos.

Ayúdanos a crecer en el amor
y en el servicio a nuestra Iglesia.

Danos el entusiasmo
y la energía de tu Espíritu
para preparar nuestro futuro.

Danos líderes llenos de fe
que abracen la misión de Cristo
en amor y en justicia.

Bendice a la Iglesia
con líderes salidos de nuestras propias familias
que dediquen sus vidas
al servicio de su pueblo
como sacerdotes, religiosos,
diáconos o ministros laicos.

Inspíranos a conocerte mejory
y abre nuestros corazones
para oir tu llamada.
Amén.

⁕

¡Virgen de Guadalupe,
Evangelizadora de las Américas,
Madre de Dios, Madre de la Iglesia
y Madre nuestra! Tú eres el orgullo
de nuestra gente. Jesús, tu Hijo, cambió
el agua en vino, porqúe tú se lo pediste.
Te imploramos, Madre Misericordiosa,
que obtengas para nosotros todas las
gracias que necesitamos de tu Hijo.
Intercede ante Él para que bendiga a las
Américas con muchas vocaciones al
sacerdocio, a la vida religiosa, al
matrimonio cristiano y a la vida laical,
Madre de Dios, ruega por nostros ahora
y siempre.
Amén

✻

SEÑOR, JESÚS,
te pedimos que envíes a tu pueblo
los servidores que necesita.
Escoge de nuestras parroquias,
de nuestros hogares,
de nuestras escuelas y universidades
una abundante cosecha
de ardientes apóstoles para tu Reino:
sacerdotes, religiosos, religiosas,
diáconos, misioneros y
apóstoles seglares;
y haz que los llamados por Ti
nunca pierdan conciencia de la
grandeza y necesidad de su vocación.

¡Oh!, Virgen María,
Madre de la Iglesia,
enseña a decir a todos los llamados
por el Señor,
un sí con alegría,
como aquel que tú dijiste en la Anunciación.

Oh Dios, Todopoderoso y Eterno,
en tu inagotable amor haz proveído
ministros para tu Iglesia.
Concédenos en nuestros días
excelentes y adecuados sacerdotes
para que sirvan y santifiquen a tu pueblo.
Inspira una respuesta generosa y valiente
en los corazones de tu pueblo,
para así aumentar el número
de sacerdotes.
Confirma y sostén a aquellos
que se han comprometido
a llevar la obra de Cristo,
el Buen Pastor,
predicando el Evangelio y uniendo
a tu Santo pueblo

en uno solo en Cristo.
Ésto te lo pedimos en el nombre
de Cristo nuestro Señor.
Amén.

*

Padre, tú llamas a cada uno de
nosotros por nombre y nos pides
que te sigamos.

Bendice a tu Iglesia y danos dedicados
y generosos líderes salidos de nuestras propias familias
y amigos, quienes puedan servir a
tu pueblo como religiosos, (religionsas,) sacerdotes,
diáconos y ministros laicos.

Inspíranos mientras crecemos en tu
amor y abre nuestros corazones
para oír tu llamada.

Te lo pedimos en
nombre de Cristo.
Amén.

Blessing of Those Discerning a Vocation

+In the name of the Father and of the Son and of the Holy Spirit. Amen.

V. Our help is in the name of the Lord.
R. Who made heaven and earth.

V. The Lord be with you.
R. And with your spirit.

Scripture Reading

Now the word of the LORD came to me saying, "Before I formed you in the womb I knew you, and before you were born I consecrated you; I appointed you a prophet to the nations." Then I said, "Ah, Lord GOD! Behold, I do not know how to speak, for I am only a youth." But the LORD said to me, "Do not say, 'I am only a youth'; for to all to whom I send you, you shall go, and whatever I command you, you shall speak."

—Jeremiah 1:4-7

Prayer of Blessing

Almighty God, we ask you to send your blessing + upon these servants of yours who seek to discern your will in their lives. As once you called Jeremiah, help them to clearly hear your voice and respond with generous hearts, saying, "Here I am, I come to do your will." Give all of your people a sure and certain sense of their vocations, as you draw us into the mystery of your life. We ask this in the name of Jesus the Lord. Amen.

Blessing of New Seminarians

+In the name of the Father and of the Son and of the Holy Spirit. Amen.

V. Our help is in the name of the Lord.
R. Who made heaven and earth.

V. The Lord be with you
R. And with your spirit.

Scripture Reading

O come, let us worship and bow down,
let us kneel before the LORD, our Maker!
For he is our God,
and we are the people of his pasture,
and the sheep of his hand.
O that today you would hearken to his voice!

—Psalm 95:6-7

Prayer of Blessing

God our Father, from the beginning of time you have called men to serve you at your altars. In the ancient covenant you gave the sons of Aaron the sacred charge to perpetuate your sacrifices and to sanctify your people through rites and prayers. In the new covenant, you gave your only Son, our Lord Jesus Christ, as the Lamb of Sacrifice and the priest to offer the perfect oblation on the altar of the cross. Bless + these men whom you have called to consider their vocations as priests. Be with them in times of difficulty and struggle. Help them to clearly hear your voice speaking to them as they discern their vocations in the seminary. Guide them to follow in the steps of your Son, Jesus, who lives and reigns with you and the Holy Spirit, one God forever and ever. Amen.

Blessing and Sending of Those Departing for the Seminary

+In the name of the Father and of the Son and of the Holy Spirit. Amen.

V. Our help is in the name of the Lord.
R. Who made heaven and earth.

V. The Lord be with you.
R. And with your spirit.

Scripture Reading

Then Elijah said to him, "Tarry here, I pray you; for the LORD has sent me to the Jordan." But he said, "As the LORD lives, and as you yourself live, I will not leave you." So the two of them went on. Fifty men of the sons of the prophets also went, and stood at some distance from them, as they both were standing by the Jordan.

Then Elijah took his mantle, and rolled it up, and struck the water, and the water was parted to the one side and to the other, till the two of them could go over on dry ground. When they had crossed, Elijah said to Elisha, "Ask what I shall do for you, before I am taken from you." And Elisha said, "I pray you, let me inherit a double share of your spirit."

—2 Kings 2:7-9

Prayer of Blessing

Lord God, you called the prophets of old as witnesses to your power active in the lives of your faithful people. Bless + these men as they depart for their seminary formation. Guide and direct their paths that they may discern your will in their lives. Give all of us a double portion of your Spirit. Enliven and encourage us to call forth vocations from our families and our communities. Give depth and persistence to our prayer for these men and draw us all into that Kingdom where you live with the Son and Holy Spirit, forever and ever. Amen.

Novena for Seminarians

This novena may be prayed in parishes with seminarians preparing for ministries or ordination, or in anticipation of a new formation year. It is prayed for nine consecutive days.

Lord God, remember our seminarian (N) or our seminarians (N&N). You have called them to discern your will in their lives. Help them to respond courageously to their vocations. Help us to encourage and strengthen them through our prayers that they may be good priests to serve your Church in holiness. We ask this in the name of our high priest, Jesus, who is Lord forever and ever. Amen.

Blessing and Welcoming Seminarians to Parish Assignments

+In the name of the Father and of the Son and of the Holy Spirit. Amen.

V. Our help is in the name of the Lord.
R. Who made heaven and earth.

V. The Lord be with you.
R. And with your spirit.

Scripture Reading

The LORD said to Moses, "Say to Aaron and his sons, 'Thus you shall bless the people of Israel': you shall say to them, 'The LORD bless you and keep you: The LORD make his face to shine upon you, and be gracious to you: The LORD lift up his countenance upon you, and give you peace.' So shall they put my name upon the people of Israel, and I will bless them."

—Numbers 6:22-27

Prayer of Blessing

Lord Jesus Christ, in your love for us, you have given us men from among us to consider their call as priests. Today we ask you to bless + (N) as he begins his service to the people of (N) parish. May his time among us be a blessing to him. May we profit from his example and may he be enriched by our prayers and support. Give him courage in times of doubt and a thankful heart in times of rejoicing, for you live and reign with the Father and the Holy Spirit, one God forever and ever. Amen.

The parishioners welcome the seminarian with the acclamation: Thanks be to God! *or another appropriate gesture.*

PRAYERS FOR SEMINARIANS IN THE SEMINARY

Short Prayers for Seminarians

O good Jesus, grant that I may become a priest after thine own Heart.

O bone Iesu, fac ut sacerdos fiam secundum Cor tuum.

Clothe me, O Lord, with the new man who was created according to God in justice and the holiness of truth. Amen.

Indue me, Domine novum hominem qui secundum Deum creatus est in iustitia et sanctitate veritatis. Amen.

Prayer of St. Thomas Aquinas for Seminarians

Creator of all things,
true source of light and wisdom,
origin of all being,
graciously let a ray of your light penetrate
the darkness of my understanding.

Take from me the double darkness
in which I have been born,
an obscurity of sin and ignorance.

Give me a keen understanding,
a retentive memory, and
the ability to grasp things
correctly and fundamentally.

Grant me the talent
of being exact in my explanations
and the ability to express myself
with thoroughness and charm.
Point out the beginning,
direct the progress,
and help in the completion.

I ask this through Christ our Lord.
Amen.

Prayers for Those Entering Religious Life

+In the name of the Father and of the Son and of the Holy Spirit. Amen.

V. Our help is in the name of the Lord.
R. Who made heaven and earth.

V. The Lord be with you.
R. And with your spirit.

Scripture Reading

So he departed from there, and found Elísha the son of Shaphat, who was plowing, with twelve yoke of oxen before him, and he was with the twelfth. Elíjah passed by him and cast his mantle upon him. And he left the oxen, and ran after Elíjah, and said, "Let me kiss my father and my mother, and then I will follow you." And he said to him, "Go back again; for what have I done to you?" And he returned from following him, and took the yoke of oxen, and slew them, and boiled their flesh with the yokes of the oxen, and gave it to the people, and they ate. Then he arose and went after Elíjah, and ministered to him.

—1 Kings 19:19-21

Prayer of Blessing

God our Father, from the beginning of time you have blessed the servants who have given everything away in your service. Bless our brother (sister) who now seeks to consecrate himself (herself) to your service in religious life. May he (she) always know of the prayers and support of his (her) family in faith in this parish community. May your blessing and our encouragement be a source of guidance and strength always. We ask this in the name of Jesus the Lord. Amen.

Prayers for Spiritual Direction

Preparing for Spiritual Direction

Prayer before the Blessed Sacrament

+In the Name of the Father and the Son and the Holy Spirit. Amen.

Gentle Lord, you fill my heart with love for you. Help me to see myself as you see me. Help me to be completely open to you and to my spiritual director. Give me courage to face the things in my life that I must face. Help me also to see the gifts and talents I bring to this community. Be present with me throughout this day as you are present to me now. May every action of my body, every thought of my mind, every stirring of my heart bring me closer to you, that I may more faithfully proclaim your presence to the world. Amen.

Prayer to Begin the Spiritual Direction Conversation

+In the Name of the Father and the Son and the Holy Spirit. Amen.

God our Father, you open our hearts and minds to the wonder of your love in all the events of this day. Be with us now as we explore the depth of that love acting in our lives. Be with us in our conversation here. May our words have effect and may our discernment draw us closer to you.We ask this in the name of Jesus the Lord. Amen

Mary, Mother of the Church … Pray for us!
Saint Joseph … Pray for us!

+In the Name of the Father and the Son and the Holy Spirit. Amen.

Closing Prayer and Blessing for Spiritual Direction

Lord God, you have given us this blessed time together. May our conversation here strengthen our resolve to follow your Son more closely. May all we do in thought, word, and deed aim at doing what is pleasing in your sight. Grant this through Christ our Lord. Amen.

Spiritual direction concludes with a blessing.

Blessing of Those Leaving the Seminary

+In the name of the Father and of the Son and of the Holy Spirit. Amen.

V. Our help is in the name of the Lord.
R. Who made heaven and earth.

V. The Lord be with you.
R. And with your spirit.

Scripture Reading

Now the eleven disciples went to Galilee, to the mountain to which Jesus had directed them. And when they saw him they worshipped him; but some doubted.

And Jesus came and said to them, "All authority in heaven and on earth has been given to me. Go therefore and make disciples of all nations, baptizing them in the name of the Father and of the Son and of the Holy Spirit, teaching them to observe all that I have commanded you; and lo, I am with you always, to the close of the age."

—Matthew 28:16-20

Prayer of Blessing

God Our Father, you show us all of the times and seasons of our lives. Be with your brother (N) as he leaves this community. Give him the strength to follow your will in this life. May he be encouraged by the continual friendship, prayers, and support of this seminary community. Let him know of your presence in his life and help him as he continues to discern your will. Bless + his journey. May he prosper in all that he does. We ask this in the name of Jesus the Lord. Amen.

Blessing for Pastoral Internships

+In the name of the Father and of the Son and of the Holy Spirit. Amen.

V. Our help is in the name of the Lord.
R. Who made heaven and earth.

V. The Lord be with you.
R. And with your spirit.

Scripture Reading

And he said to them, "The kings of the Gentiles exercise lordship over them; and those in authority over them are called benefactors. But not so with you; rather let the greatest among you become as the youngest, and the leader as one who serves. For which is the greater, one who sits at table, or one who serves? Is it not the one who sits at table? But I am among you as one who serves."

—Luke 22:25-27

Prayer of Blessing

Lord our God, you are the source of all life and all tasks. Bless our brothers as they begin a time of pastoral internship. May the wisdom and guidance of their mentors be a source of learning and strength. Help them to grow in holiness. May this year be a productive time spent in the service of your holy people. Help them to know of our prayers and support for them. We ask this through our Lord Jesus Christ, your son who lives and reigns with you and the Holy Spirit, one God forever and ever.

Novena for Diaconate Ordination

At the conclusion of the petitions at Mass each day for nine days before the Ordination, the following prayer is recited by the assembly. The principal celebrant concludes the prayer and the assembly responds in the usual fashion.

Almighty God, giver of every grace, who apportion every order and assign every office, who remain unchanged, but make all things new, send your Holy Spirit into our midst to make our brothers preparing for ordination to the diaconate ready to offer themselves forever in the ministry of the word, of the altar, and of charity, servants to all.

Grant them wisdom when they are unsure, knowledge when they are afraid, counsel when they are confused, fortitude when they are fragile, understanding when they are troubled, piety when they are indifferent, and fear of you when they are proud.

Help them to receive the Gospel of Christ: convince them to believe what they read; train them to teach what they believe; strengthen them to practice what they teach.

Hear the prayers of all your faithful servants and in the eternal charity that you have shown us, draw us all to that heavenly kingdom where all are made perfectly one at the eternal banquet of Christ, the Good Shepherd and Eternal King.

Priest: Grant this through the same Jesus Christ, our Lord. Amen.

Blessing of Those About to Be Ordained Deacons

+In the name of the Father and of the Son and of the Holy Spirit. Amen.

V. Our help is in the name of the Lord.
R. Who made heaven and earth.

V. The Lord be with you.
R. And with your spirit.

Scripture Reading

Now in these days when the disciples were increasing in number, the Hellenists murmured against the Hebrews because their widows were neglected in the daily distribution. And the twelve summoned the body of the disciples and said, "It is not right that we should give up preaching the word of God to serve tables. Therefore, brethren, pick out from among you seven men of good repute, full of the Spirit and of wisdom, whom we may appoint to this duty. But we will devote ourselves to prayer and to the ministry of the word." And what they said pleased the whole multitude, and they chose Stephen, a man full of faith and of the Holy Spirit, and Philip, and Prochorus, and Nicanor, and Timon, and Parmenas, and Nicholas, a proselyte of Antioch. These they set before the apostles, and they prayed and laid their hands upon them. And the word of God increased; and the number of the disciples multiplied greatly in Jerusalem, and a great many of the priests were obedient to the faith.

—Acts 6:1-7

Prayer of Blessing

Those to be ordained are called forward by the pastor or rector and stand facing the assembly.

Pastor or Rector:
What do you ask of this community today?

Those to be ordained:
As our diaconal ordination draws very near,
we ask the community to support us with their prayers
and to encourage us with their fraternal charity,
that in all things, God may be glorified.

Then the ordinandi kneel in place, facing the assembly.
From the center aisle, the pastor or rector prays the blessing:

Almighty and ever-living God,
from the beginning of time
you have called your people
to serve you in various ways
for the good of all and for your glory.
Bless these chosen men
with peace and courage and firm resolve
as they prepare for ordination (tomorrow).
Bless us, their brothers and sisters,
with the grace to support them in prayer
and to encourage them in charity.
Bless all your pilgrim people
with the wisdom to be attentive
to the Word they will proclaim.
Grant this through Jesus Christ our Lord. Amen.

Novena for Priesthood Ordination

At the conclusion of the petitions at Mass each day for nine days before the Ordination, the following prayer is recited by the assembly. The principal celebrant concludes the prayer and the assembly responds in the usual fashion.

Almighty God, giver of every grace, who apportion every order and assign every office, who remain unchanged, but make all things new, send your Holy Spirit into our midst to make our brothers preparing for ordination to the priesthood ready to offer themselves forever in the ministry of the word, of the altar, and of charity, servants to all.

Grant them wisdom when they are unsure, knowledge when they are afraid, counsel when they are confused, fortitude when they are fragile, understanding when they are troubled, piety when they are indifferent, and fear of you when they are proud.

Help them to receive the Gospel of Christ: convince them to believe what they read; train them to teach what they believe; strengthen them to practice what they teach.

Hear the prayers of all your faithful servants and in the eternal charity that you have shown us, draw us all to that heavenly kingdom where all are made perfectly one at the eternal banquet of Christ, the Good Shepherd and Eternal King.

Priest:
Grant this through the same Jesus Christ, our Lord. Amen.

Blessing of Those About to Be Ordained Priests

+In the name of the Father and of the Son and of the Holy Spirit. Amen.

V. Our help is in the name of the Lord.
R. Who made heaven and earth.

V. The Lord be with you.
R. And with your spirit.

Scripture Reading

And Jesus went about all the cities and villages, teaching in their synagogues and preaching the gospel of the kingdom, and healing every disease and every infirmity. When he saw the crowds, he had compassion for them, because they were harassed and helpless, like sheep without a shepherd. Then he said to his disciples, "The harvest is plentiful, but the laborers are few; pray therefore the Lord of the harvest to send out laborers into his harvest."

—Matthew 9:35-38

Prayer of Blessing

Those to be ordained are called forward by the pastor or rector and stand facing the assembly.

Pastor or Rector:
What do you ask of this community today?

Those to be ordained:
As our priesthood ordination draws very near,
we ask the community to support us with their prayers
and to encourage us with their fraternal charity,
that in all things, God may be glorified.

Then the ordinandi kneel in place, facing the assembly.
From the center aisle, the pastor or rector prays the blessing:

Almighty and ever-living God,
from the beginning of time
you have called your people
to serve you in various ways
for the good of all and for your glory.
Bless these chosen men
with peace and courage and firm resolve
as they prepare for ordination (tomorrow).
Bless us, their brothers and sisters,
with the grace to support them in prayer
and to encourage them in charity.
Bless all your pilgrim people
with the wisdom to be attentive
to the Word they will proclaim.
Grant this through Jesus Christ our Lord. Amen.

Prayers for Ordinations and Daily Prayers

Blessing of Clerical Clothing

+In the name of the Father and of the Son and of the Holy Spirit. Amen.

V. Our help is in the name of the Lord.
R. Who made heaven and earth.

V. The Lord be with you.
R. And with your spirit.

Scripture Reading

"Then you shall bring Aaron and his sons to the door of the tent of meeting, and shall wash them with water, and put upon Aaron the holy garments, and you shall anoint him and consecrate him, that he may serve me as priest. You shall bring his sons also and put coats on them, and anoint them, as you anointed their father that they may serve me as priests: and their anointing shall admit them to a perpetual priesthood throughout their generations."

—Exodus 40:12-15

Prayer of Blessing

Lord Jesus Christ, who condescended to clothe yourself in our mortal nature, we beg you in your boundless goodness to bless + these garments which your holy Church has given as suitable for clerics, in token of the innocence and humility which should be theirs. May this servant of yours, who is to wear these garments, likewise put on you, and be recognized as a man dedicated to your service. For you live and reign with the Father and the Holy Spirit, one God forever and ever. Amen.

The garments are then sprinkled with holy water.

Blessing of a Cassock

+In the name of the Father and of the Son and of the Holy Spirit. Amen.

V. Our help is in the name of the Lord.
R. Who made heaven and earth.

V. The Lord be with you.
R. And with your spirit.

Scripture Reading

Remember, O LORD, in David's favor,
all the hardships he endured;
how he swore to the LORD
and vowed to the Mighty One of Jacob,
"I will not enter my house
or get into my bed;
I will not give sleep to my eyes
or slumber to my eyelids,
until I find a place for the LORD,
a dwelling place for the Mighty One of Jacob."
Lo, we heard of it in Ephrathah,
we found it in the fields of Jaar.
"Let us go to his dwelling place;
let us worship at his footstool!"
Arise, O LORD, and go to thy resting place,
thou and the ark of thy might.
Let thy priests be clothed with righteousness,
and let thy saints shout for joy.

—Psalm 132:1-9

Prayer of Blessing

Lord Jesus Christ, who condescended to clothe yourself in our mortal nature, we beg you in your boundless goodness to bless + this cassock which your holy Church has given as the garb for clerics, in token of the innocence and humility which should be theirs. May this servant of yours, who is to wear the cassock, likewise put on you, and be recognized as a man dedicated to your service. For you live and reign with the Father and the Holy Spirit, one God forever and ever. Amen.

The cassock may then be sprinkled with holy water.

BLESSING OF AN ALB OR SURPLICE

+In the name of the Father and of the Son and of the Holy Spirit. Amen.

V. Our help is in the name of the Lord.
R. Who made heaven and earth.

V. The Lord be with you.
R. And with your spirit.

Scripture Reading

Thus did Moses and Aaron and all the congregation of the people of Israel to the Levites; according to all that the LORD commanded Moses concerning the Levites, the people of Israel did to them. And the Levites purified themselves from sin, and washed their clothes; and Aaron offered them as a wave offering before the LORD, and Aaron made atonement for them to cleanse them. And after that the Levites went in to do their service in the tent of meeting in attendance upon Aaron and his sons; as the LORD had commanded Moses concerning the Levites, so they did to them.

—Numbers 8:20-22

Prayer of Blessing

Almighty everlasting God, giver of all good things and bountiful bestower of all graces, we humbly beg you to endow us with the power of your blessing. May it also please you to bless, + by the work of the Holy Spirit, this alb (surplice) made ready for divine worship. Kindly let the grace of your holy mysteries descend on all who are to use it, so that they may appear holy, pure, and blameless in your presence, and may be aided by your mercy; through Christ our Lord. Amen.

It is sprinkled with holy water.

BLESSING OF A DEACON'S VESTMENTS

+In the name of the Father and of the Son and of the Holy Spirit. Amen.

V. Our help is in the name of the Lord.
R. Who made heaven and earth.

V. The Lord be with you.
R. And with your spirit.

Scripture Reading

And Moses brought Aaron and his sons, and washed them with water. And he put on him the coat, and girded him with the girdle, and clothed him with the robe, and put the ephod upon him, and girded him with the skillfully woven band of the ephod, binding it to him therewith. And he placed the breastpiece on him, and in the breastpiece he put the Urim and the Thummim. And he set the turban upon his head, and on the turban, in front, he set the golden plate, the holy crown, as the LORD commanded Moses.

—Leviticus 8:5-9

Prayer of Blessing

Almighty everlasting God, who decreed through Moses, your servant, that the vesture of high-priest, priest, and Levite, used in fulfilling their ministry in your sight, should be worn to dignify and beautify the worship rendered to your holy name; mercifully heed our prayers, and be pleased, through our lowly ministry, to bless + these diaconal vestments, bestowing upon them your grace, so that they become hallowed and suitable for divine worship and the sacred mysteries. Let every deacon clothed in these sacred vestments be strengthened and defended from all assault or temptation of evil spirits; let them perform and celebrate your mysteries reverently and well; and let them always carry out their ministry in a devout and pleasing manner; through Christ our Lord. Amen.

They are sprinkled with holy water.

BLESSING OF PRIESTLY VESTMENTS

+In the name of the Father and of the Son and of the Holy Spirit. Amen.

V. Our help is in the name of the Lord.
R. Who made heaven and earth.

V. The Lord be with you.
R. And with your spirit.

Scripture Reading

And Moses brought Aaron and his sons, and washed them with water. And he put on him the coat, and girded him with the girdle, and clothed him with the robe, and put the ephod upon him, and girded him with the skillfully woven band of the ephod, binding it to him therewith. And he placed the breastpiece on him, and in the breastpiece he put the Urim and the Thummim. And he set the turban upon his head, and on the turban, in front, he set the golden plate, the holy crown, as the LORD commanded Moses.

—Leviticus 8:5-9

Prayer of Blessing

Almighty everlasting God, who decreed through Moses, your servant, that the vesture of high-priest, priest, and Levite, used in fulfilling their ministry in your sight, should be worn to dignify and beautify the worship rendered to your holy name; mercifully heed our prayers, and be pleased, through our lowly ministry, to bless + these priestly vestments, bestowing upon them your grace, so that they become hallowed and suitable for divine worship and the sacred mysteries. Let every priest clothed in these sacred vestments be strengthened and defended from all assault or temptation of evil spirits; let them perform and celebrate your mysteries reverently and well; and let them always carry out their ministry in a devout and pleasing manner; through Christ our Lord. Amen.
They are sprinkled with holy water.

Ordination Meal Prayers

God our Father, the giver of all good gifts, you nourish our bodies with your creation. Bless the food of this table. May it be nourishment for us and for our brother (N) as he celebrates his ordination. May this food strengthen him in body, mind, and spirit, that he may be always faithful to your service. Grant this through Christ our Lord. Amen.

Gracious God, you are the source of life, breath, and all good things. Bless us and bless our brother (N) as he celebrates his ordination. May the food of this meal nourish us in our discipleship and nourish him in his ministry. Keep him always faithful to you as he celebrates the mysteries of our faith. We ask this in the name of Jesus the Lord. Amen.

God our Creator, you have given us this day of rejoicing as your Church celebrates the ordination of our brother (N). Give us strength by what we receive from the bounty of this table. Draw us ever closer to your Son Jesus through the nourishment we take and the mysteries we celebrate. Through the same Christ our Lord. Amen.

God the giver of all good things, you have blessed your Church today with the ordination of our brother (N). Keep him steadfast in his promises and strong in his perseverance and so draw us, through his leadership, into the mystery of that Kingdom where you live and reign forever and ever. Amen.

Morning Prayer for the Day of Ordination

These versions of the traditional morning prayers may be suitable for the day of ordination.

Arising from Sleep

O Master and holy God, who are beyond our understanding: at your word, light came forth out of darkness. In your mercy, you gave us rest through nightlong sleep, and raised us up to glorify your goodness and to offer our supplication to you. Now, in your own tender love, accept us who adore you and give thanks to you with all our heart. Grant us all our requests, if they lead to salvation; give us the grace of manifesting that we are children of light and day, and heirs to your eternal reward. In the abundance of your mercies, O Lord, remember all your people; all those present who pray with us; all our brethren on land, at sea, or in the air, in every place of your domain, who call upon your love for mankind. In particular this day, I ask you to bless the work of our bishop as he calls and ordains me to the (priesthood or diaconate). Fill me with your grace this day as I fulfill your will in my life. Upon all, pour down your great mercy, that we, saved in body and in soul, may persevere unfailingly; and that, in our confidence, we may extol your exalted and blessed Name, Father, Son, and Holy Spirit, always, now and forever. Amen.

Morning Offering

Most Holy and Adorable Trinity, one God in three Persons, I firmly believe that you are here present; I adore you with the most profound humility; I praise you and give you thanks with all my heart for the favors you have bestowed on me. Your goodness has brought me safely to the beginning of this day. Behold, O Lord, I offer you my whole being and in particular all my thoughts, words, and actions, together with such crosses and contradictions as I may meet with in the course of this day. Today, I give you in a special way my whole soul as I am ordained (a priest or a deacon). Give me, O Lord, your blessing; may your divine love animate me and may we all tend to the greater honor and glory of your sovereign majesty. Amen.

Morning Offering to the Sacred Heart

O Jesus, through the Immaculate Heart of Mary, I offer you my prayers, works, joys, and sufferings of this day of my ordination as a (priest or deacon) for all the intentions of your Sacred Heart, in union with the holy sacrifice of the Mass throughout the world, in reparation for my sins, for the intentions of all our associates, and in particular for the intentions of our Holy Father for this month. Amen.

Prayers Before Ordination to the Diaconate

Lord God, grant me the grace to accept whatever challenges, disappointments, and successes come my way so that I may grow in wisdom and experience as I strive to serve you and your Church. Through the obedience I will promise to the Bishop at ordination, make me ever more attentive to the unfolding of your will for me and for the people I serve. Grant this through Christ our Lord. Amen.

✳

Lord Jesus, as I draw near to ordination, strengthen my hands for service and give me a clear voice to proclaim your word. Be my example and guide. Be my strength and inspiration. Help me always to know my place as one who comes to serve and not to be served, for you live and reign with the Father and the Holy Spirit, one God forever and ever. Amen.

Prayer Before Ordination to the Priesthood

Almighty Father, as that day of ordination draws near, I lay before you all that I am; everything that I have; what I know and what I don't know. Accept it, transform it, bless it; use it all for the glory of your Name. Make me worthy of the trust and confidence placed in me, and guard me in the ways of integrity and truth. I ask this through Christ the Lord. Amen.

Thanksgiving Prayer After Ordinaton to the Diaconate

O God, I thank you for having called me to serve your people as deacon. Grant me the grace to firmly believe what I read, boldly teach what I believe, and always practice what I teach, through Christ our Lord. Amen.

Thanksgiving Prayer After Ordinaton to the Priesthood

Almighty God, thank you for guiding me to this awesome moment. Bless all those who have formed and taught me, supported and loved me along the way to ordination. Keep me ever mindful of the sacred character imprinted on me, so that everything I say and do may always present to the world an *alter Christus*. In his name we pray. Amen.

Blessing of Chalices and Vessels

+In the name of the Father and of the Son and of the Holy Spirit. Amen.

V. Our help is in the name of the Lord.
R. Who made heaven and earth.

V. The Lord be with you.
R. And with your spirit.

Scripture Reading

For I received from the Lord what I also delivered to you, that the Lord Jesus on the night when he was betrayed took bread, and when he had given thanks, he broke it, and said, "This is my body which is for you. Do this in remembrance of me." In the same way also the cup, after supper, saying, "This cup is the new covenant in my blood. Do this, as often as you drink it, in remembrance of me." For as often as you eat this bread and drink the cup, you proclaim the Lord's death until he comes.

—1 Corinthians 11:23-26

Prayer of Blessing

Almighty God, in ancient times you sanctified for holy use the vessels of the altar. The priests of the ancient covenant used these vessels to signify your presence in sacred rites and sacrifices. In our day, we ask you to bless + and sanctify these vessels for use in the sacrifice of the altar of the new and eternal covenant. Made holy by the body and blood of your Son, may they always be a sign for us of the sacred trust given to your priest at ordination. Bless our brother (N) as he uses this chalice (or another vessel). May he always be a good and holy priest, announcing without compromise the mystery of faith to your people. We ask this through Christ our Lord, who lives and reigns with you and the Holy Spirit, one God forever and ever. Amen.

The chalice or vessels may then be sprinkled with holy water.

The Blessing for Chalices and Vessels from the *Book of Blessings* may also be used, particularly if a bishop is present.

Blessing of the Manuturgium and Stole

+In the name of the Father and of the Son and of the Holy Spirit. Amen.

V. Our help is in the name of the Lord.
R. Who made heaven and earth.

V. The Lord be with you.
R. And with your spirit.

Scripture Reading

Children, obey your parents in the Lord, for this is right. "Honor your father and mother" (this is the first commandment with a promise), "that it may be well with you and that you may live long on the earth."

—Ephesians 6:1-3

Or

Behold, as your life was precious this day in my sight, so may my life be precious in the sight of the LORD, and may he deliver me out of all tribulation.

—1 Samuel 26:24

Prayer of Blessing

The prayer of blessing should be prayed by someone other than the newly ordained priest.

Lord God, you sanctify the life of your holy priests with the gift of ordination. Bless today the family of (N) your newly ordained priest. May this cloth + and this stole +, imbued with the chrism of ordination and the graces of the sacraments of Holy Orders and Penance be signs of Father (N)'s love of his family. May (father) and (mother) always cherish the tokens of this day. May this stole and this cloth remind our Lord that these parents gave the world the greatest gift of all, the gift of a priest. We ask this in the name of Jesus, the Lord. Amen.

The boxes containing the maniturgium and stole may then be given to the parents.

The prayer should be adapted according to the circumstances of the priest.

Prayer Before Celebrating the Mass of Thanksgiving

Father, my purpose is to celebrate Mass and to make the body and blood of our Lord Jesus Christ according to the rite of the holy Roman Church, to your praise and of the whole Church triumphant in heaven, for my own welfare and that of the whole Church militant on earth, for all who in general and in particular have commended themselves to my prayers, and for the well-being of the holy Roman Church. May joy and peace, amendment of life, room for true penitence, the grace and comfort of the Holy Spirit, and steadfastness in good works be granted me in this my Mass of thanksgiving by the almighty and merciful Lord, who lives and reigns with you forever and ever. Amen.

Blessing of Servers Before the Mass of Thanksgiving

This blessing may be given to those assisting the newly ordained priest at his Mass of Thanksgiving.

+In the name of the Father and of the Son and of the Holy Spirit. Amen.

V. Our help is in the name of the Lord.
R. Who made heaven and earth.

V. The Lord be with you.
R. And with your spirit.

Scripture Reading

Make a joyful noise to the LORD, all the lands!
Serve the LORD with gladness!
Come into his presence with singing!
Know that the LORD is God!
It is he that made us, and we are his;
we are his people, and the sheep of his pasture.
Enter his gates with thanksgiving,
and his courts with praise!
Give thanks to him, bless his name!
For the LORD is good;
his steadfast love endures for ever,
and his faithfulness to all generations.

—Psalm 100

Prayer of Blessing

God our Father, you have given us this day of rejoicing and faithful service as I celebrate the Eucharistic sacrifice in thanksgiving for the gift of my ordination to the priesthood. Bless + these ministers who assist me today in offering this Mass. May we celebrate this liturgy with the dignity and recollection that it deserves. May the mysteries offered here draw us all into that Kingdom where you live and reign with the Son and Holy Spirit, one God forever and ever. Amen.

Prayers on the Anniversary of Ordination

Prayers for the Priest Himself

Merciful God, today as I remember the day of my ordination to the priesthood, renew in me a spirit of fervor and service. May the worship and prayer of this day increase my desire to be a priest and inflame in my heart an unwavering love of your Word and awe for the sacrifice of the altar. Create in me, Lord, a spirit of righteousness and remove from my heart all that hinders me from serving you and your holy people. Grant this though Christ our Lord. Amen.

✳

God our Father, today as I remember the great gift you have given me in my ordination to the priesthood, I ask for a renewal of that grace as I strive each day to serve your people. Increase my love for Holy Scripture, my fervor for preaching and my sense of dignity as I renew each day the sacrifice of your Son, Jesus. Grant this through Christ our Lord. Amen.

✳

Lord, make me a better priest today than I was yesterday. May each new day be an opportunity to strengthen my love for you and my desire to serve your people in the ministry of the Word and the sacrifice of the altar. May each person I meet today be you, Lord, present to me in the mystery of the Body of Christ, your Son, in whose name we pray. Amen.

✳

Father of Mercy, although I am not worthy, you have called me to share in the priesthood of your Son, Jesus Christ. May my service be pleasing to you. Renew in me a spirit of humility and gratitude for the great mysteries I celebrate on behalf of your holy people. Through the same Christ our Lord. Amen.

Prayers on Behalf of the Priest

Lord Jesus, give new life to your priest, Father (N), who today celebrates the anniversary of his ordination. May your Spirit enliven him with new hope and strengthen him to continue to serve you as a holy and passionate priest. May his service to your holy body the Church never waver. We ask this in the name of Jesus the Lord. Amen.

Father, you appointed your Son the High Priest of the new covenant. Guide Father (N), whom you have chosen to be a minister of Word and Sacrament. Keep him faithful to your service. Grant this though Christ our Lord. Amen.

Prayers for a Priest About to Be Ordained a Bishop

Lord God, you are the Eternal Shepherd and guide of your people. Grant mercy and peace to Father (N), whom you have called through the voice of the Church for service as bishop of the (arch) diocese of (N). Help him always to prefer you above all things and through his episcopal ministry, draw all of the faithful to everlasting life. We ask this in the name of the High Priest, Jesus, who is Lord forever and ever. Amen.

⁕

God of Power and Might, you have called Father (N) to serve you in the office of bishop. Help him to be a good and holy pastor of his flock in the (arch) diocese of (N). Make him a faithful teacher of your Word and the Tradition of the Church, a sure guide and a wise leader. We ask this through Christ our Lord. Amen.

Blessing Upon Rising

+In the name of the Father and of the Son and of the Holy Spirit. Amen.

V. Our help is in the name of the Lord.
R. Who made heaven and earth.

V. The Lord be with you.
R. And with your spirit.

Scripture Reading

A Reading from the Book of Psalms

Blessed be the name of the LORD from this time on and for evermore. From the rising of the sun to its setting the name of the Lord is to be praised.

—Psalm 113:2-3

Or

A Reading from the Book of the prophet Isaiah

Arise, shine; for your light has come,
and the glory of the LORD has risen upon you.

—Isaiah 60:1

Prayer of Blessing

Lord, our God, you are the giver of day and the giver of night. You guard our resting and our rising. I praise you as I rise today. Sanctify my priesthood today and may all of my actions be for the glory of your name. May all my works today begin with your inspiration, continue with your saving help, and be brought to fulfillment in that kingdom where you live and reign forever and ever. Amen.

Bow to the icon of Christ or crucifix that may be in your room, or use holy water as you conclude with the sign of the cross.

Blessing and Sanctification of the Day

+In the name of the Father and of the Son and of the Holy Spirit. Amen.

V. Our help is in the name of the Lord.
R. Who made heaven and earth.

V. The Lord be with you.
R. And with your spirit.

Scripture Reading

O LORD, who shall sojourn in your tent?
Who shall dwell on your holy mountain?
He who walks blamelessly, and does what is right, and speaks truth from his heart; who does not slander with his tongue, and does no evil to his friend, nor takes up a reproach against his neighbor.

—Psalm 15:1-3

Prayer of Blessing

Lord Jesus Christ, you admonish us to love others as you have loved us. You call us to serve others as you have served us. Give life to my priestly ministry today. Conform me ever more generously into your likeness that I may serve your people in your person. Guided by your example, may I journey through this day with a generous heart. Grant me the grace to remain pure in thought, word, and deed, that I might lead others to you and be worthy of your kingdom, where you live and reign forever and ever. Amen.

Blessing at the End of the Day

+In the name of the Father and of the Son and of the Holy Spirit. Amen.

V. Our help is in the name of the Lord.
R. Who made heaven and earth.

V. The Lord be with you.
R. And with your spirit.

Scripture Reading

'Come to me, all you that are weary and are carrying heavy burdens, and I will give you rest. Take my yoke upon you, and learn from me; for I am gentle and humble in heart, and you will find rest for your souls. For my yoke is easy, and my burden is light.'

—Matthew 11:28-30

Prayer of Blessing

O God, before I sleep, I ask your forgiveness for the times I have failed you this day through my life as a priest. I ask your blessing for the times I have been a reflection of your love for humankind. Bless my sleeping that I may be refreshed and renewed so that at my rising I may be filled with the courage and strength to do your will. And, if this night should be my last, welcome me into your heavenly kingdom, that with your angels and saints I may praise you forever. Amen.

Make the sign of the cross to end.

Blessing to Sanctify the Work of the Day

+In the name of the Father and of the Son and of the Holy Spirit. Amen.

A Reading from Colossians

Whatever your task, put yourselves into it, as done for the Lord and not for your masters, since you know that from the Lord you will receive the inheritance as your reward; you serve the Lord Christ.

—Colossians 3:23-24

Prayer

Gracious God, in your wisdom, you created all the world, and blessed us through the work of your hands. As I begin my work this day, bless my priestly work and keep me holy. Guide my actions, my thoughts, and my words that they might give glory and praise to your name. I ask this in the name of Jesus, your Son. Amen.

Bow to the icon of Christ or crucifix that may be in your office, or use holy water as you conclude with the sign of the cross.

Prayer During the Day

+In the name of the Father and of the Son and of the Holy Spirit. Amen.

A Reading from the Book of Psalms

Cry out with joy to the LORD, all the earth.
Serve the LORD with gladness.
Come before God singing for joy.

—Psalm 100:1-3

Prayer

Lord God, you are the source of my strength. Keep me ever mindful of your presence in my day. You are the Spirit that guides my life as a priest. Help me to conduct myself in such a way that I might make your presence known. Bless my work and grant that I might bring it to completion to the glory of your name. Amen.

Bow to the icon of Christ or crucifix that may be in your office, or use holy water as you conclude with the sign of the cross.

Prayer at the End of the Workday

+In the name of the Father and of the Son and of the Holy Spirit. Amen.

A Reading from the Book of Psalms

Blessed be the name of the Lord from this time on and for evermore. From the rising of the sun to its setting the name of the Lord is to be praised.

—Psalm 113:2-3

Prayer

Lord, our God, you are the giver of all work. Thank you for the work of this day. May these priestly labors be a source of sanctification and salvation for the world. May each day's work serve you in that kingdom where you live and reign forever and ever. Amen.

Bow to the icon of Christ or crucifix that may be in your office, or use holy water as you conclude with the sign of the cross.

Prayer to Begin a Time of Study

+In the name of the Father and of the Son and of the Holy Spirit. Amen.

A Reading from the Book of Proverbs

And now, my children, listen to me: happy are those who keep my ways. Hear instruction and be wise, and do not neglect it.

—Proverbs 8:32-36

Prayer

Lord, our God, you are the source of all wisdom. Bless this time of study. May my labours give glory to your name and be of service to your people. May my mind and heart be enriched by this reading. May I truly learn to believe what I read, teach what I believe, and practice what I teach. I ask this in the name of Jesus the Lord. Amen.

Bow to the icon of Christ or crucifix that may be in your office, or use holy water as you conclude with the sign of the cross.

Prayers for Times of Study

Come Holy Spirit, fill my heart with your holy gifts.

Let my weakness be penetrated with your strength this very day that I may fulfill all the duties of my priestly life conscientiously, that I may do what is right and just.

Let my charity be such as to offend no one, and hurt no one's feelings; so generous as to pardon sincerely any wrong done to me.

Assist me, O Holy Spirit, in all the trials of the priesthood, enlighten me in my ignorance, advise me in my doubts, strengthen me in my weakness, help me in all my needs, protect me in temptations, and console me in afflictions.

Graciously hear me, O Holy Spirit, and pour your light into my heart, my soul, and my mind.

Assist me to live a holy life as a priest and to grow in goodness and grace. Amen.

⁎

O Lord, thou greatest and most true Light,
whence the light of the day doth spring!
O Light,
which dost lighten every man that cometh into the world!
O thou Wisdom of the eternal Father,
enlighten my mind,
that I may see only those things that please thee,
and may be blinded to all other things.
Grant that I may walk in thy ways,
and that nothing else may be light and pleasant. Amen.

—John Bradford

⁎

Father,
May everything we do
begin with your inspiration
and continue with your saving help.
Let our work always find its origin in you
and through you reach completion.
We ask this through our Lord Jesus Christ, your Son,
who lives and reigns with you and the Holy Spirit,
one God, for ever and ever. Amen.

*

Give me O Lord, I pray thee,
firm faith, unwavering hope,
perfect charity.
Pour into my heart
the Spirit of wisdom and understanding,
the Spirit of counsel and spiritual strength,
the Spirit of knowledge and true godliness,
and the Spirit of thy holy fear.
Light eternal, shine in my heart.
Power eternal, deliver me from evil.
Wisdom eternal, scatter the darkness of my ignorance.
Might eternal, pity me.
Grant that I may ever seek thy face
with all my heart and soul and strength;
and, in thine infinite mercy,
bring me at last to thy holy presence,
where I shall behold thy glory
and possess thy promised joys.

—St. Alcuin of York

Direct, O Lord, we beseech you, all our actions by your holy inspirations, and carry them on by your gracious assistance, that every prayer and work of ours may begin always from you, and by you be happily ended. Through Christ our Lord. Amen.

Creator past all telling, you have appointed from the treasures of your wisdom the hierarchies of angels, disposing them in wondrous order above the bright heavens, and have so beautifully set out all parts of the universe. You we call the true fount of wisdom and the noble origin of all things. Be pleased to shed on the darkness of mind in which I was born, the twofold beam of your light and warmth to dispel my ignorance and sin. You make eloquent the tongues of children. Then instruct my speech and touch my lips with graciousness. Make me keen to understand, quick to learn, able to remember; make me delicate to interpret and ready to speak. Guide my going in and going forward, and lead home my going forth. You are true God and true man, and live for ever and ever. Amen.

*

God be in my head and in my understanding. God be in my eyes and in my looking. God be in my mouth and in my speaking. God be in my heart and in my thinking. God be at my end and my departing.

✳

Lord, inspire us to read your Scriptures and to meditate upon them day and night. We beg you to give us real understanding of what we need, that we in turn may put its precepts into practice. Yet we know that understanding and good intentions are worthless, unless rooted in your graceful love. So we ask that the words of Scripture may be not just signs on a page, but channels of grace into our hearts.

✳

I thank you, my God, for the good resolutions, affections, and inspirations that you have communicated to me in this meditation. I beg your help in putting them into effect. My Immaculate Mother, Saint Joseph my father, my guardian angel, intercede for me.

✳

Take, Lord, and receive all my liberty, my memory, my understanding, and my entire will, all that I have and possess. You have given all to me; to you, O Lord, now I return it; all is yours. Dispose of me wholly according to your will. Give me only your love and your grace, for this is enough for me.

✳

God, grant me the serenity to accept the things I cannot change, courage to change the things I can, and the wisdom to know the difference. Living one day at a time; enjoying one moment at a time; accepting hardship as the pathway to peace. Taking as Jesus did this sinful world as it is, not as I would have it; trusting that he will make all things right if I surrender to his will; that I may be reasonably happy in this life and supremely happy with him forever in the next.

✳

O my God, I present myself before you at the end of another day, to offer you anew the homage of my heart. I humbly adore you, my Creator, my Redeemer, and my Judge! I believe in you, because you are Truth itself; I hope in you, because you are faithful to your promises; I love you with my whole heart, because you are infinitely worthy of being loved; and for your sake I love my neighbor as myself. Enable me, O my God, to return you thanks as I ought of all your inestimable blessings and favors. You have formed me out of nothing; You have delivered up your beloved Son to the ignominious death of the Cross for my redemption; You have made me a member of your holy Church; You have preserved me from falling into the abyss of eternal misery, when my sins had provoked you to punish me; and You have graciously continued to spare me, even though I have not ceased to offend you. What return, O my God, can I make for your innumerable blessings, and particularly for the favors of this day? O all ye saints and angels, unite with me in praising the God of mercy, who is so bountiful to so unworthy a creature.

PRAYERS FOR THE PREPARATION OF HOMILIES

Before the multitude of heavenly witnesses, I offer myself, soul and body, to you, eternal Spirit of God. Help me as I prepare to preach to your holy people.

I adore the brightness of your purity, the unerring keenness of your justice, and the power of your love. You are the strength and light of my soul. In you I live and move and have my being.

I desire never to grieve you by infidelity to your grace, and I pray wholeheartedly to be preserved from the slightest sin against you.

Make me faithful in my every thought, and grant that I may always listen to your voice, watch for your light, and follow your gracious inspirations.

I cling to you, and beg you, in your compassion, to watch over me in my weakness.

Holding the pierced feet of Jesus, gazing at his five wounds, trusting the Precious Blood, and adoring his open side and stricken Heart, I implore you, adorable Spirit, so to keep me in your grace that I may never sin against you.

Grant me the grace that I may never sin against you. Grant me the grace, O Holy Spirit of the Father and the Son to say to you always and everywhere: *"Speak, Lord, for your servant is listening."*

*

O, God,
Grant us in all our duties your help;
in all our perplexities, your guidance;
in all our dangers, your protection;
and in all our sorrows, your peace.
Through Jesus Christ our Lord,
our body, and our blood,
our life and our nourishment. Amen.

—St. Augustine of Hippo

Lord our God, open my heart and my mind as I prepare to preach to your holy people. May the words I speak be your words, the insights I bring, your insights, the spirit I call upon, your Spirit. Give me the words that will build up the Church and give glory to you, who live and reign forever and ever.

PRAYERS TO SAINT JOSEPH FOR THE SANCTIFICATION OF THE PRIEST'S WORK

O God, the creator of all things, you framed the law of labor for the human race. Graciously grant, by the example and patronage of St. Joseph, that we may do the priestly work you provide us and earn the reward you promise. Sustain us with your grace to live up to our duties in charity and justice. Amen.

⁕

O glorious St. Joseph, you were chosen by God to be the foster father of Jesus, the most pure spouse of Mary ever Virgin, and the head of the holy family. You have been chosen by Christ's Vicar as the heavenly patron and protector of the Church founded by Christ. Therefore it is with great confidence that I implore your powerful assistance for the whole Church on earth. Protect in a special manner, with true fatherly love, the Pope and all bishops and priests. Be the protector of all who labor for souls amid the trials and tribulations of this life, and grant that all peoples of the world may follow Christ and the Church he founded. Amen.

⁕

Dear St. Joseph, accept the offering of myself which I now make to you. I dedicate myself to your service, that you may ever be my father, my protector, and my guide in the way of salvation. In my priestly life, make me a true father, protector, and guide to those whom I serve. Obtain for me great purity of heart and a fervent love for the spiritual life. May all my actions, after your example, be directed to the greater glory of God, in union with the Divine Heart of Jesus, the Immaculate Heart of Mary, and your own paternal heart. Finally, pray for me that I may share in the peace and joy of your holy death. Amen.

⁕

Glorious St. Joseph, model of all those who are devoted to labor, obtain for me the grace to live my priestly life in a spirit of penance for the expiation of my many sins; to work conscientiously, putting the call of duty above my inclinations; to work with gratitude and joy, considering it an honor to employ and develop, by means of labor, the gifts received from God; to work with order, peace, moderation, and patience, without ever recoiling before weariness or difficulties; to work, above all, with purity of intention, and with detachment from self, having always death before my eyes and the account which I must render of time lost, of talents wasted, of good omitted, of vain complacency in success, so fatal to the work of God. All for Jesus, all for Mary, all after your example, O Patriarch Joseph. Such shall be my watchword in life and in death. Amen.

✻

St. Joseph, whose protection is so great, so strong, so prompt before the throne of God, I place in you all my interest and desires. Oh, St. Joseph, do assist me by your powerful intercession, and obtain for me from your divine Son all spiritual blessings, through Jesus Christ, our Lord. So that, having engaged here below your heavenly power, I may offer my thanksgiving and homage to the most loving of fathers. St. Joseph, I never weary contemplating you, and Jesus asleep in your arms; I dare not approach while he reposes near your heart. Press him close in my name and kiss his fine head for me and ask him to return the kiss when I draw my dying breath. St. Joseph, patron of departing souls, pray for me.

Prayers for Meals

Blessing Before Meals

Bénedic, Dómine, nos et haec
tua dona quae de tua largitate sumus sumpturi.
Per Christum Dóminum nostrum. Amen.

Bless us, O Lord, and these
thy gifts which we are about
to receive from thy bounty,
through Christ our Lord. Amen.

Grace After Meals

Ágimus tibi gratias, omnípotens Deus,
pro universis beneficiis tuis,
qui vivis et regnas in
sæcula sæculórum. Amen.

Deus det nobis suam pacem.
Et vitam æternum. Amen.

Alternate conclusion:
Fidelium animae, per misericordiam Dei,
requiescant in pace. Amen.

✻

We give thee thanks, almighty God,
for all your benefits,
who livest and reignest forever
and ever. Amen.

May the Lord grant us his peace.
And life everlasting. Amen.

Alternate conclusion:
And may the souls of the faithful departed, through the mercy of God, rest in peace. Amen.

Morning Prayers

Arising from Sleep

O Master and holy God, who are beyond our understanding: at your word, light came forth out of darkness. In your mercy, you gave us rest through nightlong sleep, and raised us up to glorify your goodness and to offer our supplication to you. Now, in your own tender love, accept us who adore you and give thanks to you with all our heart. Grant us all our requests, if they lead to salvation; give us the grace of manifesting that we are children of light and day, and heirs to your eternal reward. In the abundance of your mercies, O Lord, remember all your people; all those present who pray with us; all our brethren on land, at sea, or in the air, in every place of your domain, who call upon your love for mankind. Upon all, pour down your great mercy, that we, saved in body and in soul, may persevere unfailingly; and that, in our confidence, we may extol your exalted and blessed name, Father, Son, and Holy Spirit, always, now and forever. Amen.

Fatima Morning Offering

O Jesus, through the Immaculate Heart of Mary, I offer you my prayers, works, joys, and sufferings, all that this day may bring, be they good or bad: for the love of God, for the conversion of sinners, and in reparation for all the sins committed against the Sacred Heart of Jesus and the Immaculate Heart of Mary.

Morning Offering

Most Holy and Adorable Trinity, one God in three Persons, I firmly believe that you are here present; I adore you with the most profound humility; I praise you and give you thanks with all my heart for the favors you have bestowed on me. Your goodness has brought me safely to the beginning of this day. Behold, O Lord, I offer you my whole being and in particular all my thoughts, words, and actions, together with such crosses and contradictions as I may meet with in the course of this day. Give them, O Lord, your blessing; may your divine love animate them and may they tend to the greater honor and glory of your sovereign majesty. Amen.

Morning Offering to the Sacred Heart

O Jesus, through the Immaculate Heart of Mary, I offer you my prayers, works, joys, and sufferings of this day for all the intentions of your Sacred Heart, in union with the Holy Sacrifice of the Mass throughout the world, in reparation for my sins, for the intentions of all our associates, and in particular for the intentions of our Holy Father for this month.

Shorter Prayers at the Day's Beginning

Lord, one more day to love you!

—Bl. Charles de Foucauld

⁂

O Jesus, watch over me always, especially today, or I shall betray you like Judas.

—St. Philip Neri

⁂

Lord, today is the day I begin!

—St. Philip Neri

⁂

Jesus, shine through me and be so in me that every person I come in contact with may feel your presence in my soul.

—Bl. John Henry Newman

⁂

My God, send me your Holy Spirit to teach me what I am and what you are!

—St. John Vianney

Act of Faith

O my God, I firmly believe that you are one God in three divine Persons, Father, Son, and Holy Spirit. I believe that your divine Son became man, and died for our sins, and that he will come to judge the living and the dead. In my priestly life, I believe these and all the truths which the Holy Catholic Church teaches, because you have revealed them, who can neither deceive nor be deceived. Amen.

Act of Hope

O my God, relying on your almighty power and infinite mercy and promises, in my priestly life, I hope to obtain pardon of my sins, the help of your grace, and life everlasting, through the merits of Jesus Christ, my Lord and Redeemer. Amen.

Act of Charity

O my God, as a priest, I love you above all things, with my whole heart and soul, because you are all-good and worthy of all love. I love my neighbor as myself for the love of you. I forgive all who have injured me, and ask pardon of all whom I have injured. Amen.

Offering of Daily Actions

Eternal Father, by virtue of your generosity and love, I ask that you accept all my actions of my life as a priest, and that you multiply their value in favor of every soul in purgatory. Through Christ our Lord. Amen.

Shorter Morning Offerings

My loving Jesus, out of the grateful love I bear you as a priest, and to make reparation for my unfaithfulness to grace, I give you my heart, and I consecrate myself wholly to you; and with your help I hope never to sin again. Dear Lord, I could never equal your generosity, but I love you; accept my poor heart, and though it is worth nothing, yet it may become something by your grace. Since it loves you, make it good and take it for yourself.

✳

I will extol you, O God, my King, and I will bless your name forever and ever.

✳

Take O Lord, all my liberty, receive my memory, my understanding, and my whole will. All that I am, all that I have, you have given me, and I restore it all to you, to be disposed of according to your good pleasure. Give me only your love and your grace; with these I am rich enough, and I desire nothing more.

Offering to the Holy Trinity

Most Holy and Adorable Trinity, one God in three Persons, I praise you and give you thanks for all the favors you have given me. Your goodness has preserved me until now, I offer you my whole being and in particular, my priesthood, all my thoughts, words, and deeds, together with all the trials I may undergo this day. Give them your blessing. May your divine love enliven them and may they serve your greater glory.

I make this morning offering as a priest in union with the divine intentions of Jesus Christ, who offers himself daily in the Holy Sacrifice of the Mass, and in union with Mary, his Virgin Mother and our Mother, who was always the faithful handmaid of the Lord.

Evening Prayers

Evening Prayer to God the Father

O eternal God and Ruler of all creation, you have allowed me to reach this hour. Forgive the sins I have committed this day by word, deed, or thought. Purify me, O Lord, from every spiritual and physical stain. Grant that I may rise from this sleep to glorify you by my deeds throughout my entire lifetime, and that I be victorious over every spiritual and physical enemy. Deliver me, O Lord, from all vain thoughts and from evil desires, for yours is the kingdom, and the power, and the glory, Father, Son, and Holy Spirit, now and ever, and forever. Amen.

Evening Prayer to the Holy Spirit

O Holy Spirit, most merciful Comforter: you proceed from the Father in a manner beyond our understanding. Come, I beseech you, and take up your abode in my heart. Purify and cleanse me from all sin, and sanctify my soul. Cleanse it from every impurity, water its dryness, melt its coldness, and save it from its sinful ways. Make me truly humble and resigned, that I may be pleasing to you, and that you might abide with me forever. Most Blessed Light, most Amiable Light, enlighten me. O Rapturous Joy of Paradise, Fount of Purest Delight, my God, give yourself to me and kindle in my innermost soul the fire of your love. My Lord, instruct, direct, and defend me in all things. Give me strength against all immoderate fears and against despondency. Bestow upon me a true faith, a firm hope, and a sincere and a perfect love. Grant that I always do your most gracious will. Amen.

Evening Prayer to the Son of God

O Only-Begotten Word of the Father, Jesus Christ, who alone is perfect: according to the greatness of your mercy, do not abandon me, your servant, but ever rest in my heart. O sweet Jesus, Good Shepherd of your flock, deliver me from the attacks of the Enemy. Do not allow me to become the prey of Satan's evil intent, even though I have within me the seed of eternal damnation. Instead, O Lord Jesus Christ, Adorable God, Holy King, while I sleep, protect me by your Holy spirit, through whom you sanctified your apostles. Enlighten my mind by the light of the Holy Gospel, my soul by the love of your Cross, my heart by the purity of your teaching. Protect my body by your sacred passion, my senses by your humility, and awaken me in due time for your glorification. For you, above all, are adorable, together with your eternal Father, and the Holy Spirit, now and ever, and forever. Amen.

✳

Ah, Lord,
how many nights have I slept in enmity with thee?
O God!
in what a miserable state was my soul during that time!
It was hated by thee,
and wished to be hated by thee.
I was condemned to hell;
there was nothing wanting
but the execution of the sentence.
But thou, my God,
hast never ceased to seek after me,
and invite me to pardon.
But who can assure me
that thou hast pardoned me?
Must I, O my Jesus!
live in this uncertainty
till thou dost judge me?
But the sorrow which I feel
for having offended thee,
my desire to love thee,
and still more,
thy passion,
O my beloved Redeemer!
make me hope that thy grace dwells in my soul.
I am sorry for having offended thee,
O Sovereign Good!
and I love thee above all things.
I resolve to forfeit everything
rather than lose thy grace and thy love.
Thou dost wish that the heart
which seeks thee should be full of joy.
"Let the heart of them rejoice that seek the Lord."
Lord, I detest all the injuries
I have offered to thee.

Give me courage and confidence;
do not upbraid me with my ingratitude;
for I myself know and detest it.
Thou hast said that thou willest not
the death of a sinner,
but that he be converted and live.
Yes, my God,
I leave all things and turn to thee.
Give me thy love;
I ask nothing else.
O Mary! thou, after Jesus, art my hope;
obtain for me holy perseverance.

⁜

Watch, O Lord, with those who wake,
or watch, or weep tonight,
and give your angels and saints charge over those who sleep.
Tend your sick ones, O Lord Christ.
Rest your weary ones,
Bless your dying ones,
Soothe your suffering ones,
pity your afflicted ones,
Shield your joyous ones,
And all for your love's sake. Amen.

⁜

O my God,
I believe that thou art here present;
and that thou observest all my actions,
all my thoughts,
and the most secret motions of my heart.
I adore thee,
and I love thee with my whole heart.
I return thee thanks for all the benefits
which I have ever received from thee,
and particularly this day.
Give me light, O my God,
to see what sins I have committed this day,
and grant me grace to be truly sorry for them.

Here examine whether you have offended God during the day, by any thought, word, or deed, or by neglect of any duty.

O my God,
who art infinitely good in thyself,
and infinitely good to me,
I am sorry,
and beg pardon for all my sins,
and detest them above all things,
because they deserve thy dreadful punishments,
because they have crucified my loving Savior Jesus Christ,
and, most of all,
because they offend thine infinite goodness;
and I firmly resolve,
by the help of thy grace,
never to offend thee again,
and carefully to avoid the occasions of sin.

Here put yourself in the disposition you desire to be found at the hour of death.

O my God,
I accept of death as an act of homage and adoration
which I owe to thy Divine Majesty,
as a punishment justly due to my sins,
in union with the death of my dear Redeemer,
and as the only means of coming to thee,
my beginning and last end.

Into thy hands, O Lord, I commend my spirit;
Lord Jesus, receive my soul.

O holy Mary,
be a mother to me.

May the blessed Virgin Mary,
Saint Joseph,
and all the saints,
pray for us to our Lord,
that we may be preserved this night from sin and all evils.
Amen.

O my good angel,
whom God has appointed to be my guardian,
watch over me during this night.

All ye angels and saints of God,
pray for me.

May our Lord bless us,
and preserve us from all evil,
and bring us to life everlasting.

Amen.

And may the souls of the faithful departed,
through the mercy of God, rest in peace.

Amen.

A Short Road to Perfection by Bl. John Henry Newman

It is the saying of holy men that, if we wish to be perfect, we have nothing more to do than to perform the ordinary duties of the day well. A short road to perfection—short, not because easy, but because pertinent and intelligible. There are no short ways to perfection, but there are sure ones.

I think this is an instruction which may be of great practical use to persons like ourselves. It is easy to have vague ideas what perfection is, which serve well enough to talk about, when we do not intend to aim at it; but as soon as a person really desires and sets about seeking it himself, he is dissatisfied with anything but what is tangible and clear, and constitutes some sort of direction towards the practice of it.

We must bear in mind what is meant by perfection. It does not mean any extraordinary service, anything out of the way, or especially heroic—not all have the opportunity of heroic acts, of sufferings—but it means what the word perfection ordinarily means. By perfect we mean that which has no flaw in it, that which is complete, that which is consistent, that which is sound—we mean the opposite to imperfect. As we know well what *im*perfection in religious service means, we know by the contrast what is meant by perfection.

He, then, is perfect who does the work of the day perfectly, and we need not go beyond this to seek for perfection. You need not go out of the *round* of the day.

I insist on this because I think it will simplify our views, and fix our exertions on a definite aim. If you ask me what you are to do in order to be perfect, I say, first—Do not lie in bed beyond the due time of rising; give your first thoughts to God; make a good visit to the Blessed Sacrament; say the Angelus devoutly; eat and drink to God's glory; say the rosary well; be recollected; keep out bad thoughts; make your evening meditation well; examine yourself daily; go to bed in good time, and you are already perfect.

Prayer for the Light of Truth

I should like an enquirer to say continually:

O my God, I confess that *thou canst* enlighten my darkness. I confess that thou *alone* canst. I *wish* my darkness to be enlightened. I do not know whether thou wilt: but that thou canst and that I wish, are sufficient reasons for me to *ask*, what thou at least hast not forbidden my asking. I hereby promise that by thy grace which I am asking, I will embrace whatever I at length feel certain is the truth, if ever I come to be certain. And by thy grace I will guard against all self-deceit which may lead me to take what nature would have, rather than what reason approves.

Prayer for a Happy Death

O my Lord and Savior, support me in that hour in the strong arms of thy sacraments, and by the fresh fragrance of thy consolations. Let the absolving words be said over me, and the holy oil sign and seal me, and thy own Body be my food, and thy Blood my sprinkling; and let my sweet Mother, Mary, breathe on me, and my angel whisper peace to me, and my glorious saints . . . smile upon me; that in them all, and through them all, I may receive the gift of perseverance, and die, as I desire to live, in thy faith, in thy Church, in thy service, and in thy love. Amen.

Prayers During the Holy Hour by Bl. John Henry Newman

A Short Visit to the Blessed Sacrament before Meditation

+In the Name of the Father, and of the Son, and of the Holy Spirit. Amen.

I place myself in the presence of him, in whose Incarnate Presence I am before I place myself there.

I adore thee, O my Savior, present here as God and man, in soul and body, in true flesh and blood.

I acknowledge and confess that I kneel before that Sacred Humanity, which was conceived in Mary's womb, and lay in Mary's bosom; which grew up to man's estate, and by the Sea of Galilee called the Twelve, wrought miracles, and spoke words of wisdom and peace; which in due season hung on the cross, lay in the tomb, rose from the dead, and now reigns in heaven.

I praise, and bless, and give myself wholly to him, who is the true Bread of my soul, and my everlasting joy.

Sunday

O Sapientia, quæ ex ore Altissimi prodiisti, attingens à fine usque ad finem, fortiter suaviterque disponens omnia: Veni ad docendum nos viam prudentiæ.

Monday

O Adonai, et Dux domus Israel, qui Moysi in igne flammæ rubi apparuisti, et ei in Sina legem dedisti: Veni ad redimendum nos in brachio extento.

Tuesday

O Radix Jesse, qui stas in signum populorum, super quem continebunt reges os suum, quem Gentes deprecabuntur: Veni ad liberandum nos, jam noli tardare.

Wednesday

O Clavis David, et Sceptrum domus Israel, qui aperis et nemo claudit, claudis et nemo aperit: Veni, et educ vinctum de domo carceris, sedentem in tenebris et umbrâ mortis.

Thursday

O Oriens, Splendor lucis æternæ, et sol justitiæ: Veni et illumina sedentes in tenebris et umbrâ mortis.

Friday

O Rex Gentium, et desideratus earum, lapisque angularis, qui facis utraque unum: Veni et salva hominem, quem de limo formasti.

Saturday

O Emmanuel, Rex et Legifer noster, Expectatio gentium, et Salvador earum: Veni ad salvandum nos, Domine Deus noster.

The Divine Praises

Blessed be God.
Blessed be His Holy Name.
Blessed be Jesus Christ, true God and true man.
Blessed be the name of Jesus.
Blessed be His Most Sacred Heart.
Blessed be Jesus in the Most Holy Sacrament of the Altar.
Blessed be the Holy Spirit, the paraclete.
Blessed be the great Mother of God, Mary most holy.
Blessed be her holy and Immaculate Conception.
Blessed be her glorious Assumption.
Blessed be the name of Mary, Virgin and Mother.
Blessed be Saint Joseph, her most chaste spouse.
Blessed be God in His angels and in His saints.

May the heart of Jesus, in the Most Blessed Sacrament, be praised, adored, and loved with grateful affection, at every moment, in all the tabernacles of the world, even to the end of time. Amen.

Additional Prayers During the Holy Hour

O Sacrum Convivium

O sacred banquet,
in which Christ is received,
the memory of his Passion is renewed,
the mind is filled with grace,
and a pledge of future glory is given to us.

Tantum Ergo

Down in adoration falling
Lo! the sacred Host we hail;
Lo! o'er ancient forms departing,
newer rites of grace prevail;
Faith for all defects supplying,
where the feeble senses fail.
To the everlasting Father,
and the Son who reigns on high,
with the Holy Spirit proceeding
forth from each eternally,
be salvation, honor, blessing,
might and endless majesty. Amen.

V. You have given them bread from heaven,

R. Having all delight within it.

Let us pray.

O God, who in this wonderful Sacrament
left us a memorial of your Passion:
grant, we implore you,
that we may so venerate
the sacred mysteries of your Body and Blood,
as always to be conscious of the fruit of your Redemption.
You who live and reign forever and ever. Amen.

Anima Christi

Soul of Christ, sanctify me.
Body of Christ, save me.
Blood of Christ, inebriate me.
Water from the side of Christ, wash me.
Passion of Christ, strengthen me.
O good Jesus, hear me.
Within your wounds conceal me.
Do not permit me to be parted from you.
From the evil foe protect me.
At the hour of my death call me.
And bid me come to you,
to praise you with all your saints
for ever and ever.
Amen.

En Ego, O Bone et Dulcissime Iesu

Here,
O good and gentle Jesus,
I kneel before you,
and with all the fervor of my soul
I pray that you engrave within my heart
lively sentiments of faith, hope, and love,
true repentance for my sins,
and a firm purpose of amendment.
While I see and I ponder your five wounds
with great affection and sorrow in my soul,

I have before my eyes those words of yours
that David prophesied about you:
"They have pierced my hands and feet;
I can count all my bones." (*Ps 22:17*)
Amen.

Angel's Prayer At Fatima

"Most Holy Trinity; Father, Son, and Holy Spirit—I adore thee profoundly. I offer thee the most precious body, blood, soul and divinity of Jesus Christ, present in all the tabernacles of the world, in reparation for the outrages, sacrileges, and indifferences whereby He is offended. And through the infinite merits of His Most Sacred Heart and the Immaculate Heart Of Mary, I beg of thee the conversion of poor sinners."

Sanctity of Life

My God, we adore you here in the Blessed Sacrament.
As we kneel before you, we recognize you as the Creator of all life. We thank you and praise you for the lives you have given to us and to those we love. Give us a true and lasting respect for all life, for we recognize it as coming from you. We pray for all who have suffered or died as a result of disrespect, whether that suffering and death has come as a result of abuse, war, gossip, or abortion. We pray for an end for all disrespect of life. As we kneel before you we ask you to forgive all those who do not respect the sanctity of life. We repeat the words you spoke as you hung on the cross, "Father, forgive them, for they know not what they do."

Stay with us

"Stay with us today, and stay from now on, every day, according to the desire of my heart, which accepts the appeal of so many hearts from various parts, sometimes far away... Stay that we may meet you in prayers of adoration and thanksgiving, in prayers of expiation and petition to which all those who visit this basilica are invited...
May the unworthy successor of Peter and all those who take part in the adoration of your Eucharistic Presence attest with every visit and make ring out again the truth contained in the Apostle's words: 'Lord, you know everything. You know that I love you.' Amen."

—St. John Paul II

Consecration to the Sacred Heart of Jesus

Adorable Heart of Jesus, the tenderest, the most amiable, the most generous of all hearts, penetrated with gratitude at the sight of thy benefits, I come to consecrate myself wholly and unreservedly to thee! I wish to devote all my energies to propagating thy worship and winning, if possible, all hearts to thee. Receive my heart this day, O Jesus!

Or rather take it, change it, purify it, to render it worthy of thee; make it humble, gentle, patient, faithful, and generous like thine, by inflaming it with the fire of thy love. Hide it in thy Divine Heart with all hearts that love thee and are consecrated to thee; never permit me to take my heart from thee again. Let me rather die than grieve thy Adorable Heart. Thou knowest O Heart of Jesus, that the desire of my heart is to love thee always, to be wholly thine in life and in death, in time and eternity. Most Sacred Heart of Jesus, have mercy on us. Sacred Heart of Jesus, I trust in thee.

Hail to Thee, True Body

Hail to thee, true body born
from Virgin Mary's womb!
The same that on the cross was nailed
and bore for man the bitter doom.

Thou, whose side was pierced and flowed
both with water and with blood;
Suffer us to taste of thee,
in our life's last agony.

O kind, O loving one!
O sweet Jesus, Mary's Son!

Consecration to the Immaculate Heart of Mary

I, (N), a priest and a faithless sinner, renew and ratify today in thy hands, O Immaculate Mother, the vows of my baptism; I renounce Satan, his pomps and works; and I give myself entirely to Jesus Christ, the Incarnate Wisdom, to carry my cross after him all the days of my life, and to be more faithful to him than I have ever been before.

In the presence of all the heavenly court I choose thee this day for my Mother and Mistress. I deliver and consecrate to thee, as thy slave, my body and soul, my goods, both interior and exterior, and even the value of all my good actions, past, present, and future; leaving to thee the entire and full right of disposing of me, and all that belongs to me, without exception, according to thy good pleasure, for the greater glory of God, in time and in eternity. Amen.

Prayer to the Eucharistic Heart of Jesus

Heart of Jesus in the Eucharist,
I adore you.
Sweet Companion of our exile,
I seek you.
Holy God become man,
I beat with your Heart.

Eucharistic Heart of Jesus,
solitary, abandoned,
humiliated, cursed,
despised, outraged,
ignored by men,
have mercy on us.
Lover of our hearts,
pleading for your beloved,
patiently waiting for us,
eager to hear our confidences,
desirous of our devotion,
have mercy on us.
Heart of grace,
silent and wishing to speak,
refuge of the hidden life,
sharer of the secrets of union with God,
Eucharistic Heart of Jesus,
have mercy on us.

Jesus, Victim, I want to comfort you.
I unite myself with you.
I offer myself in union with you.
I count myself as nothing before you.

I desire to forget myself and think only of you,
to be forgotten and rejected for love of you,
not to be understood, not to be loved, except by you.
I will hold my peace that I may listen to you.
I will forsake myself in order to be lost in you.
Grant that I may quench your thirst for my salvation,
your burning thirst for my sanctification,
and that, being purged, I may give you a true and pure love.
I no longer want to deny your expectations.
Take me. I give myself to you.
I entrust to you all my actions and thoughts—
my mind, that you may enlighten it,
my heart, that you may fill it,
my will, that you may establish it,
my soul and body, that you may feed and sustain them.
Eucharistic Heart of Jesus,
whose Blood is the life of my soul,
may it no longer be I who live,
but you alone who lives in me.

Prayer for the Spread of Perpetual Adoration

Heavenly Father, increase our faith in the Real Presence of your Son Jesus Christ in the Holy Eucharist.
We are obliged to adore him, to give him thanks and to make reparation for sins.
We need your peace in our hearts and among nations.
We need conversion from our sins and the mercy of your forgiveness.
May we obtain this through prayer and our union with the Eucharistic Lord.
Please send down the Holy Spirit upon all peoples to give them the love,
courage, strength, and willingness to respond to the invitation to Eucharistic Adoration.
We beseech you to spread Perpetual Adoration of the Most Blessed Sacrament in parishes around the world.
We ask this in the name of Jesus the Lord. Amen.

Our Lady of the Most Blessed Sacrament,
help us to spread the glory of your Son through Perpetual Adoration.

At the Feet of Christ in the Eucharist

O Jesus, Divine Prisoner of Love, when I consider your love and how you emptied yourself for me, my senses deaden. You hide your inconceivable majesty and lower yourself to miserable me. O King of Glory, though you hide your beauty, yet the eye of my soul rends the veil. I see the angelic choirs giving you honor without cease, and all the heavenly powers praising you without cease, and without cease they are saying: Holy, Holy, Holy.

Oh, who will comprehend your love and your unfathomable mercy toward us! O Prisoner of Love, I lift up my poor heart in this tabernacle that it may adore you without cease night and day. I know of no obstacle in this adoration: and even though I be physically distant, my heart is always with you. Nothing can put a stop to my love for you. No obstacles exist for me. . . .

O Holy Trinity, One and Indivisible God, may you be blessed for this great gift and testament of mercy. Amen.

I adore you, Lord and Creator, hidden in the Most Blessed Sacrament. I adore you for all the works of your hands, that reveal to me so much wisdom, goodness, and mercy, O Lord. You have spread so much beauty over the earth and it tells me about your beauty, even though these beautiful things are but a faint reflection of you, incomprehensible beauty. And although you have hidden yourself and concealed your beauty, my eye, enlightened by faith, reaches you and my souls recognizes its Creator, its Highest Good, and my heart is completely immersed in prayer of adoration.

My Lord and Creator, your goodness encourages me to converse with you. Your mercy abolishes the chasm which separates the Creator from the creature. To converse with you, O Lord, is the delight of my heart. In you I find everything that my heart could desire. Here your light illumines my mind, enabling it to know you more and more deeply. Here streams of grace flow down upon my heart. Here my soul draws eternal life. O my Lord and Creator, you alone, beyond all these gifts, give your own self to me and unite yourself intimately with your miserable creature.

O Christ, let my greatest delight be to see you loved and your praise and glory proclaimed, especially the honor of your mercy. O Christ, let me glorify your goodness and mercy to the last moment of my life, with every drop of my blood and every beat of my heart. Would that I be transformed into a hymn of adoration of you. When I find myself on my deathbed, may the last beat of my heart be a loving hymn glorifying your unfathomable mercy. Amen.

—St. Faustina Kowalska

✳

"Do grant, oh my God,
that when my lips approach yours to kiss you,
I may taste the gall that was given to you;
when my shoulders lean against yours,
make me feel your scourging;
when my flesh is united with yours, in the Holy Eucharist,
make me feel your passion;
when my head comes near yours,
make me feel your thorns;
when my heart is close to yours,
make me feel your spear."

—St. Gemma Galgani

A Prayer to Our Lady of the Most Blessed Sacrament

O Virgin Mary, Our Lady of the Most Blessed Sacrament, the glory of Christians, the joy of the universal Church, and the hope of the world, pray for us. Kindle in all the faithful a lively devotion to the most Holy Eucharist, so that they may all be made worthy to receive Holy Communion every day.

V. Pray for us, O Virgin Immaculate, our Lady of the Most Blessed Sacrament.
R. That the Eucharistic Kingdom of Jesus Christ may come among us!

Litany of the Blessed Sacrament

Christ, have mercy.
Lord, have mercy.

Christ, hear us.
Christ, graciously hear us.

God the Father of heaven,

(Response for below: *Have mercy on us*.)

God the Holy Spirit,
Holy Trinity, one God,
Living Bread, that came down from heaven,
Hidden God and Savior,
Corn of the elect,
Wine whose fruit are virgins,
Bread of fatness, and royal delicacies,
Perpetual Sacrifice,
Clean oblation,
Lamb without spot,
Most pure Feast,
Food of Angels,
Hidden Manna,
Memorial of the wonders of God,
Supersubstantial Bread,
Word made flesh,
Sacred Host,
Mystery of faith,
Most high and adorable Sacrament,
Most holy of all sacrifices,
True Propitiation for the living and the dead,
Heavenly Antidote against the poison of sin,
Most wonderful of all miracles,
Most holy commemoration of the passion of Christ,
Gift transcending all fullness,
Special memorial of divine love,
Affluence of divine bounty,
Most august and holy mystery,
Medicine of immortality,
Tremendous and life-giving sacrament,

Bread made flesh by the omnipotence of the word,
Unbloody sacrifice,
Our feast at once and our fellow-guest,
Sweetest banquet, at which angels minister,
Sacrament of piety,
Bond of charity,
Priest and victim,
Spiritual sweetness tasted in its proper source,
Refreshment of holy souls,
Viaticum of those who die in the Lord,
Pledge of future glory,

Be merciful, spare us, O Lord.
Be merciful, graciously hear us, O Lord.

(Response for below: *O Lord, deliver us.*)

From an unworthy reception of your body and blood,
From the lust of the flesh,
From the lust of the eyes,
From the pride of life,
From every occasion of sin,
Through the desire by which you desired to eat this passover with your disciples,
Through the profound humility by which you washed their feet,
Through that ardent charity by which you instituted this divine sacrament,
Through your precious blood which you have left us on our altars,
Through the five wounds of this your most holy body which you received for us, we sinners,

(Response for below: *We beseech you, hear us.*)

That you would preserve and increase our faith, reverence, and devotion toward this sacrament,
That you would conduct us, through a true confession of our sins, to a frequent reception of the Holy Eucharist,
That you would deliver us from all heresy, evil, and blindness of heart,
That you would impart to us the precious and heavenly fruits of this most holy sacrament,
That at the hour of death you would strengthen and defend us by this heavenly Viaticum,

Son of God, Lamb of God, you take away the sins of the world: Spare us, O Lord.
Lamb of God, you take away the sins of the world: Graciously hear us, O Lord.
Lamb of God, you take away the sins of the world: Have mercy on us, O Lord.

Christ, hear us.
Christ, graciously hear us.

V. You gave them bread from heaven,
R. Containing in itself all sweetness.

Let us pray.

O God, in this wonderful sacrament you left us a memorial of your passion. Grant us so to venerate the sacred mysteries of your body and blood that we may ever continue to feel within us the blessed fruit of your redemption. Who live and reign forever and ever. Amen.

Lauda Sion

Lauda Sion Salvatórem	Sion, lift up thy voice and sing:
Lauda ducem et pastórem	Praise thy Savior and thy King,
In hymnis et cánticis.	Praise with hymns thy shepherd true.
Quantum potes, tantum aude:	All thou canst, do thou endeavour:
Quia major omni laude,	Yet thy praise can equal never
Nec laudáre súfficis.	Such as merits thy great King.
Laudis thema speciális,	See today before us laid
Panis vivus et vitális,	The living and life-giving Bread,
Hódie propónitur.	Theme for praise and joy profound.
Quem in sacræ mensa cœnæ,	The same which at the sacred board
Turbæ fratrum duodénæ	Was, by our incarnate Lord,
Datum non ambígitur.	Giv'n to His Apostles round.
Sit laus plena, sit sonóra,	Let the praise be loud and high:
Sit jucúnda, sit decóra	Sweet and tranquil be the joy
Mentis jubilátio.	Felt today in every breast.
Dies enim solémnis ágitur,	On this festival divine
In qua mensæ prima recólitur	Which records the origin
Hujus institútio.	Of the glorious Eucharist.
In hac mensa novi Regis,	On this table of the King,
Novum Pascha novæ legis,	Our new Paschal offering
Phase vetus términat.	Brings to end the olden rite.
Vetustátem nóvitas,	Here, for empty shadows fled,
Umbram fugat véritas,	Is reality instead,
Noctem lux elíminat.	Here, instead of darkness, light.
Quod in cœna Christus gessit,	His own act, at supper seated
Faciéndum hoc expréssit	Christ ordain'd to be repeated
In sui memóriam.	In His memory divine;
Docti sacris institútis,	Wherefore now, with adoration,
Panem, vinum, in salútis	We, the host of our salvation,
Consecrámus hóstiam.	Consecrate from bread and wine.
Dogma datur Christiánis,	Hear, what holy Church maintaineth,
Quod in carnem transit panis,	That the bread its substance changeth
Et vinum in sánguinem.	Into Flesh, the wine to Blood.
Quod non capis, quod non vides,	Doth it pass thy comprehending?
Animósa firmat fides,	Faith, the law of sight transcending
Præter rerum ordinem.	Leaps to things not understood.
Sub divérsis speciébus,	Here beneath these signs are hidden
Signis tantum, et non rebus,	Priceless things, to sense forbidden,
Latent res exímiæ.	Signs, not things, are all we see.
Caro cibus, sanguis potus:	Flesh from bread, and Blood from wine,

Manet tamen Christus totus,	Yet is Christ in either sign,
Sub utráque spécie.	All entire, confessed to be.
A suménte non concísus,	They, who of Him here partake,
Non confráctus, non divísus:	Sever not, nor rend, nor break:
Integer accípitur.	But, entire, their Lord receive.
Sumit unus, sumunt mille:	Whether one or thousands eat:
Quantum isti, tantum ille:	All receive the self-same meat:
Nec sumptus consúmitur.	Nor the less for others leave.
Sumunt boni, sumunt mali:	Both the wicked and the good
Sorte tamen inæquáli,	Eat of this celestial Food:
Vitæ vel intéritus.	But with ends how opposite!
Mors est malis, vita bonis:	Here ’tis life: and there ’tis death:
Vide paris sumptiónis	The same, yet issuing to each
Quam sit dispar éxitus.	In a difference infinite.
Fracto demum Sacraménto,	Nor a single doubt retain,
Ne vacílles, sed memento,	When they break the Host in twain,
Tantum esse sub fragménto,	But that in each part remains
Quantum toto tégitur.	What was in the whole before.
Nulla rei fit scissúra:	Since the simple sign alone
Signi tantum fit fractúra:	Suffers change in state or form:
Qua nec status nec statúra	The signified remaining one
Signáti minúitur.	And the same for evermore.
Ecce panis Angelórum,	Lo! bread of the Angels broken,
Factus cibus viatórum:	For us pilgrims food, and token
Vere panis fíliórum,	Of the promise by Christ spoken,
Non mittendus cánibus.	Children’s meat, to dogs denied.
In figúris præsignátur,	Shewn in Isaac’s dedication,
Cum Isaac immolátur:	In the manna’s preparation:
Agnus paschæ deputátur	In the Paschal immolation,
Datur manna pátribus.	In old types pre-signified.
Bone pastor, panis vere,	Jesu, shepherd of the sheep:
Jesu, nostri miserére:	Thou thy flock in safety keep,
Tu nos pasce, nos tuére:	Living bread, thy life supply:
Tu nos bona fac vidére	Strengthen us, or else we die,
In terra vivéntium.	Fill us with celestial grace.
Tu, qui cuncta scis et vales:	Thou, who feedest us below:
Qui nos pascis hic mortales:	Source of all we have or know:
Tuos ibi commensáles,	Grant that with thy Saints above,
Cohærédes et sodales,	Sitting at the feast of love,
Fac sanctórum cívium.	We may see thee face to face.
Amen. Allelúja.	Amen. Alleluia.

Litany of the Most Precious Blood of Jesus

V. Lord, have mercy.
R. Lord, have mercy.

V. Christ, have mercy.
R. Christ, have mercy.

V. Lord, have mercy.
R. Lord, have mercy.

V. Jesus, hear us.
R. Jesus, graciously hear us.

V. God, the Father of Heaven,
R. have mercy on us.

V. God, the Son, Redeemer of the world,
R. have mercy on us.

V. God, the Holy Spirit,
R. have mercy on us.

V. Holy Trinity, One God,
R. have mercy on us.

(Response for below: *Save us.*)

Blood of Christ, only-begotten Son of the Eternal Father,
Blood of Christ, Incarnate Word of God,
Blood of Christ, of the New and Eternal Testament,
Blood of Christ, falling upon the earth in the Agony,
Blood of Christ, shed profusely in the Scourging,
Blood of Christ, flowing forth in the Crowning with Thorns,
Blood of Christ, poured out on the Cross,
Blood of Christ, price of our salvation,
Blood of Christ, without which there is no forgiveness.
Blood of Christ, Eucharistic drink and refreshment of souls,
Blood of Christ, stream of mercy,
Blood of Christ, victor over demons,
Blood of Christ, courage of Martyrs,
Blood of Christ, strength of Confessors,
Blood of Christ, bringing forth Virgins,
Blood of Christ, help of those in peril,
Blood of Christ, relief of the burdened,
Blood of Christ, solace in sorrow,

Blood of Christ, hope of the penitent,
Blood of Christ, consolation of the dying,
Blood of Christ, peace and tenderness of hearts,
Blood of Christ, pledge of eternal life,
Blood of Christ, freeing souls from purgatory,
Blood of Christ, most worthy of all glory and honor,

Lamb of God, who take away the sins of the world,
R. spare us, O Lord.

Lamb of God, who take away the sins of the world,
R. graciously hear us, O Lord.

Lamb of God, who take away the sins of the world,
R. have mercy on us.

You have redeemed us, O Lord, in your Blood,
R. and made us, for our God, a kingdom.

Let us pray.

Almighty and eternal God, you have appointed your only-begotten Son the Redeemer of the world, and willed to be appeased by his blood. Grant we beg of you, that we may worthily adore this price of our salvation, and through its power be safeguarded from the evils of the present life, so that we may rejoice in its fruits forever in heaven. Through the same Christ our Lord. *Amen.*

Prayers Before and After Celebrating the Liturgy of the Hours

Merciful Father, you have given us a task that is easy and a burden that is light. Help me now as I fulfill my priestly duties in celebrating with and on behalf of your Church, the Liturgy of the Hours. Guide by prayer and direct my heart that in all my thoughts, words, and deeds, I may be more faithful to your service. Grant this in the name of Jesus the Lord. Amen.

God our Father, I praise your name as I complete my priestly responsibilities in celebrating the Liturgy of the Hours. May my meditation on your Word bear fruit in the lives of your people. I ask this through Christ our Lord.

O Lord, open thou my mouth to bless thy holy name; cleanse my heart also from all vain, evil, and wandering thoughts; enlighten my understanding, kindle my affections, that I may be able to recite this Office worthily, attentively, and devoutly, and may deserve to be heard in the presence of thy divine Majesty. Through Christ our Lord. Amen.

Lord, in union with that divine intention, wherewith thou thyself didst praise God whilst thou wast on earth, I offer these Hours (*or* this Hour) unto thee.

The Priest's Examination of Conscience

A helpful pattern for examination of conscience is to review the Commandments of God and the Precepts of the Church in light of priestly service and living:

1. Have God and the pursuit of sanctity in Christ been the goal of my life as a priest? Have I denied my faith or neglected the proclamation of the Gospel in my daily life? Have I placed my trust in false teachings or substitutes for God? Did I despair of God's mercy?
2. Have I avoided the profane use of God's name in my speech? Have I given scandal to God's people? Have I broken any of my priestly promises?
3. Have I celebrated Mass faithfully and with dignity and recollection? Was I inattentive to the needs of others at Mass? Have I neglected my responsibility to pray the *Liturgy of the Hours*? Have I been faithful in fulfilling my Mass intentions?

4. Have I shown Christlike respect to parents and family members, to my bishop and brother priests, to my staff? Have I been attentive to the religious education and formation of those entrusted to my care?
5. Have I cared for the bodily health and safety of myself and all others? Did I abuse drugs or alcohol? Have I supported in any way a disrespect for life at all stages?
6. Was I impatient, angry, envious, proud, jealous, revengeful, lazy? Have I forgiven others? Have I been disrespectful to those with whom I work?
7. Have I been just in my responsibilities to employer and employees? Have I discriminated against others because of race or other reasons?
8. Have I been chaste in thought and word? Have I used inappropriate sexual humor? Have I given myself sexual gratification? Did I deliberately look at impure television, pictures, reading, or websites?
9. Have I stolen anything from another, from my the parish, from government? If so, am I ready to repay it? Did I fulfill my financial obligations, pay my bills, use my credit responsibly? Did I rashly gamble?
10. Have I spoken ill of any other person? Have I always told the truth? Have I kept secrets and confidences?
11. Have I permitted sexual thoughts about another person?
12. Have I desired what belongs to other people? Have I wished ill on another? Have I spoken harshly about parishioners or staff members?
13. Have I been faithful to the Sacrament of Penance?
14. Have I helped make my parish community stronger and holier? Have I contributed to the support of the Church financially? Have I been generous with my time?
15. Have I done penance by abstaining and fasting on obligatory days? Have I fasted before receiving and celebrating Mass?
16. Have I been mindful of the poor? Do I accept God's will for me?

Receive my confession, O most loving and gracious Lord Jesus Christ, only hope for the salvation of my soul. Grant to me true contrition of soul, so that day and night I may by penance make satisfaction for my many sins. Savior of the world, O good Jesus, who gave yourself to the death of the Cross to save sinners, look upon me, a priest; have pity on me, and give me the light to know my sins, true sorrow for them, and a firm purpose of never committing them again.

O gracious Virgin Mary, Immaculate Mother of Jesus, I implore you to obtain for me by your powerful intercession these graces from your Divine Son.

St. Joseph, pray for me.

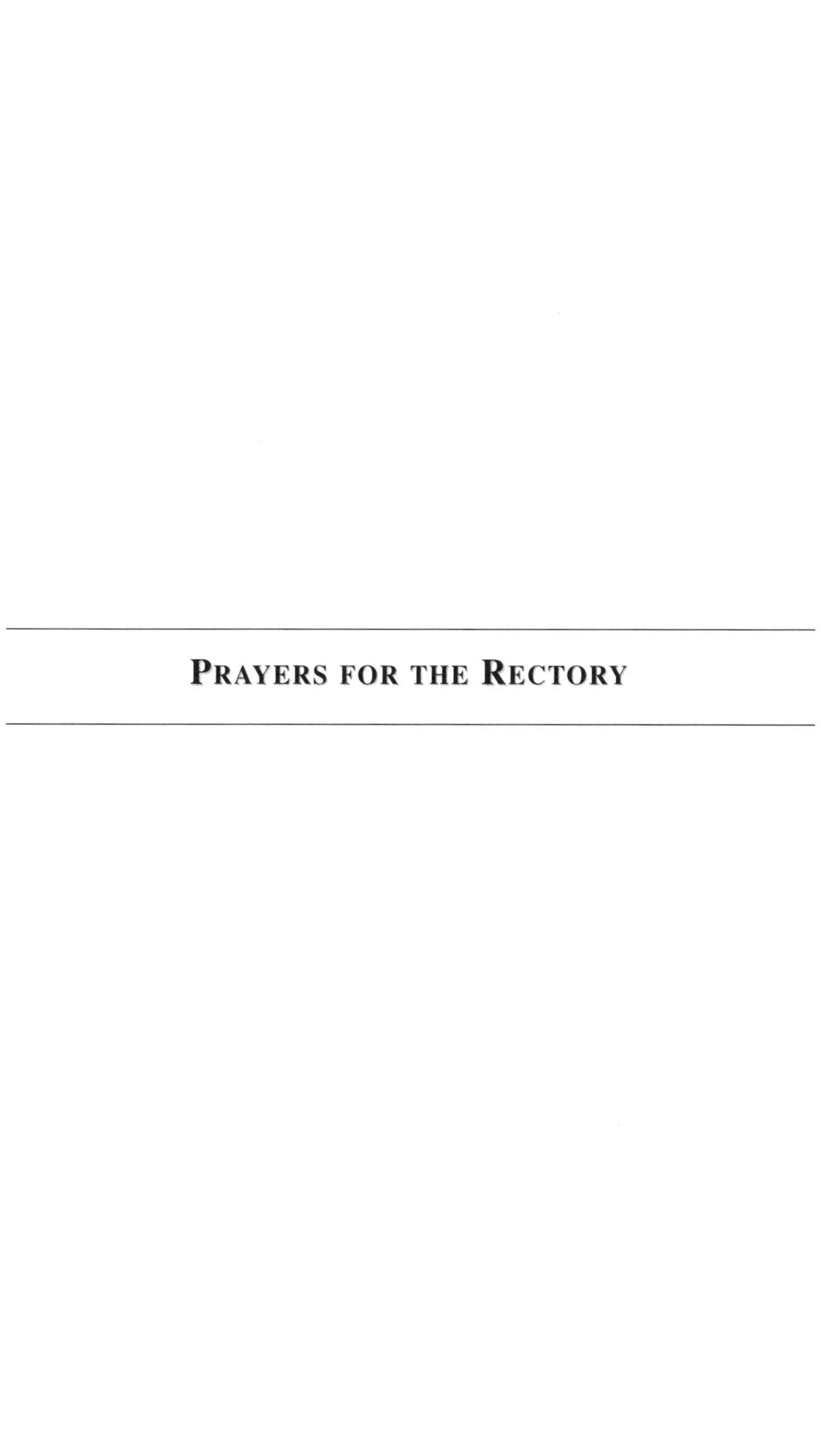

Prayers for the Rectory

Blessing of a New Rectory

+In the name of the Father and of the Son and of the Holy Spirit. Amen

V. Our help is in the name of the Lord.
R. Who made heaven and earth.

V. The Lord be with you.
R. And with your spirit.

Scripture Reading

"Now therefore fear the LORD, and serve him in sincerity and in faithfulness; put away the gods which your fathers served beyond the River, and in Egypt, and serve the LORD. And if you be unwilling to serve the LORD, choose this day whom you will serve, whether the gods your fathers served in the region beyond the River, or the gods of the Amorites in whose land you dwell; but as for me and my house, we will serve the LORD." Then the people answered, "Far be it from us that we should forsake the LORD, to serve other gods; for it is the LORD our God who brought us and our fathers up from the land of Egypt, out of the house of bondage, and who did those great signs in our sight, and preserved us in all the way that we went, and among all the peoples through whom we passed; and the LORD drove out before us all the peoples, the Amorites who lived in the land; therefore we also will serve the LORD, for he is our God."

—Joshua 24:14-18

Prayer of Blessing

At the front doors of the new rectory

V. Open to me the gates of righteousness.
R. And I will enter and give thanks.

V. This is the Lord's own house.
R. Where the just may enter.

Lord God, bless the threshold of this house with your grace. May those who enter here find perfect peace, an abundance of faith, and sincere love for you. May the doors of this house be a portal of charity. Bless the poor and the needy who will find refuge here. Bless all who will live and work here with your love. Through Christ our Lord. Amen.

The rectory is sprinkled from room to room.

Concluding Prayer

Lord God, look with favor on this house and sanctify it for your glory. May the lives of the priests who live here mirror the example of Christ. May this dwelling be a house of prayer after the example of the Holy Family. May all who enter here find a home. We ask this through Christ our Lord. Amen.

Blessing of Parish Offices

+In the name of the Father and of the Son and of the Holy Spirit. Amen.

V. Our help is in the name of the Lord.
R. Who made heaven and earth.

V. The Lord be with you.
R. And with your spirit.

Scripture Reading

Let love be genuine; hate what is evil, hold fast to what is good; love one another with brotherly affection; outdo one another in showing honor. Never flag in zeal, be aglow with the Spirit, serve the Lord. Rejoice in your hope, be patient in tribulation, be constant in prayer. Contribute to the needs of the saints, practice hospitality. Bless those who persecute you; bless and do not curse them. Rejoice with those who rejoice, weep with those who weep. Live in harmony with one another; do not be haughty, but associate with the lowly; never be conceited. Repay no one evil for evil, but take thought for what is noble in the sight of all. If possible, so far as it depends upon you, live peaceably with all.

—Romans 12:9-18

Prayer of Blessing

God our Father, bless + these places of work which we offer for the glory of your name. May the ministry offered here be genuine and filled with zeal. May all who enter here find a welcome as Christ. May all who labor here be filled with contentment and joy. May your servants rejoice here with those who rejoice and weep with those who weep and in their mission find the compassion of Christ in their service to their brothers and sisters. Grant this through Christ our Lord. Amen.

The offices are then sprinkled with holy water.

Blessing of a Rectory Kitchen

+In the name of the Father and of the Son and of the Holy Spirit. Amen.

V. Our help is in the name of the Lord.
R. Who made heaven and earth.

V. The Lord be with you.
R. And with your spirit.

Scripture Reading

Then the word of the LORD came to him, "Arise, go to Zarephath, which belongs to Sidon, and dwell there. Behold, I have commanded a widow there to feed you." So he arose and went to Zarephath; and when he came to the gate of the city, behold, a widow was there gathering sticks; and he called to her and said, "Bring me a little water in a vessel, that I may drink." And as she was going to bring it, he called to her and said, "Bring me a morsel of bread in your hand." And she said, "As the LORD your God lives, I have nothing baked, only a handful of meal in a jar, and a little oil in a jug; and now, I am gathering a couple of sticks, that I may go in and prepare it for myself and my son, that we may eat it, and die." And Elijah said to her, "Fear not; go and do as you have said; but first make me a little cake of it and bring it to me, and afterward make something for yourself and your son. For thus says the LORD the God of Israel, 'The jar of meal shall not be spent, and the jug of oil shall not fail, until the day that the LORD sends rain upon the earth.' " And she went and did as Elijah said; and she, and he, and her household ate for many days.

—1 Kings 17:8-15

Prayer of Blessing

Lord God, bless + this kitchen that we dedicate to your work. In this place may the hungry be fed and the sorrowful find joy. May this kitchen always be a warm hearth for the needy and the lonely. May it be a source of nourishment for your servants and a fountain of hope and an opportunity to love for those who work here. We ask this though Christ our Lord. Amen.

The kitchen is then sprinkled with holy water.

Blessing of a Rectory Oratory

+In the name of the Father and of the Son and of the Holy Spirit. Amen.

V. Our help is in the name of the Lord.
R. Who made heaven and earth.

V. The Lord be with you.
R. And with your spirit.

Scripture Reading

And when you pray, you must not be like the hypocrites; for they love to stand and pray in the synagogues and at the street corners, that they may be seen by men. Truly, I say to you, they have received their reward. But when you pray, go into your room and shut the door and pray to your Father who is in secret; and your Father who sees in secret will reward you. And in praying do not heap up empty phrases as the Gentiles do; for they think that they will be heard for their many words. Do not be like them, for your Father knows what you need before you ask him.
Pray then like this:

Our Father who art in heaven,
Hallowed be thy name.
Thy kingdom come.
Thy will be done,
On earth as it is in heaven.
Give us this day our daily bread;
And forgive us our debts,
As we also have forgiven our debtors;
And lead us not into temptation,
But deliver us from evil.
For if you forgive men their trespasses, your heavenly Father also will forgive you;
but if you do not forgive men their trespasses, neither will your Father forgive your trespasses.

—**Matthew 6:5-15**

Prayer of Blessing

God of all consolation, you teach your holy people to pray without ceasing and you admonish your priests to be foremost men of prayer for the life of your Church. Bless + this room dedicated to priestly prayer. May it serve as a powerhouse for this community of faith and an endless font of petition and thanksgiving. May the priests who pray here daily be filled with zeal for your holy Word and the salvation of souls. Grant this though Christ our Lord. Amen.

The room may be sprinkled with holy water.

Chapels where the Blessed Sacrament is reserved or where Mass is offered should be consecrated according to the prescriptions of the Roman Pontifical.

Blessing of a Rectory Library

+In the name of the Father and of the Son and of the Holy Spirit. Amen.

V. Our help is in the name of the Lord.
R. Who made heaven and earth.

V. The Lord be with you.
R. And with your spirit.

Scripture Reading

And he said to me, "Son of man, eat what is offered to you; eat this scroll, and go, speak to the house of Israel." So I opened my mouth, and he gave me the scroll to eat. And he said to me, "Son of man, eat this scroll that I give you and fill your stomach with it." Then I ate it; and it was in my mouth as sweet as honey.

—Ezekiel 3:1-3

Prayer of Blessing

Merciful God, you enlighten the human mind with your holy Word. Bless + this place of study where your priests find refuge in sacred learning. Inspire their hearts and minds to find you more fully each day in the traditions and teachings of your Holy Church. Give them a greater love of Scripture through their labors in this place and make them fonts of your Wisdom to serve the Body of Christ in fidelity and holiness. Grant this through Christ our Lord. Amen.

Prayers for Gatherings of Priests

BLESSING FOR A SUPPORT GROUP MEETING

+In the name of the Father and of the Son and of the Holy Spirit. Amen.

V. Our help is in the name of the Lord.
R. Who made heaven and earth.

V. The Lord be with you.
R. And with your spirit.

Scripture Reading

So when they had come together, they asked him, "Lord, will you at this time restore the kingdom to Israel?" He said to them, "It is not for you to know times or seasons which the Father has fixed by his own authority. But you shall receive power when the Holy Spirit has come upon you; and you shall be my witnesses in Jerusalem and in all Judea and Samaria and to the end of the earth." And when he had said this, as they were looking on, he was lifted up, and a cloud took him out of their sight. And while they were gazing into heaven as he went, behold, two men stood by them in white robes, and said, "Men of Galilee, why do you stand looking into heaven? This Jesus, who was taken up from you into heaven, will come in the same way as you saw him go into heaven." Then they returned to Jerusalem from the mount called Olivet, which is near Jerusalem, a sabbath day's journey away; and when they had entered, they went up to the upper room, where they were staying, Peter and John and James and Andrew, Philip and Thomas, Bartholomew and Matthew, James the son of Alphaeus and Simon the Zealot and Judas the son of James. All these with one accord devoted themselves to prayer, together with the women and Mary the mother of Jesus, and with his brothers.

—Acts 1:6-14

Prayer of Blessing

Father, we ask you to bless + and sanctify the time we spend together here, supporting one another as priests. You have called us to this ministry and you will give us the grace to live our vocations with conviction and joy. May we be a source of prayer and encouragement for one another. Give each of us the light of your wisdom as we respond to the needs of our brother priests. Help us to pray for one another. We ask this in the name of Jesus, the great High Priest, who is Lord forever and ever. Amen.

Prayers for Cooking

Blessed are you Lord, God of all creation. You give us the fruits of land and sea to nourish and sustain us. Be with me now as I prepare this meal. Bless this food and the fellowship we will share for the nourishment of both body and soul.

Lord, as you flavor our days with grace and love in good measure, help me to blend season and spice with attention and care, so that this meal may be pleasing and good for all who share it.

Prayers for Cleaning

Lord God, out of chaos you brought forth the beauty and order of creation. Be with me now as I sort through my things and bring order to my surroundings. Help me to make a clean and welcoming place for all whom you bring into my life.

Prayers for the Parish Offices

God ever patient and loving, help me to greet all who come to the door with patience and kindness. Help me to see Christ in them and to be Christ for them.

Father, give me the wisdom to use technology prudently and effectively in my work today. Guard me from wasting time so that everything I do may serve good purpose and be of benefit to others.

Prayers for Support Groups

Lord Jesus, as we gather for this time together, help us to truly listen to each other, challenge and encourage each other, and above all cherish each other as brothers in the sacred ministry you have entrusted to us.

Prayers for Brother Priests

Lord Jesus, be close to my brother priests who know hard times, especially (N). Give them the grace of believing anew, for themselves, the words they have so often spoken to comfort others.

Lord Jesus, we pray you to mold and conform us unto yourself a bit more each day. Give us always the joy of your help, and with a spirit of fervor sustain us.

Prayers for Sick and Aging Priests

Loving Father, look kindly on your priests who bear the burdens of advancing years. Sustain the vitality of their souls even as physical strength may fade, so that they may always know the joy of your help and continue to give faith-filled witness to your people.

Prayers for Departed Priests

Almighty and Eternal God, look kindly on the souls of our departed priests. As they devoted themselves to drawing others into the experience of your sacred mysteries here on earth, draw them now into the glory of the never-ending liturgy of heaven.

Merciful Father, on the day of his ordination you conformed (N) more closely to the image of your Son. Bring to completion that good work begun in him so long ago, and grant him the joy of seeing you face to face.

General Prayers for Priests

Prayer for Priests

O Jesus, our great High Priest, hear my humble prayers on behalf of your priests. Give them a deep faith, a bright and firm hope, and a burning love which will ever increase in the course of their priestly life.

In their loneliness, comfort them. In their sorrows, strengthen them. In their frustrations, point out to them that it is through suffering that the soul is purified, and show them that they are needed by the Church; they are needed by souls; they are needed for the work of redemption.

O loving Mother Mary, Mother of Priests, take to your heart your sons who are close to you because of their priestly ordination and because of the power which they have received to carry on the work of Christ in a world which needs them so much. Be their comfort, be their joy, be their strength, and especially help them to live and to defend the ideals of consecrated celibacy.

—*Cardinal John Carberry*

Prayer for Priests by St. Thérèse of Lisieux

O Jesus, Eternal Priest,
keep your priests within the shelter of your Sacred Heart,
where none may touch them.

Keep unstained their anointed hands,
which daily touch your Sacred Body.

Keep unsullied their lips,
daily purpled with your Precious Blood.

Keep pure and unearthly their hearts,
sealed with the sublime mark of the priesthood.

Let your holy love surround them and
shield them from the world's contagion.

Bless their labors with abundant fruit and
may the souls to whom they minister be their joy and consolation here
and in heaven their beautiful and everlasting crown. Amen.

Remember...

If the priest is a saint, his people will be holy.
If the priest is holy, his people will be good.
If the priest is good, his people will be fair.
If the priest is fair, his people will be mediocre.
If the priest is mediocre, his people will be bad.

—*Anonymous*

A Good Priest by Catherine de Hueck Doherty

A priest is a lover of God. A priest is a lover of men.
A priest is a holy man because he walks before the face of the All Holy.
A priest understands all things.
A priest forgives all things.
A priest encompasses all things.

The heart of a priest, like Christ's, is pierced with the lance of love.
The heart of a priest is open, like Christ's, for the whole world to walk through.
The heart of a priest is a vessel of compassion.
The heart of a priest is a chalice of love.
The heart of a priest is the trysting place of human and divine love.

A priest is a man whose goal is to be another Christ.
A priest is a man who lives to serve.
A priest is a man who has crucified himself, so that he too may be lifted up and draw all things to Christ.

A priest is a man in love with God.
A priest is the gift of God to man, and of man to God.
A priest is a symbol of the Word made flesh.
A priest is the naked sword of God's justice.
A priest is the hand of God's mercy.
A priest is the reflection of God's love.

A Parish Priest's Prayer to Mary Most Holy

O Mary, Mother of Jesus Christ, crucified and risen,
Mother of the Church, a priestly people
Mother of priests, ministers of your Son:
accept the humble offering of myself,
so that in my pastoral mission
the infinite mercy of the Eternal High Priest
may be proclaimed:
O "Mother of Mercy."

You who share the "priestly obedience" (Hebrews 10:5-7; Luke 1:38) of your Son,
and who prepared for him a worthy receptacle
by the anointing of the Holy Spirit,
keep my priestly life in the ineffable mystery
of your divine maternity,
"Holy Mother of God."

Grant me strength in the dark hours of this life,
support me in the exertions of my ministry,
entrust me to Jesus,
so that, in communion with you,
I may fulfill the ministry with fidelity and love,
O Mother of the Eternal Priest.

"Queen of Apostles and Help of Priests,"
make me faithful to the flock
entrusted to me by the Good Shepherd.
You silently accompanied Jesus

on his mission to proclaim
the Gospel to the poor.

May I always guide it with patience, sweetness,
firmness and love, caring for the sick, the weak,
thc poor, and sinners,
O "Mother, Help of the Christian People."

I consecrate and entrust myself to you, Mary,
who shared in the work of redemption
at the Cross of your Son,
you who "are inseparably linked to the work of salvation."

Grant that in the exercise of my ministry
I may always be aware of the "stupendous and penetrating dimension
of your maternal presence,"
in every moment of my life, in prayer, and action,
in joy and sorrow, in weariness and in rest,
O "Mother of Trust."

Grant, Holy Mother, that in the celebration of the Eucharist,
source and center of the priestly ministry,
I may live my closeness to him,
so that as "we celebrate Holy Eucharist
you will be present with us"
and introduce us to the redemptive mystery of your divine Son's offering.
"O Mediatrix of all grace flowing from this sacrifice to the Church
and to all the faithful."

O "Mother of Our Savior."

O Mary, I earnestly desire to place my person
and my desire for holiness
under your maternal protection and inspiration
so that you may bring me to that "conformity with Christ, Head and Shepherd"
which is necessary for the ministry of every parish priest.

Make me aware
that "you are always close to priests"
in your mission of servant
of the One Mediator, Jesus Christ,
O "Mother of Priests,"
"Benefactress and Mediatrix" of all graces. Amen.

A Prayer for All Priests

Heavenly Father,
grant that all priests
be strengthened and healed by the
power of the Eucharist they celebrate.
May the Word they proclaim give them
courage and wisdom.

We pray that all those whom they
seek to serve may see in them
the love and care of Jesus,
our Eternal High Priest, who is Lord
for ever and ever. Amen.

Mary, Mother of the Church,
Look tenderly upon your sons, our priests.

Joseph, patron of the universal Church,
pray for us all.

***Prayer to the Virgin Mary for Priests* by Saint John Paul II**

O Mary,
Mother of Jesus Christ and Mother of priests,
accept this title which we bestow on you
to celebrate your motherhood
and to contemplate with you the priesthood
of your Son and of your sons,
O holy Mother of God.

O Mother of Christ,
to the Messiah-priest you gave a body of flesh
through the anointing of the Holy Spirit
for the salvation of the poor and the contrite of heart;
guard priests in your heart and in the Church,
O Mother of the Savior.

O Mother of Faith,
you accompanied to the temple the Son of Man,
the fulfillment of the promises given to the fathers;
give to the Father for his glory
the priests of your Son,
O Ark of the Covenant.

O Mother of the Church,
in the midst of the disciples in the upper room
you prayed to the Spirit
for the new people and their shepherds;
obtain for the Order of Presbyters
a full measure of gifts,
O Queen of the Apostles.

O Mother of Jesus Christ,
you were with him at the beginning
of his life and mission,
you sought the Master among the crowd,
you stood beside him when he was lifted up from the earth
consumed as the one eternal sacrifice,
and you had John, your son, near at hand;
accept from the beginning those who have been called,
protect their growth,
in their life ministry accompany your sons,
O Mother of Priests. Amen.

Prayer for Priests

Eternal God,
please bless our priests,
who represent you on this earth.
Make them more greatly aware of the grace
that you pour out through them
when they minister the sacraments,
and help them to fall more deeply in love with you
after each and every Mass that they celebrate.
Please strengthen our priests,
who shepherd your flock,
when they are in doubt of their faith,
that they may be examples of your truth
and guide us always on the path to you.
We ask these things of you our Eternal Priest. Amen.

A Prayer for Priests

Most gracious Heavenly Father,

We thank you for our faithful priests and bishops, whose spiritual fatherhood and example of fidelity, self-sacrifice, and devotion is so vital to the faith of your people.

May our spiritual fathers be guided by the examples of saints Peter and Paul, all the apostles and their saintly successors. Give them valiant faith in the face of confusion and conflict, hope in time of trouble and sorrow, and steadfast love for you, for their families, and for all your people throughout the world. May the light of your truth shine through their lives and their good works.

Assist all spiritual fathers, that through your grace they may steadily grow in holiness and in knowledge and understanding of your truth. May they generously impart this knowledge to those who rely on them.

Through Christ, our Lord. Amen.

✳

O Almighty, Eternal God, look upon the face of your Son and for love of him, who is the Eternal High Priest, have pity on your priests. Remember, O most compassionate God, that they are but weak and frail human beings. Stir up in them the grace of their vocation which is in them by the imposition of the bishop's hands. Keep them close to you, lest the enemy prevail against them, so that they may never do anything in the slightest degree unworthy of their sublime vocation.

—Cardinal Richard Cushing

✳

Lord our God, you guide your people by the ministry of priests.
Keep them faithful in obedient service to you
that by their life and ministry they may bring you glory in Christ.
We ask this through our Lord Jesus Christ, your Son,
Who lives and reigns with you and the Holy Spirit, one God, for ever and ever. Amen.

✳

Lord Jesus, Chief Shepherd of the flock, we pray that in the great love and mercy of your Sacred Heart you attend to all the needs of your priest-shepherds throughout the world. We ask that you draw back to your Heart all those priests who have seriously strayed from your path, that you rekindle the desire for holiness in the hearts of those priests who have become lukewarm, and that you continue to give your fervent priests the desire for the highest holiness. United with your Heart and Mary's Heart, we ask that you take this petition to your heavenly Father in the unity of the Holy Spirit. Amen.

***The Beautiful Hands of a Priest* (poem by an unknown author)**

We need them in life's early morning,
We need them again at its close;
We feel their warm clasp of true friendship,
We seek them when tasting life's woes.

At the altar each day we behold them,
and the hands of a king on his throne
are not equal to them in their greatness;
Their dignity stands all alone;

And when we are tempted and wander,
to pathways of shame and of sin,
it's the hand of a priest that will absolve us,
not once, but again and again.

And when we are taking life's partner,
other hands may prepare us a feast,
but the hand that will bless and unite us
is the beautiful hand of a priest.

God bless them and keep them all holy,
for the Host which their fingers caress;
When can a poor sinner do better
than to ask Him to guide thee and bless?

When the hour of death comes upon us,
may our courage and strength be increased,
by seeing raised over us in blessing
the beautiful hands of a priest.

Blessing at the Beginning of a Retreat

+In the name of the Father and of the Son and of the Holy Spirit. Amen.

V. Our help is in the name of the Lord.
R. Who made heaven and earth.

V. The Lord be with you.
R. And with your spirit.

Scripture Reading

He came out, and went, as was his custom, to the Mount of Olives; and the disciples followed him. And when he came to the place he said to them,

"Pray that you may not enter into temptation." And he withdrew from them about a stone's throw, and knelt down and prayed, "Father, if thou art willing, remove this cup from me; nevertheless not my will, but thine, be done." And when he rose from prayer, he came to the disciples and found them sleeping for sorrow, and he said to them, "Why do you sleep? Rise and pray that you may not enter into temptation."

—Luke 22:39-46

Prayer of Blessing

God of all consolation, you call us to the activity of ministry and to times of retreat to contemplate your Spirit in our lives. Bless + these priests in their time of prayer and retreat. Refresh and renew them in their commitment to their priestly lives and ministry and draw them together into that Kingdom where you live and reign with the Son and Holy Spirit, God forever and ever. Amen.

Blessing at the Close of a Retreat

+In the name of the Father and of the Son and of the Holy Spirit. Amen.

V. Our help is in the name of the Lord.
R. Who made heaven and earth.

V. The Lord be with you.
R. And with your spirit.

Scripture Reading

Then he said to them, "These are my words which I spoke to you, while I was still with you, that everything written about me in the law of Moses and the prophets and the psalms must be fulfilled." Then he opened their minds to understand the scriptures, and said to them, "Thus it is written, that the Christ should suffer and on the third day rise from the dead, and that repentance and forgiveness of sins should be preached in his name to all nations, beginning from Jerusalem. You are witnesses of these things. And behold, I send the promise of my Father upon you; but stay in the city, until you are clothed with power from on high." Then he led them out as far as Bethany, and lifting up his hands he blessed them. While he blessed them, he parted from them, and was carried up into heaven. And they returned to Jerusalem with great joy, and were continually in the temple blessing God.

—Luke 24:44-53

Prayer of Blessing

God of beginnings and endings, fulfill in our lives the promise of your Word that we have heard and meditated on in this retreat. Bless + these priests as they return to their places of ministry. Help them to return with great joy having received in these days the Spirit of Consolation and the Presence of the One who offered himself as a sacrifice for the life of the world. Go with them as they return to your faithful people. Be their strength and guide. Grant this through Christ our Lord. Amen.

Blessing for the Opening of Study Days or Convocations

+In the name of the Father and of the Son and of the Holy Spirit. Amen.

V. Our help is in the name of the Lord.
R. Who made heaven and earth.

V. The Lord be with you.
R. And with your spirit.

Scripture Reading

The precepts of the Lord are right,
they gladden the heart.
The command of the Lord is clear,
it gives light to the eyes.

The fear of the Lord is holy,
abiding for ever.
The decrees of the Lord are truth
and all of them just.

They are more to be desired than gold,
than the purest of gold
and sweeter are they than honey,
than honey from the comb.

So in them your servant finds instruction;
great reward is in their keeping.
But can we discern all our errors?
From hidden faults acquit us.

From presumption restrain your servant
and let it not rule me.

Then shall I be blameless,
clean from grave sin.

May the spoken words of my mouth,
the thoughts of my heart,
win favor in your sight, O Lord,
my rescuer, my rock!

—Psalm 19

Prayer of Blessing

All powerful God, you give strength to those in need and wisdom to those who seek. Open our hearts and minds to receive the teaching of these days. Strengthen our fellowship with one another. Bless + your priests with righteousness and peace. May the spoken words of these days and the thoughts presented in these conferences win favor in your sight. We ask this through Christ our Lord. Amen.

Blessing for the Closing of Study Days or Convocations

+In the name of the Father and of the Son and of the Holy Spirit. Amen.

V. Our help is in the name of the Lord.
R. Who made heaven and earth.

V. The Lord be with you.
R. And with your spirit.

Scripture Reading

And he said to them, "Go into all the world and preach the gospel to the whole creation. He who believes and is baptized will be saved; but he who does not believe will be condemned. And these signs will accompany those who believe: in my name they will cast out demons; they will speak in new tongues; they will pick up serpents, and if they drink any deadly thing, it will not hurt them; they will lay their hands on the sick, and they will recover." So then the Lord Jesus, after he had spoken to them, was taken up into heaven, and sat down at the right hand of God. And they went forth and preached everywhere, while the Lord worked with them and confirmed the message by the signs that attended it. Amen.

—Mark 16:15-20

Prayer of Blessing

Almighty Father, you have given us this privileged time apart. Bless + us as we return to our parishes and workplaces. May the renewal of these days and the thoughts and ideas we have shared bear fruit in the vineyard of your service. Grant this through Christ our Lord. Amen.

Prayers for Priests on Retreat

Keep them, I pray thee, dearest Lord, keep them, for they are thine—
thy priests whose lives burn out before thy consecrated shrine.
Keep them, for they are in the world, though from the world apart;
when earthly pleasures tempt, allure—shelter them in thy heart.
Keep them, and comfort them in hours of loneliness and pain,
when all their lives of sacrifice for souls seems but in vain.
Keep them, and O remember, Lord, they have no one but thee,
yet they have only human hearts, with human frailty.
Keep them as spotless as the Host, that daily they caress;
their every thoughts and word and deed, deign, dearest Lord, to bless.
Our Father...
Hail Mary...
Glory Be...

Prayers for Parish Staffs

Blessing at the Beginning of a Parish Staff Meeting

+In the name of the Father and of the Son and of the Holy Spirit. Amen.

V. Our help is in the name of the Lord.
R. Who made heaven and earth.

V. The Lord be with you.
R. And with your spirit.

Scripture Reading

Jesus said to Simon Peter, "Simon, son of John, do you love me more than these?" He said to him, "Yes, Lord; you know that I love you." He said to him, "Feed my lambs." A second time he said to him, "Simon, son of John, do you love me?" He said to him, "Yes, Lord; you know that I love you." He said to him, "Tend my sheep." He said to him the third time, "Simon, son of John, do you love me?" Peter was grieved because he said to him the third time, "Do you love me?" And he said to him, "Lord, you know everything; you know that I love you." Jesus said to him, "Feed my sheep. Truly, truly, I say to you, when you were young, you girded yourself and walked where you would; but when you are old, you will stretch out your hands, and another will gird you and carry you where you do not wish to go." (This he said to show by what death he was to glorify God.) And after this he said to him, "Follow me."

—John 21:15-19

Prayer of Blessing

Father, you have called each of us in our various offices to fulfill the mission of our Lord Jesus Christ whom you anointed as priest, prophet, and king. Bless + the work of this parish staff. May our deliberations be holy and judicious. May our decisions be filled with charity and compassion. Give success to all our labors and joy to all our ministry. We ask this in the name of Jesus the Lord. Amen.

Blessing at the Conclusion of a Parish Staff Meeting

+In the name of the Father and of the Son and of the Holy Spirit. Amen.

V. Our help is in the name of the Lord.
R. Who made heaven and earth.

V. The Lord be with you.
R. And with your spirit.

Scripture Reading

Grace was given to each of us according to the measure of Christ's gift. Therefore it is said, "When he ascended on high he led a host of captives, and he gave gifts to men." (In saying, "He ascended," what does it mean but that he had also descended into the lower parts of the earth? He who descended is he who also ascended far above all the heavens, that he might fill all things.) And his gifts were that some should be apostles, some prophets, some evangelists, some pastors and teachers, to equip the saints for the work of ministry, for building up the body of Christ, until we all attain to the unity of the faith and of the knowledge of the Son of God, to mature manhood, to the measure of the stature of the fullness of Christ; so that we may no longer be children, tossed to and fro and carried about with every wind of doctrine, by the cunning of men, by their craftiness in deceitful wiles. Rather, speaking the truth in love, we are to grow up in every way into him who is the head, into Christ, from whom the whole body, joined and knit together by every joint with which it is supplied, when each part is working properly, makes bodily growth and upbuilds itself in love.

—Ephesians 4:7-16

Prayer of Blessing

Lord God, give growth to your people in holiness through the work this parish staff has accomplished today. You have called us all through our particular gifts to serve you and the Body of Christ in faith, love, and hope. Give maturity to our efforts and build this community of faith in your likeness. We ask this through Christ our Lord. Amen.

Blessing at the Beginning of Parish Council Meetings

+In the name of the Father and of the Son and of the Holy Spirit. Amen.

V. Our help is in the name of the Lord.
R. Who made heaven and earth.

V. The Lord be with you.
R. And with your spirit.

Scripture Reading

Jesus said to Simon Peter, "Simon, son of John, do you love me more than these?" He said to him, "Yes, Lord; you know that I love you." He said to him, "Feed my lambs." A second time he said to him, "Simon, son of John, do you love me?" He said to him, "Yes, Lord; you know that I love you." He said to him, "Tend my sheep." He said to him the third time, "Simon, son of John, do you love me?" Peter was grieved because he said to him the third time, "Do you love me?" And he said to him, "Lord, you know everything; you know that I love you." Jesus said to him, "Feed my sheep. Truly, truly, I say to you, when you were young, you girded yourself and walked where you would; but when you are old, you will stretch out your hands, and another will gird you and carry you where you do not wish to go." (This he said to show by what death he was to glorify God.) And after this he said to him, "Follow me."

—John 21:15-19

Prayer of Blessing

God of power and might, you call us from our various walks of life and with our many gifts to feed and tend your flock. Bless + the work of this parish council. May its deliberations be peaceful and productive. May their outcome give life and joy to your Church through the grace offered by the presence of this parish community. May each one of us here be enriched by our labors and follow you more closely in our lives. Through Christ our Lord. Amen.

Blessing at the Conclusion of Parish Council Meetings

+In the name of the Father and of the Son and of the Holy Spirit. Amen.

V. Our help is in the name of the Lord.
R. Who made heaven and earth.

V. The Lord be with you.
R. And with your spirit.

Scripture Reading

Do all things without grumbling or questioning, that you may be blameless and innocent, children of God without blemish in the midst of a crooked and perverse generation, among whom you shine as lights in the world, holding fast the word of life, so that in the day of Christ I may be proud that I did not run in vain or labor in vain. Even if I am to be poured as a libation upon the sacrificial offering of your faith, I am glad and rejoice with you all. Likewise you also should be glad and rejoice with me.

—Philippians 2:14-18

Prayer of Blessing

Lord Jesus Christ in our ministry to this parish community you have given us a task that is easy and a burden that is light. Through our work here, may this parish truly shine in this neighborhood as a beacon of Gospel light. Continue to bless + each one present as we run the race you have set before us in calling us to be your followers. Let us rejoice and be glad in all things. Bring us all at last to that Kingdom where you reign with the Father and the Holy Spirit, God forever and ever. Amen.

Blessing at the Beginning of Finance Council Meetings

+In the name of the Father and of the Son and of the Holy Spirit. Amen.

V. Our help is in the name of the Lord.
R. Who made heaven and earth.

V. The Lord be with you.
R. And with your spirit.

Scripture Reading

Continue steadfastly in prayer, being watchful in it with thanksgiving; and pray for us also, that God may open to us a door for the word, to declare the mystery of Christ, on account of which I am in prison, that I may make it clear, as I ought to speak. Conduct yourselves wisely toward outsiders, making the most of the time. Let your speech always be gracious, seasoned with salt, so that you may know how you ought to answer every one.

—Colossians 4:2-6

Prayer of Blessing

Lord Jesus Christ you have entrusted us with the task of serving your Church through the ministry of oversight. Help us to be worthy stewards of the gifts of time, talent, and treasure that you have given us. Bless + the conversation and decisions of this finance council. Amen.

Blessing at the Conclusion of Finance Council Meetings

+In the name of the Father and of the Son and of the Holy Spirit. Amen.

V. Our help is in the name of the Lord.
R. Who made heaven and earth.

V. The Lord be with you.
R. And with your spirit.

Scripture Reading

But we beseech you, brethren, to respect those who labor among you and are over you in the Lord and admonish you, and to esteem them very highly in love because of their work. Be at peace among yourselves. And we exhort you, brethren, admonish the idlers, encourage the fainthearted, help the weak, be patient with them all. See that none of you repays evil for evil, but always seek to do good to one another and to all. Rejoice always, pray constantly, give thanks in all circumstances; for this is the will of God in Christ Jesus for you. Do not quench the Spirit, do not despise prophesying, but test everything; hold fast to what is good, abstain from every form of evil. May the God of peace himself sanctify you wholly; and may your spirit and soul and body be kept sound and blameless at the coming of our Lord Jesus Christ. He who calls you is faithful, and he will do it.

—1 Thessalonians 5:12-24

Prayer of Blessing

God, you called us to this meeting to consider the stewardship needs of our parish. Having been open to your Spirit, we now ask to bless + the work of our minds and hands that our decisions here may be for the good of your Church, the love of our brothers and sisters, and care for the resources you have bestowed on us in your kindness and generosity. Give prosperity to the work of this parish community. Keep our spirits, souls, and bodies blameless in your sight in anticipation of the coming of our Lord Jesus Christ, who lives and reigns with you and the Holy Spirit, God forever and ever. Amen.

Blessing at the Beginning of School Board Meetings

+In the name of the Father and of the Son and of the Holy Spirit. Amen.

V. Our help is in the name of the Lord.
R. Who made heaven and earth.

V. The Lord be with you.
R. And with your spirit.

Scripture Reading

Command and teach these things. Let no one despise your youth, but set the believers an example in speech and conduct, in love, in faith, in purity. Till I come, attend to the public reading of scripture, to preaching, to teaching. Do not neglect the gift you have, which was given you by prophetic utterance when the council of elders laid their hands upon you. Practice these duties, devote yourself to them, so that all may see your progress. Take heed to yourself and to your teaching; hold to that, for by so doing you will save both yourself and your hearers.

—1 Timothy 4:11-16

Prayer of Blessing

Lord, you have entrusted to us the enrichment of our greatest resource, our young. Bless the discussions of this school board. May the decisions made here build up the children entrusted to our care, nourishing their minds, strengthening their bodies, and giving life to your Spirit living in them. Give us the wisdom of your Spirit and help us to devote this work totally to you. Through Christ our Lord. Amen.

Blessing at the Conclusion of School Board Meetings

+In the name of the Father and of the Son and of the Holy Spirit. Amen.

V. Our help is in the name of the Lord.
R. Who made heaven and earth.

V. The Lord be with you.
R. And with your spirit.

Scripture Reading

For God loves nothing so much as the one who lives with wisdom. For she is more beautiful than the sun, and excels every constellation of the stars. Compared with the light she is found to be superior, for it is succeeded by the night, but against wisdom evil does not prevail. She reaches mightily from one end of the earth to the other, and she orders all things well. I loved her and sought her from my youth.

—Wisdom 7:28-8:2a

Prayer of Blessing

Holy Spirit, enliven our hearts with your wisdom. Make us open to be vessels of your grace as we have considered the education of our children. Bless + the continuing work of this school board with your presence and draw us into that Kingdom where you live and reign with the Father and the Son, God forever and ever. Amen.

Blessing to Open Inservice Days

+In the name of the Father and of the Son and of the Holy Spirit. Amen.

V. Our help is in the name of the Lord.
R. Who made heaven and earth.

V. The Lord be with you.
R. And with your spirit.

Scripture Reading

Preserve me, O God, for in thee I take refuge.
I say to the LORD, "Thou art my Lord;
I have no good apart from thee."
As for the saints in the land, they are the noble,
in whom is all my delight.
Those who choose another god multiply their sorrows;
their libations of blood I will not pour out
or take their names upon my lips.
The LORD is my chosen portion and my cup;
thou holdest my lot.
The lines have fallen for me in pleasant places;
yea, I have a goodly heritage.
I bless the LORD who gives me counsel;
in the night also my heart instructs me.
I keep the LORD always before me;
because he is at my right hand, I shall not be moved.
Therefore my heart is glad, and my soul rejoices;
my body also dwells secure.
For thou dost not give me up to Sheol,
or let thy godly one see the Pit.
Thou dost show me the path of life;
in thy presence there is fullness of joy,
in thy right hand are pleasures for evermore.

—Psalm 16

Prayer of Blessing

God our Father, you renew us each year in our vocations as educators of our children. Bless + these ministers of education, these teachers and administrators, as they begin the work of this academic year. Help them to form your children by always giving them counsel and instructing their hearts in their service to you. Give them glad hearts in their work and joy in their vocations in the name of the great Teacher, Jesus Christ, who is Lord forever and ever. Amen.

Blessing to Close Inservice Days

+In the name of the Father and of the Son and of the Holy Spirit. Amen.

V. Our help is in the name of the Lord.
R. Who made heaven and earth.

V. The Lord be with you.
R. And with your spirit.

Scripture Reading

The word that came to Jeremiah from the Lord: "Arise, and go down to the potter's house, and there I will let you hear my words." So I went down to the potter's house, and there he was working at his wheel. And the vessel he was making of clay was spoiled in the potter's hand, and he reworked it into another vessel, as it seemed good to the potter to do. Then the word of the Lord came to me: "O house of Israel, can I not do with you as this potter has done? says the Lord. Behold, like the clay in the potter's hand, so are you in my hand, O house of Israel."

—Jeremiah 18:1-6

Prayer of Blessing

Lord Jesus, you have renewed us in this time of service and deliberation as we prepare for a new year of education and formation of your children. Bless + these teachers and administrators as they carry out the evangelization of the young, drawing them more closely this year into the light of the Gospel and the tradition of the Catholic faith. Be a source of inspiration for them in good times and in difficult times. Bring them all at last into the joy of the Kingdom where you live and reign with the Father and the Holy Spirit, one God forever and ever. Amen.

Blessing for the Opening of the School Year

+In the name of the Father and of the Son and of the Holy Spirit. Amen.

V. Our help is in the name of the Lord.
R. Who made heaven and earth.

V. The Lord be with you.
R. And with your spirit.

Scripture Reading

For the grace of God has appeared for the salvation of all men, training us to renounce irreligion and worldly passions, and to live sober, upright, and godly lives in this world, awaiting our blessed hope, the appearing of the glory of our great God and Savior Jesus Christ, who gave himself for us to redeem us from all iniquity and to purify for himself a people of his own who are zealous for good deeds. Declare these things; exhort and reprove with all authority. Let no one disregard you.

—Titus 2:11-15

The teachers will now renew their commitment to education and formation in these words:

We the teachers of (N) school renew our commitment to be men and women of integrity. We promise to give our students the best of our talents and our gifts.
We promise to set a good example for them to follow in living the Christian life.
We promise to teach them wisely the ways of discipleship that they might be strengthened in Christian holiness.
We make these promises in the name of Jesus the Lord.

The parents will now renew their commitment to support the education of their children in these words:

We parents promise to love our children with the unfailing love of Christian parents.
We promise to support the work of education carried out in this school.
We promise to be good examples of discipleship for our children to follow.
We promise to be the first and best teachers, giving wisdom and strength to our children.
We make these promises in the name of Jesus the Lord.

The children will now renew their commitment to study and be formed in ways that seem appropriate for the ages of the students.

Prayer of Blessing

God our Father, you call all people to hear your word and be taught by the example of Christ your Son. Bless + this new school year. Give holiness and wisdom to the teachers. Give prudence and the blessing of good example to our parents. Give open hearts and minds to our children as all together we strive to do your will in our lives. This we ask through Christ our Lord. Amen.

The assembly is then blessed with holy water.

Blessing of School Administrators

+In the name of the Father and of the Son and of the Holy Spirit. Amen.

V. Our help is in the name of the Lord.
R. Who made heaven and earth.

V. The Lord be with you.
R. And with your spirit.

Scripture Reading

I charge you in the presence of God and of Christ Jesus who is to judge the living and the dead, and by his appearing and his kingdom: preach the word, be urgent in season and out of season, convince, rebuke, and exhort, be unfailing in patience and in teaching. For the time is coming when people will not endure sound teaching, but having itching ears they will accumulate for themselves teachers to suit their own likings, and will turn away from listening to the truth and wander into myths. As for you, always be steady, endure suffering, do the work of an evangelist, fulfill your ministry.

—2 Timothy 4:1-5

Prayer of Blessing

Christ our Teacher, you have given us an example of patience and gentleness in your ministry. Give wisdom, understanding, and a fearless spirit to our school administrators that they may fulfill their ministry to our children and be guides and sources of encouragement for our community. May they convince, exhort, and call to conversion all who come to this school and thereby give life to your Church, drawing us all to that Kingdom where you live and reign with the Father and the Holy Spirit, God forever and ever. Amen.

The assembly may then be sprinkled with holy water.

Blessing of Teachers

+In the name of the Father and of the Son and of the Holy Spirit. Amen.

V. Our help is in the name of the Lord.
R. Who made heaven and earth.

V. The Lord be with you.
R. And with your spirit.

Scripture Reading

Who is wise and understanding among you? By his good life let him show his works in the meekness of wisdom. But if you have bitter jealousy and selfish ambition in your hearts, do not boast and be false to the truth. This wisdom is not such as comes down from above, but is earthly, unspiritual, devilish. For where jealousy and selfish ambition exist, there will be disorder and every vile practice. But the wisdom from above is first pure, then peaceable, gentle, open to reason, full of mercy and good fruits, without uncertainty or insincerity. And the harvest of righteousness is sown in peace by those who make peace.

—James 3:13-18

Prayer of Blessing

Source of all wisdom and understanding, give light to the minds and eyes of our teachers that they may be sure guides for the children of this school. Keep them ever faithful to your teaching, leading holy and righteous lives in the spirit of the Gospel. May they be true evangelists, peaceable, gentle, open to reason, and full of mercy, and thereby draw all who come to this school into the joy of that Kingdom where you live and reign forever and ever. Amen.

The teachers may then be sprinkled with holy water or come forward and have the sign of the cross traced on their foreheads as the priest says:

Show his works in the meekness of wisdom in the name of the Father and of the Son and of the Holy Spirit.

Amen.

Blessing for the Closing of the School Year

+In the name of the Father and of the Son and of the Holy Spirit. Amen.

V. Our help is in the name of the Lord.
R. Who made heaven and earth.

V. The Lord be with you.
R. And with your spirit.

Scripture Reading

My little children, I am writing this to you so that you may not sin; but if any one does sin, we have an advocate with the Father, Jesus Christ the righteous; and he is the expiation for our sins, and not for ours only but also for the sins of the whole world. And by this we may be sure that we know him, if we keep his commandments. He who says "I know him" but disobeys his commandments is a liar, and the truth is not in him; but whoever keeps his word, in him truly love for God is perfected. By this we may be sure that we are in him: he who says he abides in him ought to walk in the same way in which he walked.

—1 John 2:1-6

Prayer of Blessing

Lord Jesus Christ, you have called us into the Kingdom of Righteousness and given us the plan of perfection in the Gospel. Bless + this school. May all who go forth from this place be witnesses to the love and wisdom they have received here. Keep them safe in your love and provident care. Preserve our graduates in every good work and bless the efforts of our teachers and staff in this time of renewal and continued learning. Make us all one with you in that Kingdom where you reign with the Father and the Holy Spirit, one God forever and ever. Amen.

The school then comes forward as the priest makes the sign of the cross on their foreheads saying:

Go forth in the peace of Christ.

Amen.

Blessing for the Opening of a Religious Education Term

+In the name of the Father and of the Son and of the Holy Spirit. Amen.

V. Our help is in the name of the Lord.
R. Who made heaven and earth.

V. The Lord be with you.
R. And with your spirit.

Scripture Reading

Everyone who believes that Jesus is the Christ is a child of God, and everyone who loves the parent loves the child. By this we know that we love the children of God, when we love God and obey his commandments. For this is the love of God, that we keep his commandments. And his commandments are not burdensome. For whatever is born of God overcomes the world; and this is the victory that overcomes the world, our faith. Who is it that overcomes the world but he who believes that Jesus is the Son of God?

—1 John 5:1-5

Prayer of Blessing

Lord God, you call all Christians to learn from you after the example of your Son, Jesus Christ. Bless + your people as we begin this new religious education term. Bless the teachers, parents, and children who will teach and learn your Word this year. Keep us all on the path that leads to you. We ask this through Christ our Lord. Amen.

The assembly comes forward and the priest traces the sign of the cross on their foreheads saying:

Receive Wisdom from above, the Father and the Son and the Holy Spirit.

Amen.

Blessing of Religious Educators

+In the name of the Father and of the Son and of the Holy Spirit. Amen.

V. Our help is in the name of the Lord.
R. Who made heaven and earth.

V. The Lord be with you.
R. And with your spirit.

Scripture Reading

See what love the Father has given us, that we should be called children of God; and so we are. The reason why the world does not know us is that it did not know him. Beloved, we are God's children now; it does not yet appear what we shall be, but we know that when he appears we shall be like him, for we shall see him as he is. And everyone who thus hopes in him purifies himself as he is pure.

—1 John 3:1-3

Prayer of Blessing

Source of all wisdom and understanding, give light to the minds and eyes of our religious educators and catechists that they may be sure guides for the children of this parish. Keep them ever faithful to your teaching, leading holy and righteous lives in the spirit of the Gospel. May they be true evangelists, peaceable, gentle, open to reason, and full of mercy, and thereby draw all who come to this school into the joy of that Kingdom where you live and reign forever and ever. Amen.

Blessing of Parents

+In the name of the Father and of the Son and of the Holy Spirit. Amen.

V. Our help is in the name of the Lord.
R. Who made heaven and earth.

V. The Lord be with you.
R. And with your spirit.

Scripture Reading

A good name is to be chosen rather than great riches,
and favor is better than silver or gold.
The rich and the poor meet together;
the LORD is the maker of them all.
A prudent man sees danger and hides himself;
but the simple go on, and suffer for it.
The reward for humility and fear of the LORD
is riches and honor and life.
Thorns and snares are in the way of the perverse;
he who guards himself will keep far from them.
Train up a child in the way he should go,
and when he is old he will not depart from it.

—Proverbs 22:1-6

Prayer of Blessing

Lord God, you have called all Christian parents to be the first and best catechists for their children. Bless + these parents and give them insight into your Word and the teachings of your Church. May they be true sources of inspiration for their children. We ask this in the name of Jesus the Lord. Amen.

Blessing of New Staff Members

+In the name of the Father and of the Son and of the Holy Spirit. Amen.

V. Our help is in the name of the Lord.
R. Who made heaven and earth.

V. The Lord be with you.
R. And with your spirit.

Scripture Reading

Unless the LORD builds the house,
those who build it labor in vain.
Unless the LORD watches over the city,
the watchman stays awake in vain.
It is in vain that you rise up early
and go late to rest,
eating the bread of anxious toil;
for he gives to his beloved sleep.
Lo, sons are a heritage from the LORD,
the fruit of the womb a reward.
Like arrows in the hand of a warrior
are the sons of one's youth.
Happy is the man who has
his quiver full of them!
He shall not be put to shame
when he speaks with his enemies in the gate.

—Psalm 127

Prayer of Blessing

God the Giver of all good things, from age to age you call men and women to your service. Bless + (N) as he (she) begins his (her) service to the people of this parish community. May (he, she) be a source of blessing in his (her) work. May we be a sourcc of inspiration for him (her). Continue to build our parish community in love through the work of our hands and draw us all to that Kingdom where you live in unity with the Son and Holy Spirit, one God forever and ever. Amen.

The members of the staff may then give a sign of peace or welcome.

Blessing of Departing Staff Members

+In the name of the Father and of the Son and of the Holy Spirit. Amen.

V. Our help is in the name of the Lord.
R. Who made heaven and earth.

V. The Lord be with you.
R. And with your spirit.

Scripture Reading

"Lord, now lettest thou thy servant depart in peace,
according to thy word;
for mine eyes have seen thy salvation
which thou hast prepared in the presence of all peoples,
a light for revelation to the Gentiles,
and for glory to thy people Israel."

—Luke 2:29-32

Prayer of Blessing

Gentle Savior, you have given each of us an appointed time. Bless + (N) our brother (sister) who has labored among us and built up the Kingdom of God in this parish community. May his (her) departure from us be peaceful. Continue to bless his (her) days and inspire the life of the Gospel in everything he (she) does. May he (she) receive this token of our love and prayers and remember with fondness the days spent in our midst until we meet in the Kingdom where you live with the Father and the Holy Spirit, one God forever and ever. Amen.

The departing staff member is then given a small symbolic gift.

Blessing of an Arriving Parochial Vicar

+In the name of the Father and of the Son and of the Holy Spirit. Amen.

V. Our help is in the name of the Lord.
R. Who made heaven and earth.

V. The Lord be with you.
R. And with your spirit.

Scripture Reading

And Jesus went about all the cities and villages, teaching in their synagogues and preaching the gospel of the kingdom, and healing every disease and every infirmity. When he saw the crowds, he had compassion for them, because they were harassed and helpless, like sheep without a shepherd. Then he said to his disciples, "The harvest is plentiful, but the laborers are few; pray therefore the Lord of the harvest to send out laborers into his harvest."

—Matthew 9:35-38

Prayer of Blessing

Pastor: Our bishop has called Father (N) to serve the needs of this parish community as parochial vicar. Today we welcome him, pledging our support for his evangelical labors in this parish and our love for him as our priest.

As he begins this ministry I ask:

Are you, the members of (N) parish, resolved to give support and encouragement to the ministry and priesthood of Father (N)?

All: We are.

Are you committed to pray daily for him and for the fruitfulness of his work with the people of this community?

All: We are.

Are you resolved to labor with him to preach the Gospel to this neighborhood through the work of this community of faith?

All: We are.

Now the pastor addresses the newly arrived priest.

Father (N), are you resolved to give support and encouragement to the people of this parish and build up the Body of Christ through your life and example as a priest?

Father: I am.

Are you committed to pray without ceasing for the people of this parish and be strong and diligent in your leadership, representing the Holy Catholic Church, our bishop, and your pastor?

Father: I am.

Are you resolved to love the people of this parish and, through your spirit of generous service, inspire them to give witness to the power of Christ to this neighborhood?

Father: I am.

The parish community of (N) welcomes you with great joy

All: Thanks be to God.

Pastor: God of all Grace, you have called your priests to seek to serve rather than be served. Give life to the priestly work of Father (N), who comes to this community as your ambassador and an icon of the gentleness, wisdom, and compassion of your Son, Jesus. Bless + him and the work of his hands. May his days among us be filled with peace. We ask this through the same Christ our Lord. Amen.

Blessing of a Departing Parochial Vicar

+In the name of the Father and of the Son and of the Holy Spirit. Amen.

V. Our help is in the name of the Lord.
R. Who made heaven and earth.

V. The Lord be with you.
R. And with your spirit.

Scripture Reading

"You are the salt of the earth; but if salt has lost its taste, how shall its saltness be restored? It is no longer good for anything except to be thrown out and trodden under foot by men. You are the light of the world. A city set on a hill cannot be hid. Nor do men light a lamp and put it under a bushel, but on a stand, and it gives light to all in the house. Let your light so shine before men, that they may see your good works and give glory to your Father who is in heaven."

—Matthew 5:13-16

Prayer of Blessing

Lord God, you guard our every action. Bless + Father (N) as he departs from this parish and begins his new work. May he always have blessed memories of his time with us. May his work continue to grow and bear fruit for your Kingdom. We ask this in the name of Jesus the Lord. Amen.

Blessing of an Arriving Permanent Deacon

+In the name of the Father and of the Son and of the Holy Spirit. Amen.

V. Our help is in the name of the Lord.
R. Who made heaven and earth.

V. The Lord be with you.
R. And with your spirit.

Scripture Reading

And the LORD said to Moses, "Bring the tribe of Levi near, and set them before Aaron the priest, that they may minister to him. They shall perform duties for him and for the whole congregation before the tent of meeting, as they minister at the tabernacle; they shall have charge of all the furnishings of the tent of meeting, and attend to the duties for the people of Israel as they minister at the tabernacle. And you shall give the Levites to Aaron and his sons; they are wholly given to him from among the people of Israel."

—Numbers 3:5-9

Prayer of Blessing

Pastor: Our bishop has called Deacon (N) to serve the needs of this parish community as a permanent deacon. Today we welcome him, pledging our support for his work of service in this parish and our love for him as our deacon.

As he begins this ministry I ask:

Are you, the members of (N) parish resolved to give support and encouragement to the ministry and service of Deacon (N)?

All: We are.

Are you committed to pray daily for him and for the fruitfulness of his diaconal work with the people of this community?

All: We are.

Are you resolved to labor with him to serve the needs of the poor in this neighborhood through the work of this community of faith?

All: We are.

Now the pastor addresses the newly arrived deacon.

Deacon (N), are you resolved to give support and encouragement to the people of this parish and build up the Body of Christ through your service as a deacon?

Deacon: I am.

Are you committed to pray without ceasing for the people of this parish and be steadfast and tireless in your service, representing the Holy Catholic Church, our bishop, and your pastor?

Deacon: I am.

Are you resolved to love the people of this parish and, through your spirit of generous service, inspire them to give witness to the power of Christ to this neighborhood?

Deacon: I am.

The parish community of (N) welcomes you with great joy.

All: Thanks be to God.

Pastor: God of all Grace, you have called your deacons to seek to serve rather than be served. Give life to the work of Deacon (N) who comes to this community as an example of the generosity and ministry of your Son, Jesus. Bless + him and the work of his hands. May his days among us be filled with peace. We ask this through the same Christ our Lord. Amen.

Blessing of a Departing Permanent Deacon

+In the name of the Father and of the Son and of the Holy Spirit. Amen.

V. Our help is in the name of the Lord.
R. Who made heaven and earth.

V. The Lord be with you.
R. And with your spirit.

Scripture Reading

Now in these days when the disciples were increasing in number, the Hellenists murmured against the Hebrews because their widows were neglected in the daily distribution. And the twelve summoned the body of the disciples and said, "It is not right that we should give up preaching the word of God to serve tables. Therefore, brethren, pick out from among you seven men of good repute, full of the Spirit and of wisdom, whom we may appoint to this duty. But we will devote ourselves to prayer and to the ministry of the word." And what they said pleased the whole multitude, and they chose Stephen, a man full of faith and of the Holy Spirit, and Philip, and Prochorus, and Nicanor, and Timon, and Parmenas, and Nicholas, a proselyte of Antioch. These they set before the apostles, and they prayed and laid their hands upon them. And the word of God increased; and the number of the disciples multiplied greatly in Jerusalem, and a great many of the priests were obedient to the faith.

—Acts 6:1-7

Prayer of Blessing

Lord God, you guard our every action. Bless + Deacon (N) as he departs from this parish and begins his new work. May he always have blessed memories of his time with us. May his work continue to grow and bear fruit for your Kingdom. We ask this in the name of Jesus the Lord. Amen.

Blessing of Ministers of Social Outreach

+In the name of the Father and of the Son and of the Holy Spirit. Amen.

V. Our help is in the name of the Lord.
R. Who made heaven and earth.

V. The Lord be with you.
R. And with your spirit.

Scripture Reading

For you know the grace of our Lord Jesus Christ, that though he was rich, yet for your sake he became poor, so that by his poverty you might become rich. And in this matter I give my advice: it is best for you now to complete what a year ago you began not only to do but to desire, so that your readiness in desiring it may be matched by your completing it out of what you have. For if the readiness is there, it is acceptable according to what a man has, not according to what he has not. I do not mean that others should be eased and you burdened, but that as a matter of equality your abundance at the present time should supply their want, so that their abundance may supply your want, that there may be equality. As it is written, "He who gathered much had nothing over, and he who gathered little had no lack."

—2 Corinthians 8:9-15

Prayer of Blessing

Lord God, bless + these ministers who seek to do your will by serving the poor and needy members of this community. May their work be true comfort for those they serve, and offer an example of the presence of Christ in this community. We ask this through the same Christ our Lord. Amen.

Blessing of Liturgical Committee

+In the name of the Father and of the Son and of the Holy Spirit. Amen.

V. Our help is in the name of the Lord.
R. Who made heaven and earth.

V. The Lord be with you.
R. And with your spirit.

Scripture Reading

"No one can come to me unless the Father who sent me draws him; and I will raise him up at the last day. It is written in the prophets, 'And they shall all be taught by God.' Every one who has heard and learned from the Father comes to me. Not that anyone has seen the Father except him who is from God; he has seen the Father. Truly, truly, I say to you, he who believes has eternal life. I am the bread of life. Your fathers ate the manna in the wilderness, and they died. This is the bread which comes down from heaven, that a man may eat of it and not die. I am the living bread which came down from heaven; if anyone eats of this bread, he will live for ever; and the bread which I shall give for the life of the world is my flesh."

—John 6:44-51

Prayer of Blessing

Lord God, you call us to offer you fitting praise and worship. Guide the deliberations of this liturgy committee and bless + its members with wisdom so that our worship of you in this parish community may bear fruit in the eternal liturgy of heaven. We ask this through Christ our Lord. Amen.

Blessing of Finance Staff

+In the name of the Father and of the Son and of the Holy Spirit. Amen.

V. Our help is in the name of the Lord.
R. Who made heaven and earth.

V. The Lord be with you.
R. And with your spirit.

Scripture Reading

"If I have withheld anything that the poor desired,
or have caused the eyes of the widow to fail,
or have eaten my morsel alone,
and the fatherless has not eaten of it
(for from his youth I reared him as a father,
and from his mother's womb I guided him);
if I have seen anyone perish for lack of clothing,
or a poor man without covering;
if his loins have not blessed me,
and if he was not warmed with the fleece of my sheep;
if I have raised my hand against the fatherless,
because I saw help in the gate."

—Job 31:16-21

Prayer of Blessing

Almighty Father, bless + and guide those who consider the temporal affairs of this community with your wisdom. May our deliberations give you honor and glory and be for the good of this parish and the world. Grant this through Christ our Lord. Amen.

Blessing of Music Ministers

+In the name of the Father and of the Son and of the Holy Spirit. Amen.

V. Our help is in the name of the Lord.
R. Who made heaven and earth.

V. The Lord be with you.
R. And with your spirit.

Scripture Reading

Praise the Lord!
Praise God in his sanctuary;
praise him in his mighty firmament!
Praise him for his mighty deeds;
praise him according to his exceeding greatness!
Praise him with trumpet sound;

praise him with lute and harp!
Praise him with timbrel and dance;
praise him with strings and pipe!
Praise him with sounding cymbals;
praise him with loud clashing cymbals!
Let everything that breathes praise the LORD!
Praise the LORD!

—Psalm 150

Prayer of Blessing

Loving God, bless + those who will assist in ministering to your people in praise and worship. Guide their voices and their hands to be faithful witnesses of the heavenly worship. We ask this through Christ our Lord. Amen.

BLESSING OF HOSPITALITY MINISTERS

+In the name of the Father and of the Son and of the Holy Spirit. Amen.

V. Our help is in the name of the Lord.
R. Who made heaven and earth.

V. The Lord be with you.
R. And with your spirit.

Scripture Reading

"This is my commandment, that you love one another as I have loved you. Greater love has no man than this, that a man lay down his life for his friends. You are my friends if you do what I command you. No longer do I call you servants, for the servant does not know what his master is doing; but I have called you friends, for all that I have heard from my Father I have made known to you. You did not choose me, but I chose you and appointed you that you should go and bear fruit and that your fruit should abide; so that whatever you ask the Father in my name, he may give it to you. This I command you, to love one another."

—John 15:12-17

Prayer of Blessing

Loving God, you call all men and women into the hospitality of your Church. Bless + these ministers of hospitality, May their work be a true sign of your welcome and love for all people. Grant this through Christ our Lord. Amen.

Blessing of Youth Ministers

+In the name of the Father and of the Son and of the Holy Spirit. Amen.

V. Our help is in the name of the Lord.
R. Who made heaven and earth.

V. The Lord be with you.
R. And with your spirit.

Scripture Reading

"I am the good shepherd. The good shepherd lays down his life for the sheep. He who is a hireling and not a shepherd, whose own the sheep are not, sees the wolf coming and leaves the sheep and flees; and the wolf snatches them and scatters them. He flees because he is a hireling and cares nothing for the sheep. I am the good shepherd; I know my own and my own know me, as the Father knows me and I know the Father; and I lay down my life for the sheep. And I have other sheep, that are not of this fold; I must bring them also, and they will heed my voice. So there shall be one flock, one shepherd."

—John 10:11-16

Prayer of Blessing

Gentle Shepherd, Jesus Christ, you call our youth to be faithful to you in their lives. Bless + these youth ministers and give them your inspiration as they guide and direct our youth to that Kingdom where you live with the Father and the Holy Spirit, one God forever and ever. Amen.

Blessing of Maintenance Staff Members

+In the name of the Father and of the Son and of the Holy Spirit. Amen.

V. Our help is in the name of the Lord.
R. Who made heaven and earth.

V. The Lord be with you.
R. And with your spirit.

Scripture Reading

How lovely is thy dwelling place,
O Lord of hosts!

My soul longs, yea, faints
for the courts of the LORD;
my heart and flesh sing for joy
to the living God.
Even the sparrow finds a home,
and the swallow a nest for herself,
where she may lay her young,
at thy altars, O LORD of hosts,
my King and my God.
Blessed are those who dwell in thy house,
ever singing thy praise!
Blessed are the men whose strength is in thee,
in whose heart are the highways to Zion.
As they go through the valley of Baca
they make it a place of springs;
the early rain also covers it with pools.
They go from strength to strength;
the God of gods will be seen in Zion.
O LORD God of hosts, hear my prayer;
give ear, O God of Jacob!
Behold our shield, O God;
look upon the face of thine anointed!
For a day in thy courts is better
than a thousand elsewhere.
I would rather be a doorkeeper in the house of my God
than dwell in the tents of wickedness.
For the LORD God is a sun and shield;
he bestows favor and honor.
No good thing does the LORD withhold
from those who walk uprightly.
O LORD of hosts,
blessed is the man who trusts in thee!

—Psalm 84

Prayer of Blessing

Lord God, through the intercession of St. Joseph, bless + these workers who build up your Kingdom by assisting the work of this parish community. May their work be to your glory and for the good of your Holy Church. Grant this through Christ our Lord. Amen.

Blessing to Open a Staff Retreat

+In the name of the Father and of the Son and of the Holy Spirit. Amen.

V. Our help is in the name of the Lord.
R. Who made heaven and earth.

V. The Lord be with you.
R. And with your spirit.

Scripture Reading

The apostles returned to Jesus, and told him all that they had done and taught. And he said to them, "Come away by yourselves to a lonely place, and rest a while." For many were coming and going, and they had no leisure even to eat. And they went away in the boat to a lonely place by themselves. Now many saw them going, and knew them, and they ran there on foot from all the towns, and got there ahead of them. As he went ashore he saw a great throng, and he had compassion on them, because they were like sheep without a shepherd; and he began to teach them many things.

—Mark 6:30-34

Prayer of Blessing

God our Father, in your providence you have brought us together as a parish staff for this time of prayer and discernment. Bless + our time together and fill us with renewed zeal for the work of your Church. Grant this through Christ our Lord. Amen.

Blessing to Close a Staff Retreat

+In the name of the Father and of the Son and of the Holy Spirit. Amen.

V. Our help is in the name of the Lord.
R. Who made heaven and earth.

V. The Lord be with you.
R. And with your spirit.

Scripture Reading

So if there is any encouragement in Christ, any incentive of love, any participation in the Spirit, any affection and sympathy, complete my joy by being of the same mind, having the same love, being in full accord and of one mind. Do nothing from selfishness or conceit, but in humility count others better than yourselves. Let each of you look not only to his own interests, but also to the interests of others.

—Philippians 2:1-4

Prayer of Blessing

Loving God, in this time together you have renewed us with your Word. Continue to inspire our every thought, word, and deed, and bless + us with continued courage and creativity in doing the work of your Church. We ask this in the name of Jesus the Lord. Amen.

Blessing for Planning Days

+In the name of the Father and of the Son and of the Holy Spirit. Amen.

V. Our help is in the name of the Lord.
R. Who made heaven and earth.

V. The Lord be with you.
R. And with your spirit.

Scripture Reading

Then I saw a new heaven and a new earth; for the first heaven and the first earth had passed away, and the sea was no more. And I saw the holy city, new Jerusalem, coming down out of heaven from God, prepared as a bride adorned for her husband; and I heard a loud voice from the throne saying, "Behold, the dwelling of God is with men. He will dwell with them, and they shall be his people, and God himself will be with them; he will wipe away every tear from their eyes, and death shall be no more, neither shall there be mourning nor crying nor pain any more, for the former things have passed away." And he who sat upon the throne said, "Behold, I make all things new." Also he said, "Write this, for these words are trustworthy and true." And he said to me, "It is done! I am the Alpha and the Omega, the beginning and the end. To the thirsty I will give from the fountain of the water of life without payment."

—Revelation 21:1-7

Prayer of Blessing

Lord Jesus Christ, you called the apostles apart for times of prayer and renewal. Bless + us as we begin this time of planning for your Church. Fill us with new ideas and a renewed fervor for the work of evangelization. Grant this through Christ our Lord. Amen.

Blessing for a Retiring Staff Member

+In the name of the Father and of the Son and of the Holy Spirit. Amen.

V. Our help is in the name of the Lord.
R. Who made heaven and earth.

V. The Lord be with you.
R. And with your spirit.

Scripture Reading

On that day, when evening had come, he said to them, "Let us go across to the other side." And leaving the crowd, they took him with them in the boat, just as he was. And other boats were with him. And a great storm of wind arose, and the waves beat into the boat, so that the boat was already filling. But he was in the stern, asleep on the cushion; and they woke him and said to him, "Teacher, do you not care if we perish?" And he awoke and rebuked the wind, and said to the sea, "Peace! Be still!" And the wind ceased, and there was a great calm. He said to them, "Why are you afraid? Have you no faith?" And they were filled with awe, and said to one another, "Who then is this, that even wind and sea obey him?"

—Mark 4:35-41

Prayer of Blessing

Almighty God, bless + (N) today as he (she) leaves the service of this parish and begins his (her) retirement. May the coming days be filled with hope and praise for you. May his (her) memories of his (her) time in this parish be filled with joy. We ask this in the name of Jesus the Lord. Amen.

Blessing of a Retiring Priest

+In the name of the Father and of the Son and of the Holy Spirit. Amen.

V. Our help is in the name of the Lord.
R. Who made heaven and earth.

V. The Lord be with you.
R. And with your spirit.

Scripture Reading

Now as Solomon finished offering all this prayer and supplication to the LORD, he arose from before the altar of the LORD, where he had knelt with hands outstretched toward heaven; and he stood, and blessed all the assembly of Israel with a loud voice, saying, "Blessed be the LORD who has given rest to his people Israel, according to all that he promised; not one word has failed of all his good promise, which he uttered by Moses his servant. The LORD our God be with us, as he was with our fathers; may he not leave us or forsake us; that he may incline our hearts to him, to walk in all his ways, and to keep his commandments, his statutes, and his ordinances, which he commanded our fathers. Let these words of mine, wherewith I have made supplication before the LORD, be near to the LORD our God day and night, and may he maintain the cause of his servant, and the cause of his people Israel, as each day requires; that all the peoples of the earth may know that the LORD is God; there is no other. Let your heart therefore be wholly true to the LORD our God, walking in his statutes and keeping his commandments, as at this day."

—1 Kings 8:54-61

Prayer of Blessing

Almighty God, bless + Father (N) today as he leaves the service of this parish and begins his retirement. May the coming days be filled with hope and praise for you. May his memories of his time in this parish be filled with joy. We ask this in the name of Jesus the Lord. Amen.

Blessing of a Priest Departing for a Sabbatical

+In the name of the Father and of the Son and of the Holy Spirit. Amen.

V. Our help is in the name of the Lord.
R. Who made heaven and earth.

V. The Lord be with you.
R. And with your spirit.

Scripture Reading

The apostles returned to Jesus, and told him all that they had done and taught. And he said to them, "Come away by yourselves to a lonely place, and rest a while." For many were coming and going, and they had no leisure even to eat. And they went away in the boat to a lonely place by themselves. Now many saw them going, and knew them, and they ran there on foot from all the towns, and got there ahead of them. As he went ashore he saw a great throng, and he had compassion on them, because they were like sheep without a shepherd; and he began to teach them many things.

—Mark 6:30-34

Prayer of Blessing

God of Journeys, bless + Father (N) as he begins this time of renewal. May he return to us refreshed in spirit and mind. May the coming days be filled with joy. Renew the spirit of his priesthood and return him safely to this parish community. We ask this through Christ our Lord. Amen.

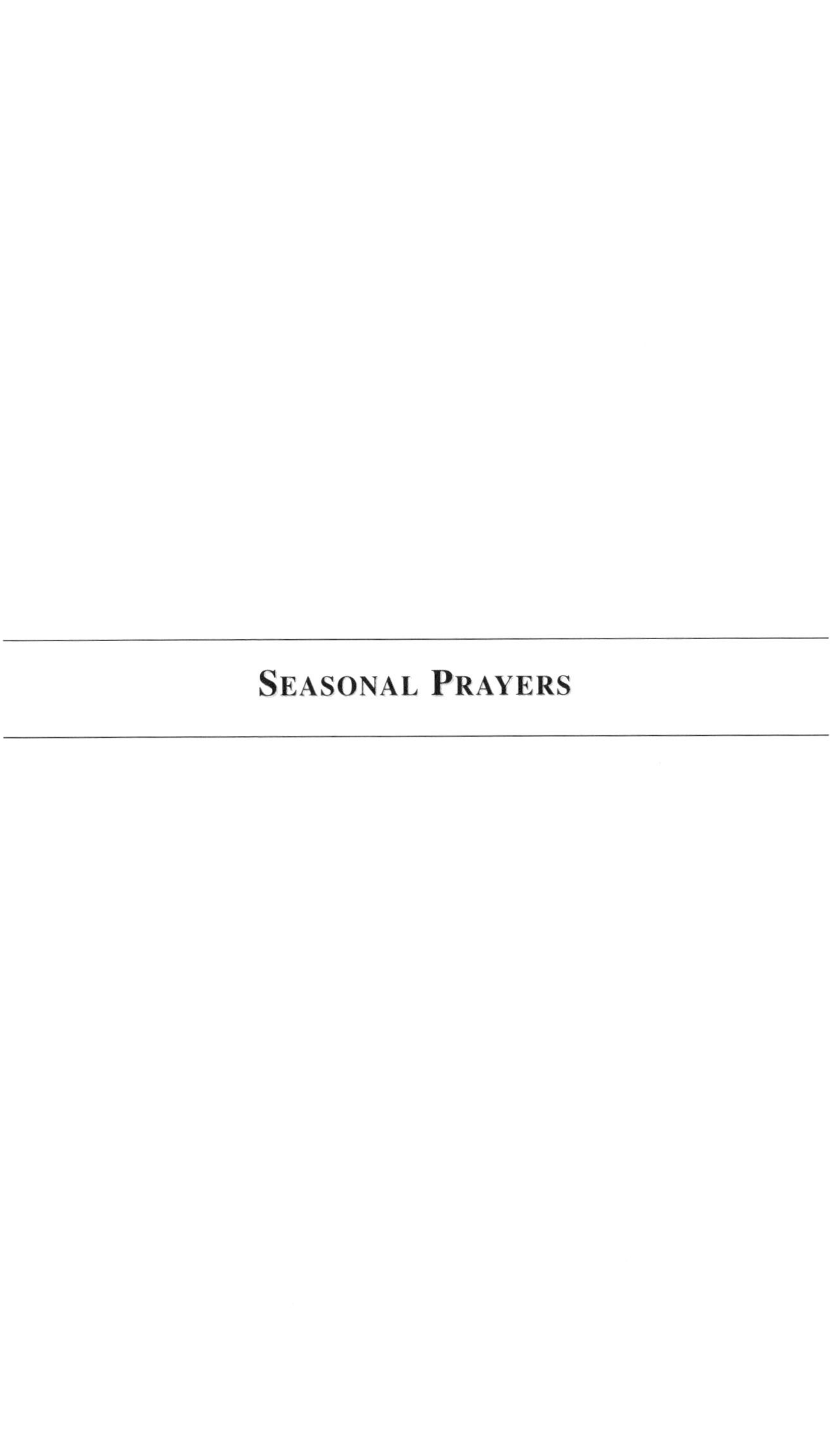

Seasonal Prayers

A Priest's Prayer for Advent

Come, long-expected Jesus. Excite in me a wonder at the wisdom and power of your Father and ours. Receive my prayer as part of my service of the Lord who enlists me in God's own work for justice.

Come, long-expected Jesus. Excite in me a hunger for peace: peace in the world, peace in my home, peace in myself.

Come, long-expected Jesus. Excite in me a joy responsive to the Father's joy. I seek his will so I can serve with gladness, singing, and love.

Come, long-expected Jesus. Excite in me the joy and love and peace it is right to bring to the manger of my Lord. Raise in me, too, sober reverence for the God who acted there, hearty gratitude for the life begun there, and spirited resolution to serve the Father and Son.

I pray in the name of Jesus Christ, whose advent I hail. Amen.

Father, all-powerful God, your eternal Word took flesh on our earth when the Virgin Mary placed her life at the service of your plan. Lift our minds in watchful hope to hear the voice which announces his glory and open our minds to receive the Spirit who prepares us for his coming. We ask this through Christ our Lord. Amen.

Blessing of a Rectory Advent Wreath

+In the name of the Father and of the Son and of the Holy Spirit. Amen.

V. Our help is in the name of the Lord.
R. Who made heaven and earth.

V. The Lord be with you.
R. And with your spirit.

Scripture Reading

There shall come forth a shoot from the stump of Jesse, and a branch
shall grow out of his roots.
And the Spirit of the LORD shall rest upon him,
the spirit of wisdom and understanding,
the spirit of counsel and might,
the spirit of knowledge and the fear of the LORD.

And his delight shall be in the fear of the LORD.
He shall not judge by what his eyes see,
or decide by what his ears hear;
but with righteousness he shall judge the poor,
and decide with equity for the meek of the earth;
and he shall smite the earth with the rod of his mouth,
and with the breath of his lips he shall slay the wicked.
Righteousness shall be the girdle of his waist,
and faithfulness the girdle of his loins.
The wolf shall dwell with the lamb,
and the leopard shall lie down with the kid,
and the calf and the lion and the fatling together,
and a little child shall lead them.
The cow and the bear shall feed;
their young shall lie down together;
and the lion shall eat straw like the ox.
The child shall play over the hole of the asp,
and the weaned child shall put his hand on the adder's den.
They shall not hurt or destroy
in all my holy mountain;
for the earth shall be full of the knowledge of the LORD
as the waters cover the sea.

In that day the root of Jesse shall stand as a sign to the peoples; him shall the nations seek, and his dwellings shall be glorious.

—Isaiah 11:1-10

Prayer of Blessing

Lord God of all expectations, bless + this advent wreath and with it our hopes for the coming of your Son Jesus, who lives and reigns with you forever and ever. Amen.

Advent Wreath Prayers for each week

The following are the Advent wreath prayers that change every week. They are prayed at the lighting of each candle every day during Advent.

Week One:

The first candle is lit, and the prayer for the first week is said.

Priest:

Let us pray.
Stir up thy might, we beg thee, O Lord,

and come, so that we may escape through thy protection
and be saved by thy help from the dangers
that threaten us because of our sins.
Who livest and reignest for ever and ever. Amen.

During the first week one candle is left burning during the evening meal, at prayers or at bedtime.

Week Two:

Two candles are lit on the second Sunday and allowed to burn as before. The prayer for the week is:

Priest:

Let us pray.
O Lord, stir up our hearts
that we may prepare for thy only begotten Son,
that through his coming
we may be made worthy to serve thee with pure souls.
Through the same Christ our Lord. Amen.

Week Three:

Three candles, including the rose candle, are lit on Gaudete, the third Sunday, and during that week. The following prayer is said:

Priest:

Let us pray.
We humbly beg thee, O Lord,
to listen to our prayers;
and by the grace of thy coming
bring light into our darkened minds.
Who livest and reignest for ever and ever. Amen.

Week Four:

All four candles are lit on the fourth Sunday and allowed to burn as before. The prayer said the fourth week is:

Priest:

Let us pray.
Stir up thy might, we pray thee, O Lord, and come;
rescue us through thy great strength so that salvation,
which has been hindered by our sins,
may be hastened by the grace of thy gentle mercy.
Who livest and reignest for ever and ever. Amen.

Father in heaven, our hearts desire the warmth of your love and our minds are searching for the light of your Word. Increase our longing for Christ our Savior and give us the strength to grow in love, that the dawn of his coming may find us rejoicing in his presence and welcoming the light of his truth. We ask this in the name of Jesus the Lord. Amen.

A Priest's Prayers for Christmas

Before Breakfast Prayer for Christmas Season

The Word was made flesh, alleluia, alleluia!
And dwelt among us, alleluia, alleluia!

Let the heavens rejoice and the earth be glad, before the face of the Lord, for he comes. Bless us, O Lord, and these thy gifts, which we are about to receive from thy bounty. Through Christ our Lord. Amen.

Prayer After Breakfast During Christmas Season

Glory to God in the highest, and on earth peace to men of good will, alleluia! The Lord has reigned, and he is clothed with beauty. Almighty God, the Savior of the world, who hast nourished us with heavenly food, we give thee thanks for the gift of this bodily refreshment which we have received from thy bountiful mercy. Through Christ our Lord. Amen.

Christmas Vigil Prayer

God of endless ages, Father of all goodness, we keep vigil for the dawn of salvation and the birth of your Son. With gratitude we recall his humanity, the life he shared with the sons of men. May the power of his divinity help us answer his call to forgiveness and life. We ask this through Christ our Lord. Amen.

God our Father, every year we rejoice as we look forward to this feast of our salvation. May we welcome Christ as our Redeemer, and meet him with confidence when he comes to be our judge, who lives and reigns with you and the Holy Spirit, one God, for ever and ever. Amen.

Prayer before Midnight Mass

Lord our God, with the birth of your Son, your glory breaks on the world. Through the night hours of the darkened earth, we your people watch for the coming of your promised Son. As we wait, give us a foretaste of the joy that you will grant us when the fullness of his glory has filled the earth, who lives and reigns with you for ever and ever. Amen.

✳

Father, you make this holy night radiant with the splendor of Jesus Christ, our light. We welcome him as Lord, the true light of the world. Bring us to eternal joy in the kingdom of heaven, where he lives and reigns with you and the Holy Spirit, one God, for ever and ever. Amen.

Christmas Prayer

Lord, in this holy season of prayer and song and laughter, we praise you for the great wonders you have sent us: for shining star and angel's song, for infant's cry in lowly manger. We praise you for the Word made flesh in a little Child. We behold his glory, and are bathed in its radiance.

Be with us as we sing the ironies of Christmas, the incomprehensible comprehended, the poetry made hard fact, the helpless Babe who cracks the world asunder. We kneel before you shepherds, innkeepers, wisemen. Help us to rise bigger than we are. Amen.

✳

Moonless darkness stands between.
Past, the Past, no more be seen!
But the Bethlehem star may lead me
to the sight of Him who freed me
from the self that I have been.
Make me pure, Lord: thou art holy;
Make me meek, Lord: thou wert lowly;
Now beginning, and always,
now begin, on Christmas day.

—Gerard Manley Hopkins

Blessing of Christmas Flowers

+In the name of the Father and of the Son and of the Holy Spirit. Amen.

V. Our help is in the name of the Lord.
R. Who made heaven and earth.

V. The Lord be with you.
R. And with your spirit.

Scripture Reading

Take off the garment of your sorrow and affliction,
O Jerusalem,

and put on for ever the beauty of the glory from God.
Put on the robe of the righteousness from God;
put on your head the diadem of the glory of the Everlasting.
For God will show your splendor everywhere under heaven.
For your name will for ever be called by God,
"Peace of righteousness and glory of godliness."

—Baruch 5:1-4

Prayer of Blessing

God our Creator, in this time of joy you give us renewed life in the birth of your Son. Bless + these flowers that we will use to celebrate the birth of Jesus. May they remind us of the new life given to us through this blessed day. We ask this through the same Christ our Lord. Amen.

Blessing of a Rectory Creche

+In the name of the Father and of the Son and of the Holy Spirit. Amen.

V. Our help is in the name of the Lord.
R. Who made heaven and earth.

V. The Lord be with you.
R. And with your spirit.

Scripture Reading

Now when the king dwelt in his house, and the LORD had given him rest from all his enemies round about, the king said to Nathan the prophet, "See now, I dwell in a house of cedar, but the ark of God dwells in a tent." And Nathan said to the king, "Go, do all that is in your heart; for the LORD is with you." But that same night the word of the LORD came to Nathan, "Go and tell my servant David, 'Thus says the LORD: Would you build me a house to dwell in?' "

—2 Samuel 7:1-5

Prayer of Blessing

God our Father, from the glories of your temple in heaven, your Son came among us to be born in a manger. Bless + this crib. May it remind us of his humble birth and make us worthy to share his glory in heaven. May this manger remind us that Jesus gave himself to us as food in the Eucharist. May our meditation on this crib draw us to that Kingdom where you live and reign forever and ever. Amen.

Epiphany Blessing of Chalk

V. Our help is in the name of the Lord.
R. Who made heaven and earth.

V. The Lord be with you.
R. And with your spirit.

Bless, O Lord God, this creature chalk
to render it helpful to your people.
Grant that they who use it in faith
and with it inscribe upon the doors of their homes
the names of your saints, Caspar, Melchior, and Balthasar,
may through their merits and intercession
enjoy health of body and protection of soul.
Through Christ our Lord. Amen.

And the chalk is sprinkled with holy water.

The chalk is then used to inscribe doors.

A Blessing of Throats for the Feast of St. Blaise on February 3

+In the name of the Father and of the Son and of the Holy Spirit. Amen.

V. Our help is in the name of the Lord.
R. Who made heaven and earth.

V. The Lord be with you.
R. And with your spirit.

Scripture Reading

Is any one among you suffering? Let him pray. Is any cheerful? Let him sing praise. Is any among you sick? Let him call for the elders of the church, and let them pray over him, anointing him with oil in the name of the Lord; and the prayer of faith will save the sick man, and the Lord will raise him up; and if he has committed sins, he will be forgiven. Therefore confess your sins to one another, and pray for one another, that you may be healed. The prayer of a righteous man has great power in its effects.

—James 5:13-16

Prayer of Blessing

Almighty and most gentle God, who didst create the multiplicity of things through thine only Word, and didst will that same Word through whom all things were made to take flesh for the refashioning of man; thou, who art great and without measure, terrible and worthy of praise, a worker of wonders: the glorious martyr and bishop Blaise, not fearing to suffer all sorts of diverse tortures because of his profession of faith in thee, was suited happily to bear the palm of martyrdom: and thou didst grant to him, among other graces, the favor that he should by thy power cure all kinds of illnesses of the throat: we humbly beg thy Majesty not to look upon our sins, but to be pleased by his merits and prayers and to deign in thy venerable kindness to bless + and sanctify + this creature of wax by the outpouring of thy grace; that all whose necks in good faith are touched by it may be freed by the merits of his sufferings from any illness of the throat, and that healthy and strong they may offer thanks to thee within thy Holy Church, and praise thy glorious name, which is blessed forever and ever. Through our Lord Jesus Christ thy Son, who liveth and reigneth with thee, in the unity of the Holy Ghost, God, world without end. Amen.

Then he will hold the two, unlit blessed candles crossed over our throats, intoning:

Per intercessionem S. Blasii liberet te Deus a malo gutteris et a quovis alio malo.

English:
May God at the intercession of St. Blaise preserve you from throat troubles and every other evil.

A Blessing of Bakers and St. Agatha Bread on February 5

+In the name of the Father and of the Son and of the Holy Spirit. Amen.

V. Our help is in the name of the Lord.
R. Who made heaven and earth.

V. The Lord be with you.
R. And with your spirit.

Scripture Reading

God is able to provide you with every blessing in abundance, so that you may always have enough of everything and may provide in abundance for every good work. As it is written, "He scatters abroad, he gives to the poor; his righteousness endures for ever." He who supplies seed to the sower and bread for food will supply and multiply your resources and increase the harvest of your righteousness. You will be enriched in every way for great generosity, which through us will produce thanksgiving to God; for the rendering of this service not only supplies the wants of the saints but also overflows in many thanksgivings to God.

—2 Corinthians 9:8-11

Prayer of Blessing

Lord God, bless + this bread we bring on this feast of your holy martyr, St. Agatha. May it protect from harm all who eat it. Bless + these bakers who provide us with the staff of life. Keep them always in your care. We ask this in the name of Jesus the Lord. Amen.

A Priest's Meditation for Lent

Lent is a very spatial season.
That is, it is a kind of geographical smorgasbord.
It is all about places.
Arid and acrid deserts, the sting of shifting sands pummeling faces.
Precipitous rock formations.
Cast yourself down.
A derelict town square and an ancient, moss-covered well.
Give me a drink of water.
A chaotic pool of stone teeming with the crippled, the broken, the forgotten.
I was blind but now I see.
A new-hewn tomb, heaped with the tribute of grief.
Friend come forth!
A garden overgrown with human fragility.
Could you not wait one hour?
A public court acrimonious with irony.
What is truth?
A temple of tattered trusts.
The curtain was torn from top to bottom.
A desolate eerily silent hill—a skull place—Adam's loins.
It is finished.

Lent is about places, lush and unkempt places, wild places, desolate places, real places, and spiritual places.

If we look carefully at the Sunday readings for the first two Sundays of Lent we see this quite dramatically laid out for us with the precision of a spiritual cartologist.

The first Sunday of Lent takes place in the desert. It is a lonely and isolated scene, particularly in Mark's spare prose. Jesus was in the desert. He was tempted. There were beasts. The angels attended him.

Hyperbolic and very dry, this deserted place. Sometimes this is the reality of our lives as priests because we are, of course, human beings. The human condition, unaided by God's presence, is dry, useless. The priestly life is the same. But, with God's presence we can overcome the temptation to live into the dead-end of the desert of our lives.

The second Sunday of Lent takes us far away from that lonely locale to a mountain. God does all of his revealing on a mountain. The mountain is the sphere for answers, just as the desert is a place of confounding. The mountain and the desert.

Two poles of experience, two extremes.

And we are a people caught somewhere between the desert and the mountaintop.

The desert.

The desert, of course, is a beautiful place. Full of exquisite, exotic flowers and cacti, lovely rock and sand formations, odd fauna that slither and slide through clefts in the cliffs. The desert is a beautiful place—that is, if you don't have to live there.

Jesus went into the desert for forty days.
Perhaps it was to share our human experience in the depth of its depravity.

Because, upon close inspection the desert, like life, is a dangerous place.

Those who venture into the desert must be prepared for it. They must pack lightly. No extra baggage, nothing useless, only the essentials.

They must plan carefully. We will need this much and not more. A bit too little and all is lost, a bit too much and the burden is too great.

Every choice counts in the desert.
Every rock is a portend of menace.
Every wind, a prophet of doom.

Every pool, a potential phantasm.
Every sound, a plea of desperation.
And so the desert is like our lives—full of risk, scorching, menacing.
But we are thrown into it and do not know the rules.
We pack too much, we carry around all our ugly attitudes, blatant bigotries, prides, and prejudices.
We get weighed down by the desert's desperate difficulties.
The sands shift into our mouths and nostrils and we are lost.

The desert is a place of death; unless of course, Jesus is there.
Wherever two or three are gathered.
When Jesus is there, there is nothing to fear.
When Jesus is there, there is hope of escape.

To the Mountain.

The air of the mountain is rarefied.

On the mountain things are clearer, easier to comprehend. This is this, and that is that.
This is my son.
That is Moses.
That is Elijah.
On the mountain there is symmetry.
You stand here; and you, here.
On the mountain there is wonder and light.
Light which the clouds cannot obscure.
Wonder that our cynicism cannot shroud.
Everything can be seen from the peak.
God's law is clear.
God's prophecy is fulfilled.
God's love is explicit.
We are known on the mountain.

Once, we were people of the desert.
One day, we will dwell in the heights.
But between the desert and the mountaintop is the road.

Ah, the road.
Now the road, well—
The road has its own challenges.
Finding the road is the first thing.
Which path should I take?

Which way am I called?
Shall I walk this way or that?
If I choose this path, the other may be closed to me,
Obscured as it were by the dense forest of alternative.
No matter which highway is chosen,
The outcome is usually the same.
Maps are few and far between and hard to come by.
Generalities, values, character, suggestion—these are the billboards of the road.
There are rules, no doubt, but as on any freeway, they are often more evident in the breach than the observance.

Sometimes the road is confusing, turning here and there, and we can become confounded.

Sometimes the road is flooded by the waters of adversity and we must wade all un-baptism-like through the muddy morass of muck and mire, waters sometimes up to our necks, but onward we go.

Sometimes the road swirls with the brittle leaves of seemingly endless autumns. The road and the field becoming indiscernible from one another.

Sometimes there are ditches along the road and we erode into the chasm of our own hopelessness, fatality, sin.

On the road we face the inevitable stumbling blocks, the satans of our own creation, landmarks of pride, conceit, guilt, and jealousy.
On the road we can become bogged down in fixating on the landscape, gazing forever at the hills and dales of our own talents, our insolence.
On the road we can step on each other's feet (or roll over each other's feet). We betray our fellow travelers, we give bad directions, we err.

But on the road we are together, for good or not.
On the road we must walk side by side through the occasionally narrow passages. We must help one another.
This one's provisions have failed. This one has fainted. This one is going in the wrong direction.
I am lost.
I am desperate.
I am destitute.
On the road we must learn to ask for help and to give it.
We sometimes are very good at this kind of journeying, and sometimes not.

But on the road, as long as we keep moving on the road, there is also some expectation, some harboring of hope, some murmur of prospect, some imperative to "Come and See" this view from the mountain that we cannot altogether fathom.

For we travel in a "between time," a time when there are wars and rumors of war, when the smoke of battle is in our eyes, when destruction's ugly hand scars the landscape of our moral consciousness, when death and violence are mere commonplaces. And yet hopefully we hang on to hope. Somewhere in the recesses of our imaginations in spite of what we see, somewhere, we envision, peep at, a world of peace, where the lion lies down with the lamb, where crescent and cross intersect in an ironic encounter of mutual respect and even love. If we can still hope, we are in a "between time," a people on the move toward the mountain, a people of the road.

And on that road we travel in a "between time," a time when religion has become a tool of rhetoric, an arguing point, a vote-getting apparatus for the right and the left. It is a time in which the magisterial word of God is wielded for power by the right and by the left. A time in which liberals and conservatives use God's word not for a better world but for the begetting of chronic agendaizing. But if we can imagine a world in which the power of God is manifested not only in rhetoric but in deeds that transform the desert of sin and self-destruction, that liberate those who are hungry for dignity and bread, then we are living in a "between time." If we can still gasp for the spirit of God in the asphyxiating plastic bags of our own destruction-drenched world, we are in a "between time" and we are a people on the move, a people of the road.

Priests are men of the road, drifting, hovering between life and death, between chaos and order, between fertility and futility, between building and utter destruction. We are men still choked and dazed by the harsh reality of the desert. But not without hope, not without dreams, not without the Spirit. Not without the promise of the mountain. Our time is a time of anticipation, a time of wondering, a time of living into the mystery of the God who is here and not here, the now and not yet. A priest's life must therefore be a kind of continuous Lent, a perpetual propulsion into the privilege of the divine.

Our dreams, our hopes, our breath are hovering in these days of Lent.
Hovering like the rain clouds that pour down incessant balm upon our souls still parched by the callousness of isolation.
Hovering like the sign of ashes on the foreheads of penitents.

Hovering like the sun in a snow-mist covered sky.
Like the moon in a clear azure sea of frozen stars.
Like a white host, hovering between heaven and earth, filled with the reality of God, yet somehow able to satisfy our hunger, our temporal desires, for what? Perhaps for the infinite, yet food for the journey.

There will be a time when the road will end.
There will be a time when all irony will cease,
a day when all heartache will be healed.
When our tired limbs will stretch out toward eternity.
When our conflicted minds will turn from the dark mirror to the reality of the living one.
When we can stand full stature on the mountaintop and sing.

Then we can face one another with pure love.
Then we can know even as we are known.
Then we can be in spirit and truth what we are now only in insinuation, that is, SAINTS.

And so it is Lent again.
And we put our tired feet on the road.
A people of the road.

The desert and the mountaintop.
Indeed, Lent, like life, is a spatial season.

—Denis Robinson, O.S.B.

+

In the Name of Our Lord Jesus Christ

The Good Works of Lent

In order to pursue without compromise a fervent conversion of life afforded by this holy season, I propose the following life-changing works:

In the area of prayer:

In the area of fasting:

In the area of almsgiving:

The following book of Holy Scripture will be my focus for reading and meditation this season:

Blessing of Fish During Lent

+In the name of the Father and of the Son and of the Holy Spirit. Amen.

V. Our help is in the name of the Lord.
R. Who made heaven and earth.

V. The Lord be with you.
R. And with your spirit.

Scripture Reading

When they had gone ashore, they saw a charcoal fire there, with fish on it, and bread. Jesus said to them, "Bring some of the fish that you have just caught." So Simon Peter went aboard and hauled the net ashore, full of large fish, a hundred and fifty-three of them; and though there were so many, the net was not torn. Jesus said to them, "Come and have breakfast." Now none of the disciples dared to ask him, "Who are you?" because they knew it was the Lord. Jesus came and took the bread and gave it to them, and did the same with the fish.

—John 21:9-13

Prayer

May this fish not only nourish our bodies but also be a sign of our resolve to follow you during this season. In the sharing of this meal, may we feel your presence among us. May your presence strengthen us in spirit as we await the joy of your resurrection. Through Christ our Lord. Amen.

A Litany for Lent by Bl. John Henry Newman

(1) From Quinquagesima (Sunday before Ash Wednesday) down to end of Second Week in Lent

Litany of Penance

LORD, have mercy.
Lord, have mercy.
Christ, have mercy.
Christ, have mercy.
Lord, have mercy.
Lord, have mercy.

Christ, hear us.
Christ, graciously hear us.
God the Father of Heaven, *Have mercy on us.*
God the Son, Redeemer of the world, "
God the Holy Ghost,
Holy Trinity, one God,
Incarnate Lord,
Lover of souls,
Savior of sinners,
Who didst come to seek those that were lost,
Who didst fast for them forty days and nights,
By thy tenderness towards Adam when he fell,
By thy faithfulness to Noah in the ark,
By thy remembrance of Lot in the midst of sinners,
By thy mercy on the Israelites in the desert,
By thy forgiveness of David after his confession,
By thy patience with wicked Achab on his humiliation,
By thy restoration of the penitent Manasses,
By thy long suffering towards the Ninevites,
when they went in sackcloth and ashes,
By thy blessing on the Maccabees,
who fasted before the battle,
By thy choice of John to go before thee as the preacher of penance,
By thy testimony to the publican,
who hung his head and smote his breast,
By thy welcome given to the returning prodigal,
By thy gentleness with the woman of Samaria,
By thy condescension towards Zacchæus,
persuading him to restitution,
By thy pity upon the woman taken in adultery,
By thy love of Magdalen, who loved much,
By thy converting look, at which Peter wept,
By thy gracious words to the thief upon the cross,

We sinners, *Beseech thee, hear us.*
That we may judge ourselves, "
and so escape thy judgment,
That we may bring forth worthy fruits of penance,
That sin may not reign in our mortal bodies,
That we may work out our salvation with fear and trembling,
Son of God,

Lamb of God, who takest away the sins of the world,
Spare us, O Lord.
Lamb of God, who takest away the sins of the world,
Graciously hear us, O *Lord.*
Lamb of God, who takest away the sins of the world,
Have mercy on us.
Christ, hear us.
Christ, graciously hear us.

O Lord, hear our prayer.
And let our cry come unto thee.

Let us Pray,

Grant, we beseech thee, O Lord, to thy faithful, pardon and peace, that they may be cleansed from all their offenses, and also serve thee with a quiet mind, through Christ our Lord. Amen.

A Priest's Prayers for Lent

Prayer for Ash Wednesday

Lord, protect us in our struggle against evil. As we begin the discipline of Lent, make this season holy by our self-denial. May the light of your truth bestow sight to the darkness of our sinful eyes and our repentance bring us the blessing of your forgiveness and the gift of new life. Grant this through our Lord Jesus Christ, your Son, who lives and reigns with you and the Holy Spirit, one God, for ever and ever. Amen.

Act of Hope for Lent

O my God, knowing your almighty power, and your infinite goodness and mercy, I hope in you that, by the merits of the passion and death of our Savior Jesus Christ, you will grant me eternal life, which you have promised to all such as shall do the works of a good Christian; and these I resolve to do, with the help of your grace. Amen.

Act of Charity for Lent

O my God, I love you above all things with my whole heart and soul because you are all good and worthy of all my love. I love my neighbor as myself for the love of you. I forgive all who have injured me and ask pardon of all whom I have injured. Amen.

Act of Charity for Lent

Almighty Father, you have called me to walk by the light of Christ, your Son, and to trust in his wisdom. During Lent, I submit myself to him completely and strive to believe in him with all my heart. With my renewed commitment to Jesus, I endeavour to continue his work here on earth in helping to build your Kingdom so that all may benefit from the message of salvation. Amen.

Act of Contrition for Lent

My God, I am sorry for my sins with all my heart. In choosing to do wrong and failing to do good, I have sinned against you whom I should love above all things. I firmly intend, with your help, to do penance, to sin no more, and to avoid whatever leads me to sin. Our Savior Jesus Christ suffered and died for us. In his name, my God, have mercy. Amen.

Act of Love for Lent

Loving God, we enter the season of Lent in the spirit of joy, giving ourselves to spiritual strife, cleansing our soul and body, controlling our passions, as we limit our food, living on the virtues of the Holy Spirit; May we persevere in our longing for Christ so as to be worthy to behold his most solemn passion and the most holy passover, rejoicing the while with spiritual joy. Amen.

Chaplet of the Seven Sorrows of Mary

Pray one Hail Mary *while meditating on each of the Seven Sorrows of Mary, which are:*

1. The prophecy of Simeon.
2. The flight into Egypt.
3. The loss of the Child Jesus in the Temple.
4. Mary meeting Jesus carrying his Cross.
5. The Crucifixion.
6. Mary receiving the Body of Jesus from the Cross.
7. The Body of Jesus being placed in the tomb.

Then pray three Hail Marys *in remembrance of the tears Mary shed because of the suffering of her Divine Son.*

Concluding prayers:

Pray for us, O Most Sorrowful Virgin, that we may be made worthy of the promises of Christ.

Lord Jesus, we now implore, both for the present and for the hour of our death, the intercession of the Most Blessed Virgin Mary, your Mother, whose Holy Soul was pierced during your passion by a sword of grief. Grant us this favor, O Savior of the world, who lives and reigns with the Father and the Holy Spirit forever and ever. Amen.

Prayer to Our Lady of Sorrows

Most holy and afflicted Virgin, Queen of Martyrs, you stood beneath the cross, witnessing the agony of your dying Son. Look with a mother's tenderness and pity on me, who kneel before you. I venerate your sorrows and I place my requests with filial confidence in the sanctuary of your wounded heart. Present them, I beseech you, on my behalf to Jesus Christ, through the merits of his own most sacred passion and death, together with your sufferings at the foot of the cross. Through the united efficacy of both, obtain the granting of my petition. To whom shall I have recourse in my wants and miseries if not to you, Mother of Mercy? You who have drunk so deeply of the chalice of your Son, only you can have compassion on me in my sorrow.

Holy Mother, your soul was pierced by a sword of sorrow at the sight of the passion of your divine Son. Intercede for me and obtain for me from our Lord {mention your petition}, if it be for his honor and glory, and for my good. Amen.

Prayer before the Crucifix

Behold, O kind and most sweet Jesus, I cast myself upon my knees in your sight, and with the most fervent desire of my soul I pray and beseech you that you would impress upon my heart, lively sentiments of faith, hope, and charity, true repentance for my sins, and a firm purpose of amendment, while with deep affection and grief of soul I ponder within myself and mentally contemplate your five most precious wounds, having before my eyes that which David spoke in prophecy of you, O good Jesus: "they have pierced my hands and feet, they have numbered all my bones."

The Seven Last Words of Jesus

1. Father, forgive them for they know not what they do.
2. Woman, behold thy Son!... Behold thy Mother!
3. Verily, I say unto thee, today thou shalt be with me in paradise.
4. *Eli, Eli, lama sabachtani.*
5. I thirst.
6. It is finished.
7. Father, into thy hands I commend my spirit.

Prayer of the Seven Last Words

O divine Jesus, incarnate Son of God, for our salvation you consented to be born in a stable, to spend your whole life amidst poverty, trials, and misery, and to die by suffering on the Cross. At the hour of my death, please tell your Father, "Father, forgive them." Tell Your Mother, "Behold your child." Tell my soul, "This day you shall be with me in paradise."

My God, my God, do not forsake me in that final hour. I thirst, yes, my soul thirsts, for you who are the fountain of living waters. My life will surely pass away like a shadow; and in a short while everything would be accomplished. Therefore, my adored Savior, from this moment to that final hour, and for all eternity, I commend my spirit into your hands. Lord Jesus, receive my heart and my soul. Amen.

Prayers in Honor of the Passion

I give you glory, O Christ, because you, the only-begotten, the Lord of all, underwent the death of the Cross to free my sinful soul from the bonds of sin. What shall I give to you, O Lord, in return for all this kindness?

Glory to you, O Lord, for your love, for your mercy, for your patience.

Glory to you, for forgiving us all our sins, for coming to save our souls, for your incarnation in the Virgin's womb.

Glory to you, for your bonds, for receiving the cut of the lash, for accepting mockery.

Glory to you, for your crucifixion, for your burial, for your resurrection.

Glory to you, for your resurrection, for being preached to men, for being taken up to heaven.

Glory to you who sit at the Father's right hand and who will return in glory.

Glory to you for willing that the sinner be saved through your great mercy and compassion. Amen.

Meditations and Intercessions for Good Friday by Bl. John Henry Newman

---

Jesus, the Lamb of God

BEHOLD the Lamb of God, behold Him who taketh away the sins of the world. So spoke St. John Baptist, when he saw our Lord coming to him. And in so speaking, he did but appeal to that title under which our Lord was known from the beginning. Just Abel showed forth his faith in Him by offering of the firstlings of his flock. Abraham, in place of his son Isaac whom God spared, offered the like for a sacrifice. The Israelites were enjoined to sacrifice once a year, at Easter time, a lamb—one lamb for each family, a lamb without blemish—to be eaten whole, all but the blood, which was sprinkled, as their protection, about their house doors. The Prophet Isaiah speaks of our Lord under the same image: "He shall be led as a sheep to the slaughter, and shall be dumb as a lamb before his shearers" (liii. 7); and all this because "He was wounded for our iniquities, He was bruised for our sins;...by His bruises we are healed" (liii. 5). And in like manner the Holy Evangelist St. John, in the visions of the Apocalypse, thus speaks of Him: "I saw,...(Apoc. v. 6), and behold a lamb standing as it were slain;" and then he saw all the blessed "fall down before the Lamb,"...(verses 8, 9), and they sung a new canticle saying, "Thou wast slain, and hast redeemed us to God in Thy blood, out of every tribe and tongue and people and nation" (verse 9)...Worthy is the Lamb that was slain, to receive power, and divinity, and wisdom, and strength, and honor, and glory, and benediction" (verse 12).

This is Jesus Christ, who when darkness, sin, guilt, and misery had overspread the earth, came down from heaven, took our nature upon Him, and shed His precious blood upon the Cross for all men.

Let us pray for all people, that they may be converted.

O Lord Jesus Christ, O King of the whole world, O Hope and Expectation of all nations, O thou who hast bought all men for thy own at the price of thy most precious blood, look down in pity upon all who are spread over the wide earth, and impart to them the knowledge of thy truth. Remember, O Lord, thy own most bitter sufferings of soul and body in thy betrayal, thy passion and thy crucifixion, and have mercy upon their souls. Behold, O Lord, but a portion of mankind has heard of thy name—but a portion even professes to adore thee—and yet thousands upon thousands in the East and the West, in the North and the South, hour after hour, as each hour comes, are dropping away from this life into eternity. Remember, O my dear Lord, and lay it to heart, that to the dishonor of thy name, and to the triumph of thine enemies, fresh victims are choking up the infernal pit, and are taking up their dwelling there for ever. Listen to the intercessions of thy saints, let thy Mother plead with thee, let not the prayers of Holy Church thy spouse be offered up in vain. Visit the earth quickly and give all men to know, to believe, and to serve thee, in whom is our salvation, life and resurrection, who with the Father, etc.

Jesus, the Author and Finisher of Faith

ST. PAUL tells us to "look on Jesus, the Author and Finisher of faith." Faith is the first step towards salvation, and without it we have no hope. For St. Paul says, "Without faith it is impossible to please God." It is a divine light; by it we are brought out of darkness into sunshine; by it, instead of groping, we are able to see our way towards heaven. Moreover, it is a great *gift*, which comes from above, and which we cannot obtain except from Him who is the object of it. He, our Lord Jesus Himself, and He alone, gives us the grace to believe in Him. Hence the Holy Apostle calls Him the author of our faith—and He finishes and perfects it also—from first to last it is altogether from Him. Therefore it was that our Lord said, "If thou canst believe, all things are possible to him that believeth" (Mark ix. 22-23). And hence the poor man to whom He spoke, who believed indeed already, but still feebly, made answer—"crying out with tears, I *do* believe, Lord; help thou my unbelief." Hence, too, on another occasion, the Apostles said to our Lord, "Increase our faith" (Luke xvii. 5). And St. Paul draws out fully the whole matter when he reminds his converts, "And you (hath He raised), when you were dead in your offenses and sins, wherein in time past you walked, according to the course of this world,...in which we all conversed in time past,...and were by nature children of wrath, even as the rest; but God (who is rich in mercy), for His exceeding charity wherewith He loved us, even when we were dead in sins hath quickened us together in Christ... By grace you are saved through faith, and that not of yourselves, for it is the gift of God" (Ephesians ii. 1-8).

Let us pray for all the scorners, scoffers, and unbelievers, all false teachers and opposers of the truth, who are to be found in this land.

O Lord Jesus Christ, upon the Cross thou didst say: "Father, forgive them, for they know not what they do." And this surely, O my God, is the condition of vast multitudes among us now; they know not what they might have known, or they have forgotten what once they knew. They deny that there is a God, but they know not what they are doing. They laugh at the joys of heaven and the pains of hell, but they know not what they are doing. They renounce all faith in thee, the Savior of man, they despise thy Word and Sacraments, they revile and slander thy Holy Church and her priests, but they know not what they are doing. They mislead the wandering, they frighten the weak, they corrupt the young, but they know not what they do. Others, again, have a wish to be religious, but mistake error for truth—they go after fancies of their own, and they seduce others and keep them from thee. They know not what they are doing, but thou canst make them know. O Lord, we urge thee by thy own dear words, "Lord and Father, forgive them, for they know not what they do." Teach them now, open their eyes here, before the future comes; give them faith in what they must see hereafter, if they will not believe in it here. Give them full and saving faith here; destroy their dreadful delusions, and give them to drink of that living water, which whoso hath shall not thirst again.

Jesus, the Lord of Armies

AMONG the visions which the beloved disciple St. John was given to see, and which he has recorded in his Apocalypse, one was that of our Lord as the commander and leader of the hosts of the Saints in their warfare with the world. "I saw," he says, "and behold a white horse, and He that sat on him had a bow, and there was a crown given Him; and He went forth conquering that He might conquer" (Apoc. vi. 2). And again, "I saw heaven opened, and behold a white horse, and He that sat upon him was called Faithful and True, and with justice doth He judge and fight" (Apoc. xix. 11)…"And he was clothed with a garment, sprinkled with blood, and His Name is called, *The Word of God.* And the armies that are in heaven followed Him on white horses, clothed in fine linen, white and clean" (verse 13). Such is the Captain of the Lord's Host, and such are His soldiers. He and they ride on white horses, which means, that their cause is innocent, and upright and pure. Warriors of this world wage *unjust* wars, but our Almighty Leader fights for a heavenly cause and with heavenly weapons—and in like manner His soldiers fight the good fight of faith; they fight against their and their Master's three great enemies, the World, the Flesh, and the Devil. He is covered with blood, but it is His own blood, which He shed for our redemption. And His followers are red with blood, but still again it is His blood, for it is written "they have washed their robes, and have made them white in the blood of the Lamb" (Apoc. vii. 14). And again He and they are certain of victory because it is said "He went forth conquering that He might conquer" (Apoc. vi. 2). So let us say with the Psalmist "Gird thy sword upon thy thigh, O thou most mighty … Because of truth and meekness and justice thy right hand shall conduct thee wonderfully" (Psalm xliv. 4-5).

Let us pray for the whole Church militant here upon earth.

O Lion of the Tribe of Judah, the root of David, who fightest the good fight, and hast called on all men to join thee, give thy courage and strength to all thy soldiers over the whole earth, who are fighting under the standard of thy Cross. Give grace to every one in his own place to fight thy battle well. Be with thy missionaries, put right words into their mouths, prosper their labors, and sustain them under their sufferings with thy consolations, and carry them on, even through torment and blood (if it be necessary), to their reward in heaven. Give the grace of wisdom to those in high station, that they may neither yield to fear, nor be seduced by flattery. Make them prudent as serpents, and simple as doves. Give thy blessing to all preachers and teachers, that they may speak thy words and persuade their hearers to love thee. Be with all faithful servants of thine, whether in low station or in high, who mix in the world; instruct them how to speak and how to act every hour of the day, so as to preserve their own souls from evil and to do good to their companions and associates. Teach us, one and all, to live in thy presence and to see thee, our Great Leader and thy Cross—and thus to fight valiantly and to overcome, that at the last we may sit down with thee in thy Throne, as thou also hast overcome and art set down with thy Father in His Throne.

Jesus, the Only Begotten Son

JESUS is the only Son of the only Father—as it is said in the Creed, "I believe in one God, the Father Almighty," and then "and in Jesus Christ, His only Son our Lord." And so He Himself says in the Gospel, "As the Father hath life in Himself, so He hath given to the Son also to have life in Himself" (John v. 26). And He said to the man whom He cured of blindness, "Dost thou believe in the Son of God? It is He that talketh with thee" (John ix. 35-37). And St. John the Evangelist says, "The Word was made flesh and dwelt among us, and we saw His glory, the glory as it were of the only begotten of the Father" (John i. 14). And St. John Baptist says, "The Father loveth the Son and He hath given all things into His hand. He that believeth in the Son, hath life everlasting" (John iii. 35, 36). And St. Paul says, "There is one body and one Spirit—as ye are called in one hope of your calling. One Lord, one faith, one baptism, One God and Father of all" (Eph. iv. 4-6).

Thus Almighty God has set up *all* things in unity—and therefore His Holy Church in a special way, as the Creed again says, "One Holy Catholic and Apostolic Church." It is His wise and gracious will that His followers should not follow their own way, and form many bodies, but one. This was the meaning of the mystery of His garment at the time of His crucifixion, which "was without seam, woven from the top throughout" (John xix. 23). And therefore was it that the soldiers were not allowed to break His sacred limbs, for like the Jewish Easter Lamb not a bone of Him was to be broken.

Let us pray for the unity of the Church and the reconciliation and peace of all Christians.

O Lord Jesus Christ, who, when thou wast about to suffer, didst pray for thy disciples to the end of time that they might all be one, as thou art in the Father, and the Father in thee, look down in pity on the manifold divisions among those who profess thy faith, and heal the many wounds which the pride of man and the craft of Satan have inflicted upon thy people. Break down the walls of separation which divide one party and denomination of Christians from another, so that as there is but one holy company in heaven above, so likewise there may be but one communion, confessing and glorifying thy holy Name here below.

Jesus, the Eternal King

OUR Lord was called Jesus, when He took flesh of the Blessed Virgin. The angel Gabriel said to her, "Behold, thou shalt bring forth a Son, and thou shalt call His name Jesus." But, though He then gained a new name, He had existed from eternity; He never was not—He never had a beginning—and His true name, therefore, is the Eternal King. He ever reigned with His Father and the Holy Ghost, three Persons, one God. And hence, shortly before His crucifixion, He said, "Glorify thou me, O Father, with thyself, with the glory which I had, before the world was, with thee" (John xvii. 5). He who was the Eternal King in heaven, came to be King, and Lord, and Lawgiver, and Judge upon earth. Hence the prophet Isaiah says, foretelling His coming, *A child* is born to us, and a Son is given to us, and the government is upon His shoulder; and His name shall be called Wonderful Counsellor, God the Mighty, the Father of the world to come, the Prince of Peace" (Isaiah ix. 6). And when He left the world, He left His power behind Him, and divided it among His followers. He gave one portion of His power to one, another to another. He gave the fullness of His power to St. Peter, and to his successors, who, in consequence, are His vicars and representatives—so that, as the Father sent the Son, so the Son has sent St. Peter. But not only St. Peter and the other apostles, but all bishops and prelates in Holy Church, all pastors of souls, all Christian kings have power from Him, and stand to us in His place.

Let us pray for our Holy Father the Pope, and all rulers in the Church.

O Emmanuel, God with us, who art the Light that enlighteneth all men, who from the time when thou camest upon earth, hast never left it to itself, who, after teaching thy apostles, gave them to teach others to succeed them, and didst especially leave St. Peter and his successors, bishops of Rome, to take thy place towards us, and to guide and rule us in thy stead age after age, till the end come; thou hast sent grievous trials for many years upon the

Holy See of Rome. We believe and confess, O Lord, without any hesitation at all, that thou hast promised a continuous duration to thy Church while the world lasts—and we confess before thee, that we are in no doubt or trouble whatever, we have not a shadow of misgiving as to the permanence and the spiritual well-being either of thy Church itself or of its rulers. Nor do we know what is best for thy Church, and for the interests of the Catholic faith, and for the Pope, or the bishops throughout the world at this time. We leave the event entirely to thee; we do so without any anxiety, knowing that everything must turn to the prosperity of thy ransomed possession, even though things may look threatening for a season. Only we earnestly entreat that thou wouldest give thy own servant and representative true wisdom and courage, and fortitude, and the consolations of thy grace in this life, and a glorious immortal crown in the life to come.

Jesus, the Beginning of the New Creation

OUR Lord Jesus Christ is said by His almighty power to have begun a new creation, and to be Himself the first fruit and work of it. Mankind were lost in sin, and were thereby, not only not heirs of heaven, but the slaves of the Evil One. Therefore He who made Adam in the beginning resolved in His mercy to make a new Adam, and by a further ineffable condescension determined that that new Adam should be Himself. And therefore, by His holy prophet Isaiah, He announced before He came, "Behold I create new heavens and a new earth" (Isaiah lxv. 17). On the other hand St. Paul calls Him "The image of the invisible God, the first-born of every creature" (Col. i. 15). And St. John calls Him "the Amen, the faithful and true witness, who is the beginning of the creation of God" (Apoc. iii. 14). The Creator came as if He were a creature, because He took upon Him a created nature—and as, at the first, Eve was formed out of the side of Adam, so now, when He hung on the cross, though not a bone of Him was broken, his side was pierced, and out of it came the grace, represented by the blood and the water, out of which His bride and spouse, His Holy Church, was made. And thus all the sanctity of all portions of that Holy Church is derived from Him as a beginning; and He feeds us with His divine flesh in the Holy Eucharist, in order to spread within us, in the hearts of all of us, the blessed leaven of the New Creation. All the wisdom of the doctors, and the courage and endurance of the martyrs, and the purity of virgins, and the zeal of preachers, and the humility and mortification of religious men, is from Him, as the beginning of the new and heavenly creation of God.

Let us pray for all ranks and conditions of men in thy Holy Church.

O Lord, who art called the Branch, the Orient, the Splendor of the eternal light, and the Sun of Justice, who art that tree, of whom thy beloved disciple speaks as the Tree of Life, bearing twelve fruits, and its leaves for the healing of the nations, give thy grace and blessing on all those various states and conditions in thy Holy Church, which have sprung from thee and live in thy Life. Give to all bishops the gifts of knowledge, discernment, prudence, and love. Give to all priests to be humble, tender, and pure; give to all pastors of thy flock to be zealous, vigilant, and unworldly; give to all religious bodies to act up to their rule, to be simple and without guile, and to set their hearts upon invisible things and them only. Grant to fathers of families to recollect that they will have hereafter to give account of the souls of their children; grant to all husbands to be tender and true; to all wives to be mindful and patient; grant to all children to be docile; to all young people to be chaste; to all the aged to be fervent in spirit; to all who are engaged in business, to be honest and unselfish; and to all of us the necessary graces of faith, hope, charity, and contrition.

Jesus, the Lover of Souls

THE inspired writer says, "Thou hast mercy upon all, because thou canst do all things, and overlookest the sins of men for the sake of repentance. For thou lovest all things that are, and hatest none of the things which thou hast made…And how could anything endure, if thou wouldst not? or be preserved, if not called by thee? But thou sparest all, because they are thine, O Lord, who lovest souls" (Wisdom xi. 24-27). This is what brought Him from heaven, and gave Him the name of Jesus—for the angel said to St. Joseph about Mary, "She shall bring forth a Son, and thou shalt call His name Jesus; for He shall save His people from their sins" (Matt. i. 21). It was His great love for souls and compassion for sinners which drew Him from heaven. Why did He consent to veil His glory in mortal flesh, except that He desired so much to save those who had gone astray and lost all hope of salvation. Hence He says Himself, "The Son of Man is come to seek and to save that which was lost" (Matt. xvii. 11, Luke xix. 10). Rather than that we should perish, He did all that even omnipotence could do consistently with its holy attributes, for He gave Himself. And He loves each of us so much that He has died for each one as fully and absolutely as if there were no one else for Him to die for. He is our best friend, our True Father, the only real Lover of our souls—He takes all means to make us love Him in return, and He refuses us nothing if we do.

Let us pray for the conversion of all sinners.

O Lord, "who didst give thyself for us, that thou mightest redeem us from all iniquity, and mightest cleanse to thyself a people acceptable, a pursuer of good works," look upon thy baptized, look on the multitude of those who once were thine and have gone from thee. Ah, for how short a time do they keep thy grace in their hearts, how soon do they fall off from thee, with what difficulty do they return; and even, though they repent and come to penance, yet how soon, in the words of Scripture, doth the dog return to his vomit, and the sow that was washed to her wallowing in the mire. O my God, save us all from the seven deadly sins, and rescue those who have been made captive by them. Convert all sinners—bring judgments down upon them, if there is no other way of reclaiming them. Touch the hearts of all proud men, wrathful, revengeful men; of the obstinate, of the self-relying, of the envious, of the slanderer, of the hater of goodness and truth; of the slothful and torpid; of all gluttons and drunkards; of the covetous and unmerciful; of all licentious talkers; of all who indulge in impure thoughts, words, or deeds. Make them understand that they are going straight to hell, and save them from themselves and from Satan.

Jesus, Our Guide and Guardian

THERE are men who think that God is so great that He disdains to look down upon *us*, our doings and our fortunes. But He who did not find it beneath His Majesty to make us, does not think it beneath Him to observe and to visit us. He says Himself in the Gospel: "Are not five sparrows sold for two farthings? and not one of them is forgotten before God. Yea, the very hairs of your head are all numbered. Fear not, therefore: you are of more value than many sparrows." He determined from all eternity that He would create us. He settled our whole fortune—and, if He did not absolutely decree to bring us to heaven, it is because we have free will, and by the very constitution of our nature He has put it in part out of His own power, for we must do *our* part, if to heaven we attain. But He has done every thing short of this. He died for us all upon the Cross, that, if it were possible to save us, we might be saved. And He calls upon us lovingly, begging us to accept the benefit of His meritorious and most Precious Blood. And those who trust Him He takes under His special protection. He marks out their whole life for them; He appoints all that happens to them; He guides them in such way as to secure their salvation; He gives them just so much of health, of wealth, of friends, as is best for them; He afflicts them only when it is for their good; He is never angry with them. He measures out just that number of years which is good for them; and He appoints the hour of their death in such a way as to secure their perseverance up to it.

Let us pray for ourselves and for all our needs.

O my Lord and Savior, in thy arms I am safe; keep me and I have nothing to fear; give me up and I have nothing to hope for. I know not what will come upon me before I die. I know nothing about the future, but I rely upon thee. I pray thee to give me what is good for me; I pray thee to take from me whatever may imperil my salvation; I pray thee not to make me rich, I pray thee not to make me very poor; but I leave it all to thee, because thou knowest and I do not. If thou bringest pain or sorrow on me, give me grace to bear it well—keep me from fretfulness and selfishness. If thou givest me health and strength and success in this world, keep me ever on my guard lest these great gifts carry me away from thee. O thou who didst die on the Cross for me, even for me, sinner as I am, give me to know thee, to believe on thee, to love thee, to serve thee; ever to aim at setting forth thy glory; to live to and for thee; to set a good example to all around me; give me to die just at that time and in that way which is most for thy glory, and best for my salvation.

Jesus, Son of Mary

WHEN our Lord came upon earth, He might have created a fresh body for Himself out of nothing—or He might have formed a body for Himself out of the earth, as He formed Adam. But He preferred to be born, as other men are born, of a human mother. Why did He do so? He did so to put honor on all those earthly relations and connections which are ours by nature; and to teach us that, though He has begun a new creation, He does not wish us to cast off the old creation, as far as it is not sinful. Hence it is our duty to love and honor our parents, to be affectionate to our brothers, sisters, friends, husbands, wives, not only not less, but even more, than it was man's duty before our Lord came on earth. As we become better Christians, more consistent and zealous servants of Jesus, we shall become only more and more anxious for the good of all around us—our kindred, our friends, our acquaintances, our neighbors, our superiors, our inferiors, our masters, our employers. And this we shall do from the recollection how our Lord loved His Mother. He loves her still in heaven with a special love. He refuses her nothing. We then on earth must feel a tender solicitude for all our relations, all our friends, all whom we know or have dealings with. And moreover, we must love not only those who love us, but those who hate us or injure us, that we may imitate Him, who not only was loving to His Mother, but even suffered Judas, the traitor, to kiss Him, and prayed for His murderers on the cross.

Let us pray God for our relations, friends, well wishers, and enemies, living and dead.

O Jesus, son of Mary, whom Mary followed to the Cross when thy disciples fled, and who didst bear her tenderly in mind in the midst of thy sufferings, even in thy last words, who didst commit her to thy best beloved disciple, saying to her, "Woman, behold thy son," and to him, "Behold thy Mother," we, after thy pattern, would pray for all who are near and dear to us, and we beg thy grace to do so continually. We beg thee to bring them all into the light of thy truth, or to keep them in thy truth if they already know it, and to keep them in a state of grace, and to give them the gift of perseverance. We thus pray for our parents, for our fathers and our mothers, for our children, for every one of them, for our brothers and sisters, for every one of our brothers, for every one of our sisters, for our cousins and all our kindred, for our friends, and our father's friends, for all our old friends, for our dear and intimate friends, for our teachers, for our pupils, for our masters and employers, for our servants or subordinates, for our associates and work-fellows, for our neighbors, for our superiors and rulers; for those who wish us well, for those who wish us ill; for our enemies; for our rivals; for our injurers and for our slanderers. And not only for the living, but for the dead, who have died in the grace of God, that He may shorten their time of expiation, and admit them into His presence above.

Jesus, Our Daily Sacrifice

OUR Lord not only offered Himself as a sacrifice on the Cross, but He makes Himself a perpetual, a daily sacrifice, to the end of time. In the Holy Mass that one sacrifice on the Cross once offered is renewed, continued, applied to our benefit. He seems to say, my Cross was raised up long ago, and only for a few hours—and very few of my servants were present there—but I intend to bring millions into my Church. For their sakes then I will perpetuate my sacrifice, that each of them may be as though they had severally been present on Calvary. I will offer myself up day by day to the Father, that every one of my followers may have the opportunity to offer his petitions to Him, sanctified and recommended by the all-meritorious virtue of my Passion. Thus I will be a Priest for ever, after the order of Melchisedech—my priests shall stand at the altar—but not they, but I rather, will offer. I will not let them offer mere bread and wine, but I myself will be present upon the altar instead, and I will offer up myself invisibly, while they perform the outward rite. And thus the Lamb that was slain once for all, though He is ascended on high, ever remains a victim from His miraculous presence in Holy Mass under the figure and appearance of mere earthly and visible symbols.

Let us pray for all who day by day have calls upon us.

My Lord Jesus Christ, thou hast given me this great gift, that I am allowed, not only to pray for myself, but to intercede for others in thy Holy Mass. Therefore, O Lord, I pray thee to give all grace and blessing upon this town and every inhabitant of it—upon the Catholic Church in it, for our bishop, and his clergy, and for all Catholic places of worship and their congregations. I pray thee to bless and prosper all the good works and efforts of all priests, religious, and pious Catholics—I pray for all the sick, all the suffering, all the poor, all the oppressed—I pray for all prisoners—I pray for all evildoers. I pray for all ranks in the community. I pray for all who are in peril and danger. I pray for all who have benefited me, befriended me, or aided me. I pray for all who have asked my prayers—I pray for all whom I have forgotten. Bring us all after the troubles of this life into the haven of peace, and reunite us all together for ever, O my dear Lord, in thy glorious heavenly kingdom.

A *Triduo* to St. Joseph for March 19 by Bl. John Henry Newman

---

First Day
Consider the Glorious Titles of St. Joseph

He was the true and worthy spouse of Mary, supplying in a visible manner the place of Mary's invisible spouse, the Holy Ghost. He was a virgin, and his virginity was the faithful mirror of the virginity of Mary. He was the cherub, placed to guard the new terrestrial paradise from the intrusion of every foe.

V. Blessed be the name of Joseph.
R. Henceforth and forever. Amen.

LET US PRAY

God, who in thine ineffable providence didst vouchsafe to choose Blessed Joseph to be the husband of thy most holy Mother, grant, we beseech thee, that we may be made worthy to receive him for our intercessor in heaven, whom on earth we venerate as our holy Protector: who livest and reignest world without end. Amen.

—See *"The Raccolta"*

Second Day
Consider the Glorious Titles of St. Joseph

His was the title of father of the Son of God, because he was the spouse of Mary, ever Virgin. He was our Lord's father, because Jesus ever yielded to him the obedience of a son. He was our Lord's father, because to him were entrusted, and by him were faithfully fulfilled, the duties of a father, in protecting Him, giving Him a home, sustaining and rearing Him, and providing Him with a trade.

V. Blessed be the name of Joseph.
R. Henceforth and for ever. Amen.

LET US PRAY

God, who in thine ineffable providence didst vouchsafe...

Third Day
Consider the Glorious Titles of St. Joseph

He is Holy Joseph, because according to the opinion of a great number of doctors, he, as well as St. John Baptist, was sanctified even before he was born. He is Holy Joseph, because his office, of being spouse and protector of Mary, specially demanded sanctity. He is Holy Joseph, because no other saint but he lived in such an intimacy and familiarity with the source of all holiness, Jesus, God incarnate, and Mary, the holiest of creatures.

V. Blessed be the name of Joseph.
R. Henceforth and for ever. Amen.

LET US PRAY

God, who in thine ineffable providence didst vouchsafe...

Blessing of St Joseph's Table

+In the name of the Father and of the Son and of the Holy Spirit. Amen.

V. Our help is in the name of the Lord.
R. Who made heaven and earth.

V. The Lord be with you.
R. And with your spirit.

Scripture Reading

"You shall not pervert the justice due to the sojourner or to the fatherless, or take a widow's garment in pledge; but you shall remember that you were a slave in Egypt and the Lord your God redeemed you from there; therefore I command you to do this. When you reap your harvest in your field, and have forgotten a sheaf in the field, you shall not go back to get it; it shall be for the sojourner, the fatherless, and the widow; that the LORD your God may bless you in all the work of your hands. When you beat your olive trees, you shall not go over the boughs again; it shall be for the sojourner, the fatherless, and the widow. When you gather the grapes of your vineyard, you shall not glean it afterward; it shall be for the sojourner, the fatherless, and the widow. You shall remember that you were a slave in the land of Egypt; therefore I command you to do this."

—Deuteronomy 24:17-22

Prayer of Blessing

All-provident God, the good things that grace this table remind us of your many good gifts.

Bless this food, and may the prayers of Saint Joseph, who provided bread for your Son and food for the poor, sustain us and all our brothers and sisters on our journey toward your heavenly kingdom. We ask this through Christ our Lord. Amen.

A Priest's Prayers for Easter

Christ is Risen: The world below lies desolate.
Christ is Risen: The spirits of evil are fallen.
Christ is Risen: The angels of God are rejoicing.
Christ is Risen: The tombs of the dead are empty.
Christ is Risen indeed from the dead,
the first of the sleepers,
Glory and power are his forever and ever.

—St. Hippolytus

*

O Jesus, King,
receive my supplication,
and consider my supplication,
as a pledge to you.
For you, O living King,
have gone forth and gone up,
out of hell,
as conqueror.

Woe to those who have rejected you;
For, to evil spirits and demons,
you are sorrow,

to Satan and to death,
you are pain,
to sin and hell,
you are mourning.

Yet, joy has come today,
for those who are born anew.
On this great day therefore,
we give great glory to you,
who died and is now alive,
that to all you may give
life and resurrection!

—St. Ephrem the Syrian

✳

God our Father,
by raising Christ your Son
you conquered the power of death
and opened for us the way to eternal life.
Let our celebration today raise us up
and renew our lives by the Spirit that is within us.
Grant this through our Lord Jesus Christ, your Son,
who lives and reigns with you and the Holy Spirit,
one God, for ever and ever. Amen.

✳

O God,
who for our redemption gave your only-begotten Son
to the death of the cross,
and by his glorious resurrection
delivered us from the power of our enemy.
Grant us so to die daily to sin,
that we may evermore live
with him in the joy of his resurrection;
through Jesus Christ your Son our Lord,
who lives and reigns with you and the Holy Spirit,
one God, now and for ever. Amen.

✳

Blessed be the God and Father
of our Lord Jesus Christ.
In his great mercy
he has given us a new birth
to a living hope through the resurrection

of Jesus Christ from the dead
and to an inheritance
that is imperishable, undefiled, and unfading.
It is reserved in heaven for you,
who because of your faith in God
are being protected by his power
until the salvation
that is ready to be revealed at the end of time.

Queen of Heaven rejoice, Alleluia;
The Son whom you merited to bear, Alleluia,
has risen as he said, Alleluia.
Pray for us to God, Alleluia.
Rejoice and be glad, O Virgin Mary, Alleluia,
For the Lord is truly Risen, Alleluia.

O God, who made this most holy night to shine
with the glory of the Lord's resurrection:
Stir up in your Church that Spirit of adoption
which is given to us in baptism,
that we, being renewed both in body and mind,
may worship your only-begotten Son Jesus Christ
who overcame death
and opened to us the gate of everlasting life:
Grant that we,
who celebrate with joy the day of the Lord's resurrection,
may be raised from the death of sin
by your life-giving Spirit;
through Jesus Christ our Lord,
who lives and reigns with you and the Holy Spirit,
one God, now and for ever. Amen.

O God,
whose blessed Son made himself known
to his disciples in the breaking of bread:
Open the eyes of our faith,
that we may behold him in all his redeeming work;
who lives and reigns with you,
in the unity of the Holy Spirit, one God,
now and for ever. Amen.

✳

God of mercy,
you wash away our sins in water,
you give us a new birth in the Spirit,
and redeem us in the blood of Christ.
As we celebrate Christ's resurrection,
increase our awareness of these blessings,
and renew your gift of life within us.
We ask this through our Lord Jesus Christ, your Son,
who lives and reigns with you and the Holy Spirit,
one God, for ever and ever. Amen.

✳

Heavenly Father and God of mercy,
we no longer look for Jesus among the dead,
for he is alive
and has become the Lord of life.
From the waters of death you raise us with him
and renew your gift of life within us.
Increase in our minds and hearts
the risen life we share with Christ
and help us to grow as your people
toward the fullness of eternal life with you.
We ask this through Christ our Lord. Amen.

✳

God our Father,
may we look forward with hope
to our resurrection,
for you have made us your sons and daughters,
and restored the joy of our youth.
We ask this through our Lord Jesus Christ, your Son,
who lives and reigns with you and the Holy Spirit,
one God, for ever and ever. Amen.

✳

Almighty and ever-living God,
give us new strength
from the courage of Christ our shepherd,
and lead us to join the saints in heaven,
where he lives and reigns with you and the Holy Spirit,
one God, for ever and ever. Amen.

God and Father of our Lord Jesus Christ,
though your people walk in the valley of darkness,
no evil should they fear;
for they follow in faith the call of the shepherd
whom you have sent for their hope and strength.
Attune our minds to the sound of his voice,
lead our steps in the path he has shown,
that we may know the strength of his outstretched arm
and enjoy the light of your presence for ever.
We ask this through Christ our Lord. Amen.

Lord,
the resurrection of your Son
has given us new life and renewed hope.
Help us to live as new people
in pursuit of the Christian ideal.
Grant us wisdom to know what we must do,
the will to want to do it,
the courage to undertake it,
the perseverance to continue to do it,
and the strength to complete it.

Blessing of Easter Flowers

+In the name of the Father and of the Son and of the Holy Spirit. Amen.

V. Our help is in the name of the Lord.
R. Who made heaven and earth.

V. The Lord be with you.
R. And with your spirit.

Scripture Reading

"Therefore I tell you, do not be anxious about your life, what you shall eat or what you shall drink, nor about your body, what you shall put on. Is not life more than food, and the body more than clothing? Look at the birds of the air: they neither sow nor reap nor gather into barns, and yet your heavenly Father feeds them. Are you not of more value than they? And which of you by being anxious can add one cubit to his span of life?

And why are you anxious about clothing? Consider the lilies of the field, how they grow; they neither toil nor spin; yet I tell you, even Solomon in all his glory was not arrayed like one of these. But if God so clothes the grass of the field, which today is alive and tomorrow is thrown into the oven, will he not much more clothe you, O men of little faith? Therefore do not be anxious, saying, 'What shall we eat?' or 'What shall we drink?' or 'What shall we wear?' For the Gentiles seek all these things; and your heavenly Father knows that you need them all. But seek first his kingdom and his righteousness, and all these things shall be yours as well."

—Matthew 6:25-33

Prayer of Blessing

Lord, you have given glory to the grasses of the field and you give us new life in this Easter season. Bless + these flowers which will decorate your altar. May they be a sign to us of the new life given to us in your Son, Jesus whose resurrection we celebrate with joy. Through the same Christ our Lord. Amen.

Blessing of Easter Foods

+In the name of the Father and of the Son and of the Holy Spirit. Amen.

V. Our help is in the name of the Lord.
R. Who made heaven and earth.

V. The Lord be with you.
R. And with your spirit.

Scripture Reading

"In this manner you shall eat it: your loins girded, your sandals on your feet, and your staff in your hand; and you shall eat it in haste. It is the Lord's passover. For I will pass through the land of Egypt that night, and I will smite all the first-born in the land of Egypt, both man and beast; and on all the gods of Egypt I will execute judgments: I am the Lord. The blood shall be a sign for you, upon the houses where you are; and when I see the blood, I will pass over you, and no plague shall fall upon you to destroy you, when I smite the land of Egypt. This day shall be for you a memorial day, and you shall keep it as a feast to the Lord; throughout your generations you shall observe it as an ordinance forever."

—Exodus 12:11-14

Prayer of Blessing

Bless, O Lord, this creation that it may be a means of salvation to the human race, and grant that, by the invocation of thy Holy Name, it may promote health of body, and salvation of soul in those who partake of it, through Christ our Lord. Amen.

An Easter Litany by Bl. John Henry Newman

Litany of the Resurrection

LORD, have mercy.
Lord, have mercy.
Christ, have mercy.
Christ, have mercy.
Lord, have mercy.
Lord, have mercy.
Christ, hear us.
Christ, graciously hear us.
God the Father of Heaven, *Have mercy on us.*
God the Son, Redeemer of the world, "
God the Holy Ghost,
Holy Trinity, one God,
Jesus, Redeemer of mankind, *Have mercy on us.*
Jesus, Conqueror of sin and Satan, "
Jesus, triumphant over Death,
Jesus, the Holy and the Just,
Jesus, the Resurrection and the Life,
Jesus, the Giver of grace,
Jesus, the Judge of the world,
Who didst lay down thy life for thy sheep,
Who didst rise again the third day,
Who didst manifest thyself to thy chosen,
Visiting thy blessed Mother,
Appearing to Magdalen while she wept,
Sending thy angels to the holy women,
Comforting the Eleven,
Saying to them, Peace,
Breathing on them the Holy Ghost,
Confirming the faith of Thomas,

Committing thy flock to Peter,
Speaking of the Kingdom of God,

We sinners *beseech thee, hear us*,
That we may walk in newness of life, *We beseech thee, hear us*.
That we may advance in the knowledge of thee, "
That we may grow in grace,
That we may ever have the bread of life,
That we may persevere unto the end,
That we may have confidence before thee at thy coming,
That we may behold thy face with joy,
That we may be placed at thy right hand in the judgment,
That we may have our lot with the saints,

Lamb of God, who takest away the sins of the world,
Spare us, O *Lord*.
Lamb of God, who takest away the sins of the world,
Graciously hear us, O *Lord*.
Lamb of God, who takest away the sins of the world,
Have mercy on us.
Christ, hear us.
Christ, graciously hear us.
Lord, have mercy.
Christ, have mercy.
Lord, have mercy.

Christ is risen, Alleluia.
He is risen indeed, and hath appeared unto Simon, Alleluia.

Let us Pray,

O God, who by thy only begotten Son hast overcome death, and opened on us the way to eternal life, vouchsafe, we beseech thee, so to confirm us by thy grace, that we may in all things walk after the manner of those who have been redeemed from their sins, through the same Jesus Christ our Lord. Amen.

A Blessing of Lilies for the Feast of St. Anthony on June 13

+In the name of the Father and of the Son and of the Holy Spirit. Amen.

V. Our help is in the name of the Lord.
R. Who made heaven and earth.

V. The Lord be with you.
R. And with your spirit.

Scripture Reading

"Therefore I tell you, do not be anxious about your life, what you shall eat or what you shall drink, nor about your body, what you shall put on. Is not life more than food, and the body more than clothing? Look at the birds of the air: they neither sow nor reap nor gather into barns, and yet your heavenly Father feeds them. Are you not of more value than they? And which of you by being anxious can add one cubit to his span of life? And why are you anxious about clothing? Consider the lilies of the field, how they grow; they neither toil nor spin; yet I tell you, even Solomon in all his glory was not arrayed like one of these. But if God so clothes the grass of the field, which today is alive and tomorrow is thrown into the oven, will he not much more clothe you, O men of little faith? Therefore do not be anxious, saying, 'What shall we eat?' or 'What shall we drink?' or 'What shall we wear?' For the Gentiles seek all these things; and your heavenly Father knows that you need them all. But seek first his kingdom and his righteousness, and all these things shall be yours as well."

—**Matthew 6:25-33**

Prayer of Blessing

O God, who art the Creator and Preserver of all mankind, the Lover of spotless purity, the Giver of all grace and everlasting life, sanctify by thy holy benediction these lilies, which in thanksgiving, and in honor of St. Anthony, thy confessor, we present for thy blessing.

Pour down upon them, by the sacred sign of the holy Cross, thy heavenly dew, thou who didst so kindly create them to gladden man by their beauty and fragrance; enrich them with such power, that to whatsoever disease they may be applied, or in whatsoever home they may be kept, or on whatsoever person they may be borne with devotion, through the intercession of thy servant, Anthony, they may cure every sickness, repel the attacks of Satan, preserve holy chastity, and bring peace and grace to all who serve thee. Through Christ Our Lord. Amen.

A Blessing of Rectory Gardens on the Solemnity of the Assumption for August 15

+In the name of the Father and of the Son and of the Holy Spirit. Amen.

V. Our help is in the name of the Lord.
R. Who made heaven and earth.

V. The Lord be with you.
R. And with your spirit.

Scripture Reading

My beloved speaks and says to me:
"Arise, my love, my fair one,
and come away;
for lo, the winter is past,
the rain is over and gone.
The flowers appear on the earth,
the time of singing has come,
and the voice of the turtledove
is heard in our land.
The fig tree puts forth its figs,
and the vines are in blossom;
they give forth fragrance.
Arise, my love, my fair one,
and come away."

—Song of Songs 2:10-13

Prayer of Blessing

Almighty and eternal God, as often as we look on this garden with our bodily eyes, so often do we consider the actions of your saints with our mind's eye, and ponder their sanctity for our imitation. Be so good, we beg of you, to bless and sanctify this garden that whoever in this garden humbly pays devout reverence and honor to your only-begotten Son and his Blessed Mother, may through their merits and intercession win grace in this life, and everlasting glory in the world to come. We ask this in the name of Jesus the Lord. Amen.

Blessing of an Altar of the Dead

+In the name of the Father and of the Son and of the Holy Spirit. Amen.

V. Our help is in the name of the Lord.
R. Who made heaven and earth.

V. The Lord be with you.
R. And with your spirit.

Scripture Reading

"All that the Father gives me will come to me; and him who comes to me I will not cast out. For I have come down from heaven, not to do my own will, but the will of him who sent me; and this is the will of him who sent me, that I should lose nothing of all that he has given me, but raise it up at the last day. For this is the will of my Father, that every one who sees the Son and believes in him should have eternal life; and I will raise him up at the last day."

—John 6:37-40

Prayer of Blessing

God our Father, bless + this altar that we use to commemorate our beloved dead. Guide them in your goodness to eternal life. May we never forget to pray for them and ask them to pray for us. Through Christ our Lord. Amen.

Prayers for the Dead

De Profundis

Out of the depths I cry to you, O Lord; Lord, hear my voice.
Let your ears be attentive to my voice in supplication.
If you, O Lord, mark iniquities, Lord, who can stand?
But with you is forgiveness, that you may be revered.
I trust in the Lord; my soul trusts in his word.
My soul waits for the Lord more than sentinels wait for the dawn.
More than sentinels wait for the dawn, let Israel wait for the Lord,
For with the Lord is kindness and with him is plenteous redemption;
And he will redeem Israel from all their iniquities.

Prayer for Mercy on the Souls in Purgatory

My Jesus, by the sorrows thou didst suffer in thine agony in the garden, in thy scourging and crowning with thorns, on the way to Calvary, in thy crucifixion and death, have mercy on the souls in purgatory, and especially on those that are most forsaken; do thou deliver them from the dire torments they endure; call them and admit them to thy most sweet embrace in paradise.

Prayer for All the Deceased

By thy resurrection from the dead, O Christ, death no longer hath dominion over those who die in holiness. So, we beseech thee, give rest to thy servants in thy sanctuary and in Abraham's bosom. Grant it to those, who from Adam until now have adored thee with purity, to our fathers and brothers, to our kinsmen and friends, to all men who have lived by faith and passed on their road to thee, by a thousand ways, and in all conditions, and make them worthy of the heavenly kingdom.

Prayer for the Holy Souls in Purgatory

O Lord, who art ever merciful and bounteous with thy gifts, look down upon the suffering souls in purgatory. Remember not their offenses and negligences, but be mindful of thy loving mercy, which is from all eternity. Cleanse them of their sins and fulfill their ardent desires that they may be made worthy to behold thee face to face in thy glory. May they soon be united with thee and hear those blessed words which will call them to their heavenly home: "Come, blessed of my Father, take possession of the kingdom prepared for you from the foundation of the world."

Sunday Prayer for the Faithful Departed

O Lord God omnipotent, I beseech thee by the Precious Blood, which thy divine Son Jesus shed in the garden, deliver the souls in purgatory, and especially that one which is the most forsaken of all, and bring it into thy glory, where it may praise and bless thee for ever. Amen.

Eternal rest grant unto them, O Lord, and let perpetual light shine upon them. May the souls of the faithful departed, through the mercy of God, rest in peace. Amen.

Monday Prayer for the Faithful Departed

O Lord God omnipotent, I beseech thee by the Precious Blood which thy divine Son Jesus shed in his cruel scourging, deliver the souls in purgatory, and among them all, especially that soul which is nearest to its entrance into thy glory, that it may soon begin to praise and bless thee forever. Amen.

Eternal rest grant unto them, O Lord, and let perpetual light shine upon them. May the souls of the faithful departed, through the mercy of God, rest in peace. Amen.

Tuesday Prayer for the Faithful Departed

O Lord God omnipotent, I beseech thee by the Precious Blood of thy divine Son Jesus that was shed in his bitter crowning with thorns, deliver the souls in purgatory, and among them all, particularly that soul which is in the greatest need of our prayers, in order that it may not long be delayed in praising thee in thy glory and blessing thee forever. Amen.

Eternal rest grant unto them, O Lord, and let perpetual light shine upon them. May the souls of the faithful departed, through the mercy of God, rest in peace. Amen.

Wednesday Prayer for the Faithful Departed

O Lord God omnipotent, I beseech thee by the Precious Blood of thy divine Son Jesus that was shed in the streets of Jerusalem whilst he carried on his sacred shoulders the heavy burden of the Cross, deliver the souls in purgatory and especially that one which is richest in merits in thy sight, so that, having soon attained the high place in glory to which it is destined, it may praise thee triumphantly and bless thee forever. Amen.

Eternal rest grant unto them, O Lord, and let perpetual light shine upon them. May the souls of the faithful departed, through the mercy of God, rest in peace. Amen.

Thursday Prayer for the Faithful Departed

O Lord God omnipotent, I beseech thee by the Precious Body and Blood of thy divine Son Jesus, which he Himself on the night before His Passion gave as meat and drink to his beloved Apostles and bequeathed to his holy Church to be the perpetual sacrifice and life-giving nourishment of his faithful people, deliver the souls in purgatory, but most of all, that soul which was most devoted to this Mystery of infinite love, in order that it may praise thee together with thy divine Son and the Holy Spirit in thy glory forever. Amen.

Eternal rest grant unto them, O Lord, and let perpetual light shine upon them. May the souls of the faithful departed, through the mercy of God, rest in peace. Amen.

Friday Prayer for the Faithful Departed

O Lord God omnipotent, I beseech thee by the Precious Blood which Jesus thy divine Son did shed this day upon the tree of the Cross, especially from his sacred hands and feet, deliver the souls in purgatory, and particularly that soul for whom I am most bound to pray, in order that I may not be the cause which hinders thee from admitting it quickly to the possession of thy glory where it may praise thee and bless thee forevermore. Amen.

Eternal rest grant unto them, O Lord, and let perpetual light shine upon them. May the souls of the faithful departed, through the mercy of God, rest in peace. Amen.

Saturday Prayer for the Faithful Departed

O Lord God omnipotent, I beseech thee by the Precious Blood which gushed forth from the sacred side of thy divine Son Jesus in the presence and to the great sorrow of his most holy Mother, deliver the souls in purgatory and among them all especially that soul which has been most devout to this noble Lady, that it may come quickly into thy glory, there to praise thee in her, and her in thee through all the ages. Amen.

Eternal rest grant unto them, O Lord, and let perpetual light shine upon them. May the souls of the faithful departed, through the mercy of God, rest in peace. Amen.

Prayer for a Departed Priest

O God, thou didst raise thy servant (N) to the sacred priesthood of Jesus Christ, according to the order of Melchisedech, giving him the sublime power to offer the Eternal Sacrifice, to bring the Body and Blood of thy Son Jesus Christ down upon the altar, and to absolve the sins of men in thine own Holy Name. We beseech thee to reward his faithfulness and to forget his faults, admitting him speedily into thy holy presence, there to enjoy forever the recompense of his labors. This we ask through Jesus Christ thy Son, our Lord. Amen.

Prayer for Deceased Priests

O heavenly Father, Father of the great high priest, your Son, Jesus Christ, we pray for the happy repose of all deceased priests. These men gave their lives to bring the love of your Son to the world. Look kindly on them and give them a share of your glory in heaven. We ask this in the name of your Son, Jesus, our Lord. Amen.

A Prayer for the Dying

Most merciful Jesus, lover of souls, I pray you, by the agony of your most Sacred Heart, and by the sorrows of your Immaculate Mother, to wash in your Most Precious Blood, the sinners of the world who are now in their agony, and who will die today.

Heart of Jesus, once in agony, have mercy on the dying. Amen.

A Prayer for a Happy Death

O God, who has doomed all men to die, but has concealed from all the hour of their death, grant that I may pass my days in the practice of holiness and justice, and that I may deserve to quit this world in the peace of a good conscience, and in the embrace of your love through the same Christ our Lord. Amen.

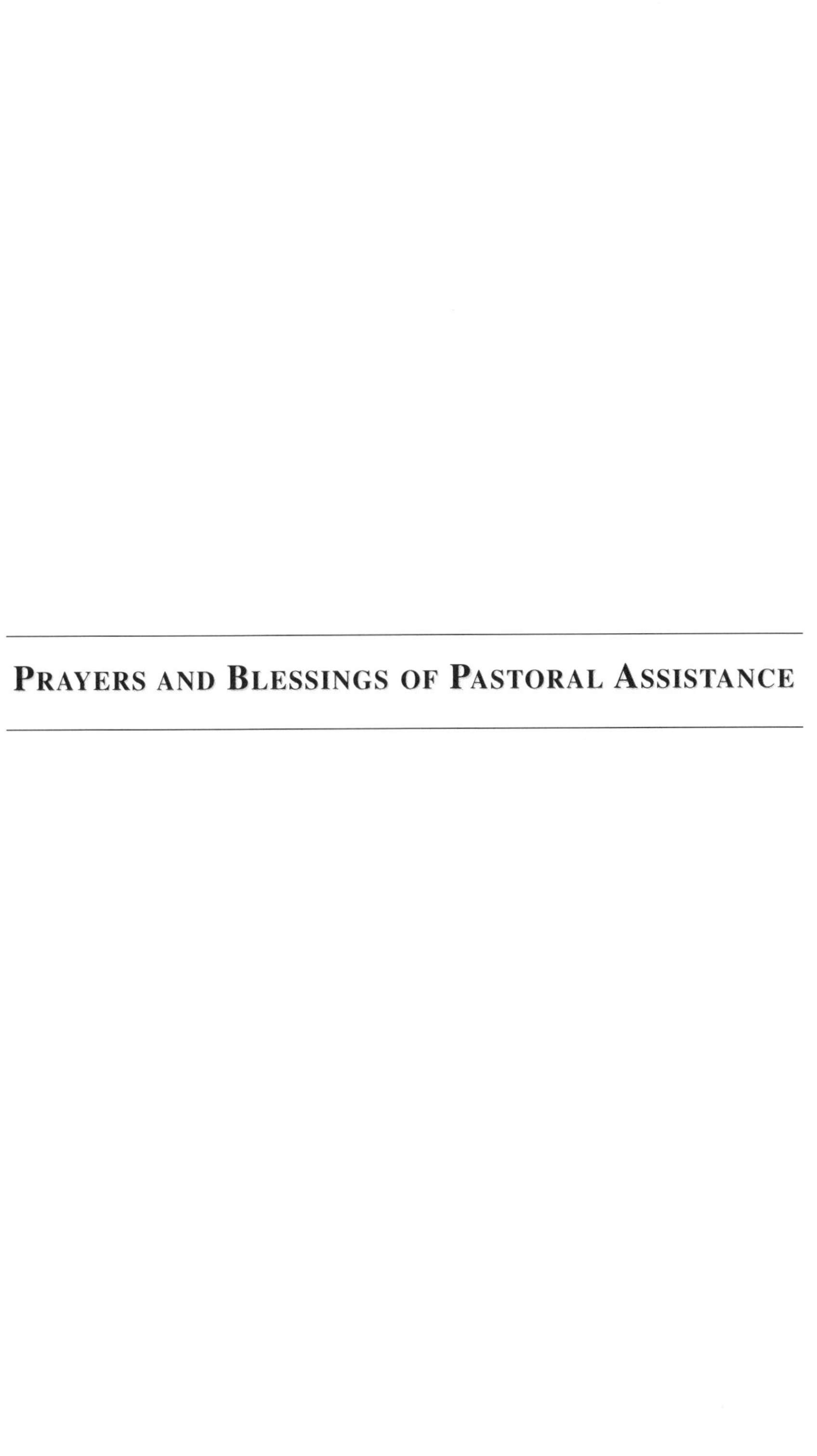

Prayers and Blessings of Pastoral Assistance

Blessing of Those Seeking Spiritual Counsel

+In the name of the Father and of the Son and of the Holy Spirit. Amen.

V. Our help is in the name of the Lord.
R. Who made heaven and earth.

V. The Lord be with you.
R. And with your spirit.

Scripture Reading

Incline your ear, and come to me;
hear, that your soul may live;
and I will make with you an everlasting covenant,
my steadfast, sure love for David.
Behold, I made him a witness to the peoples,
a leader and commander for the peoples.
Behold, you shall call nations that you know not,
and nations that knew you not shall run to you,
because of the LORD your God, and of the Holy One of Israel,
for he has glorified you.
Seek the LORD while he may be found,
call upon him while he is near.

—Isaiah 55:3-6

Prayer of Blessing

Lord God, we ask your blessing today upon our brother (sister) (N). Allow him (her) the freedom of honest conversation. Let him (her) know of your care and concern. Open his (her) heart to the joy of your presence as we begin this time of counsel together. Bless this time and give us your peace in our lives. We ask this in the name of Jesus the Lord. Amen.

Blessing of Those Seeking Spiritual Direction

+In the name of the Father and of the Son and of the Holy Spirit. Amen.

V. Our help is in the name of the Lord.
R. Who made heaven and earth.

V. The Lord be with you.
R. And with your spirit.

Scripture Reading

Jesus entered a village; and a woman named Martha received him into her house. And she had a sister called Mary, who sat at the Lord's feet and listened to his teaching. But Martha was distracted with much serving; and she went to him and said, "Lord, do you not care that my sister has left me to serve alone? Tell her then to help me." But the Lord answered her, "Martha, Martha, you are anxious and troubled about many things; one thing is needful. Mary has chosen the good portion, which shall not be taken away from her."

—Luke 10:38-42

Prayer of Blessing

Lord, you allowed Mary to sit at your feet and listen to your words. Inspire our time together today. Bless + (N) as he (she) seeks to know your will more fully in his (her) life. Give us the gifts of your Holy Spirit, and enkindle in our lives a greater love for you, who live and reign with the Father and the Holy Spirit, one God forever and ever. Amen.

Blessing of Couples Seeking Marriage Counseling

+In the name of the Father and of the Son and of the Holy Spirit. Amen.

V. Our help is in the name of the Lord.
R. Who made heaven and earth.

V. The Lord be with you.
R. And with your spirit.

Scripture Reading

Seeing the crowds, he went up on the mountain, and when he sat down his disciples came to him. And he opened his mouth and taught them, saying:
"Blessed are the poor in spirit, for theirs is the kingdom of heaven.
Blessed are those who mourn, for they shall be comforted.
Blessed are the meek, for they shall inherit the earth.
Blessed are those who hunger and thirst for righteousness, for they shall be satisfied.
Blessed are the merciful, for they shall obtain mercy.
Blessed are the pure in heart, for they shall see God.
Blessed are the peacemakers, for they shall be called sons of God.
Blessed are those who are persecuted for righteousness' sake, for theirs is the kingdom of heaven.

"Blessed are you when men revile you and persecute you and utter all kinds of evil against you falsely on my account. Rejoice and be glad, for your reward is great in heaven, for so men persecuted the prophets who were before you."

—Matthew 5:1-12

Prayer of Blessing

Lord God, you have called (N) and (N) to the blessings of married life. Be with them in their times of trial and hardship. Give them insight to see your love present in their lives and in their marriage. Renew in them the sacrament of your grace and instill in them a new hope and a new recognition that you are with them in all things. Bless + them and our time together today. We ask this in the name of Jesus the Lord. Amen.

Blessing of Those in the Annulment Process

+In the name of the Father and of the Son and of the Holy Spirit. Amen.

V. Our help is in the name of the Lord.
R. Who made heaven and earth.

V. The Lord be with you.
R. And with your spirit.

Scripture Reading

Count it all joy, my brethren, when you meet various trials, for you know that the testing of your faith produces steadfastness. And let steadfastness have its full effect, that you may be perfect and complete, lacking in nothing. If any of you lacks wisdom, let him ask God, who gives to all men generously and without reproaching, and it will be given him.

—James 1:2-5

Prayer of Blessing

God our Father, you give us life and wisdom even in times of pain and disappointment. Bless + (N) as he (she) continues the healing brought through this annulment process. Give him (her) the strength to see you walking with him (her) even in times of great trial and adversity. We ask this through Christ our Lord. Amen.

Blessing of Families Seeking Counseling

+In the name of the Father and of the Son and of the Holy Spirit. Amen.

V. Our help is in the name of the Lord.
R. Who made heaven and earth.

V. The Lord be with you.
R. And with your spirit.

Scripture Reading

Put on then, as God's chosen ones, holy and beloved, compassion, kindness, lowliness, meekness, and patience, forbearing one another and, if one has a complaint against another, forgiving each other; as the Lord has forgiven you, so you also must forgive. And above all these put on love, which binds everything together in perfect harmony. And let the peace of Christ rule in your hearts, to which indeed you were called in the one body. And be thankful. Let the word of Christ dwell in you richly; teach and admonish one another in all wisdom, and sing psalms and hymns and spiritual songs with thankfulness in your hearts to God. And whatever you do, in word or deed, do everything in the name of the Lord Jesus, giving thanks to God the Father through him.

—Colossians 3:12-17

Prayer of Blessing

Loving God, in your goodness you have called us to the joys and the challenges of family life. Be with this family and bless + them as we struggle to find your will in their lives. Help us to be open to conversation. Make us respectful of one another and draw us more fully into that love which inspired the life of the Holy Family of Nazareth. We ask this through Christ our Lord. Amen.

Blessing of Those Struggling with Addictions

+In the name of the Father and of the Son and of the Holy Spirit. Amen.

V. Our help is in the name of the Lord.
R. Who made heaven and earth.

V. The Lord be with you.
R. And with your spirit.

Scripture Reading

We are afflicted in every way, but not crushed; perplexed, but not driven to despair; persecuted, but not forsaken; struck down, but not destroyed; always carrying in the body the death of Jesus, so that the life of Jesus may also be manifested in our bodies. For while we live we are always being given up to death for Jesus' sake, so that the life of Jesus may be manifested in our mortal flesh. So death is at work in us, but life in you. Since we have the same spirit of faith as he had who wrote, "I believed, and so I spoke," we too believe, and so we speak, knowing that he who raised the Lord Jesus will raise us also with Jesus and bring us with you into his presence. For it is all for your sake, so that as grace extends to more and more people it may increase thanksgiving, to the glory of God. So we do not lose heart. Though our outer nature is wasting away, our inner nature is being renewed every day. For this slight momentary affliction is preparing for us an eternal weight of glory beyond all comparison, because we look not to the things that are seen but to the things that are unseen; for the things that are seen are transient, but the things that are unseen are eternal.

—2 Corinthians 4:8-18

Prayer of Blessing

God of mercy, we bless you in the name of your Son, Jesus Christ, who ministered to all who came to Him. Give your blessing + to (N), one of your children; enfold him (her) in your love and restore him (her) to the freedom of God's children.

Lord, look with compassion on all those who have lost their health and freedom. Restore to them the assurance of your unfailing mercy, strengthen them in the work of recovery, and help them to resist all temptation.

To those who care for them, grant patience and understanding and a love that perseveres. We ask this through Christ our Lord. Amen.

Blessing of Priests Struggling with Addictions

+In the name of the Father and of the Son and of the Holy Spirit. Amen.

V. Our help is in the name of the Lord.
R. Who made heaven and earth.

V. The Lord be with you.
R. And with your spirit.

Scripture Reading

We are afflicted in every way, but not crushed; perplexed, but not driven to despair; persecuted, but not forsaken; struck down, but not destroyed; always carrying in the body the death of Jesus, so that the life of Jesus may also be manifested in our bodies. For while we live we are always being given up to death for Jesus' sake, so that the life of Jesus may be manifested in our mortal flesh. So death is at work in us, but life in you. Since we have the same spirit of faith as he had who wrote, "I believed, and so I spoke," we too believe, and so we speak, knowing that he who raised the Lord Jesus will raise us also with Jesus and bring us with you into his presence. For it is all for your sake, so that as grace extends to more and more people it may increase thanksgiving, to the glory of God. So we do not lose heart. Though our outer nature is wasting away, our inner nature is being renewed every day. For this slight momentary affliction is preparing for us an eternal weight of glory beyond all comparison, because we look not to the things that are seen but to the things that are unseen; for the things that are seen are transient, but the things that are unseen are eternal.

—2 Corinthians 4:8-18

Prayer of Blessing

God of mercy, we bless you in the name of your Son, Jesus Christ, who ministered to all who came to him. Give your strength to (N), one of your faithful priests; enfold him in your love and restore him (her) to the freedom of God's children.

Lord, look with compassion on all those who have lost their health and freedom. Restore to them the assurance of your unfailing mercy, strengthen them in the work of recovery, and help them to resist all temptation.

To those who care for them, grant patience and understanding and a love that perseveres. We ask this through Christ our Lord. Amen.

Blessing of Men's Groups

+In the name of the Father and of the Son and of the Holy Spirit. Amen.

V. Our help is in the name of the Lord.
R. Who made heaven and earth.

V. The Lord be with you.
R. And with your spirit.

Scripture Reading

Rejoice in the Lord always; again I will say, Rejoice. Let all men know your forbearance. The Lord is at hand. Have no anxiety about anything, but in everything by prayer and supplication with thanksgiving let your requests be made known to God. And the peace of God, which passes all understanding, will keep your hearts and your minds in Christ Jesus. Finally, brethren, whatever is true, whatever is honorable, whatever is just, whatever is pure, whatever is lovely, whatever is gracious, if there is any excellence, if there is anything worthy of praise, think about these things. What you have learned and received and heard and seen in me, do; and the God of peace will be with you.

—Philippians 4:4-9

Prayer of Blessing

Loving God, you have called these men to faithful service in your Church. Bless + this men's group with your grace and fill them with the joy of service to their brothers and sisters. We ask this in the name of Jesus the Lord. Amen.

Blessing of Women's Groups

+In the name of the Father and of the Son and of the Holy Spirit. Amen.

V. Our help is in the name of the Lord.
R. Who made heaven and earth.

V. The Lord be with you.
R. And with your spirit.

Scripture Reading

So if there is any encouragement in Christ, any incentive of love, any participation in the Spirit, any affection and sympathy, complete my joy by being of the same mind, having the same love, being in full accord and of one mind. Do nothing from selfishness or conceit, but in humility count others better than yourselves. Let each of you look not only to his own interests, but also to the interests of others. Have this mind among yourselves, which is yours in Christ Jesus, who, though he was in the form of God, did not count equality with God a thing to be grasped, but emptied himself, taking the form of a servant, being born in the likeness of men. And being found in human form he humbled himself and became obedient unto death, even death on a cross. Therefore God has highly exalted him and bestowed on him the name which is above every name, that at the name of Jesus every knee should bow, in heaven and on earth and under the earth, and every tongue confess that Jesus Christ is Lord, to the glory of God the Father.

—Philippians 2:1-11

Prayer of Blessing

Loving God, you have called these women to faithful service in your Church. Bless + this women's group with your grace and fill them with the joy of service to their brothers and sisters. We ask this in the name of Jesus the Lord. Amen.

Blessing of Parishioners Departing on a Trip

+In the name of the Father and of the Son and of the Holy Spirit. Amen.

V. Our help is in the name of the Lord.
R. Who made heaven and earth.

V. The Lord be with you.
R. And with your spirit.

Scripture Reading

But an angel of the Lord said to Philip, "Rise and go toward the south to the road that goes down from Jerusalem to Gaza." This is a desert road. And he rose and went. And behold, an Ethiopian, a eunuch, a minister of the Candace, queen of the Ethiopians, in charge of all her treasure, had come to Jerusalem to worship and was returning; seated in his chariot, he was reading the prophet Isaiah. And the Spirit said to Philip, "Go up and join this chariot." So Philip ran to him, and heard him reading Isaiah the prophet, and asked, "Do you understand what you are reading?" And he said, "How can I, unless some one guides me?" And he invited Philip to come up and sit with him.

—Acts 8:26-31

Prayer of Blessing

Lord, Bless + these parishioners who are going on a journey. May they arrive safely at their destination and return to us filled with life and hope. Grant this through Christ our Lord. Amen.

Blessing of Parishioners Departing on a Pilgrimage

+In the name of the Father and of the Son and of the Holy Spirit. Amen.

V. Our help is in the name of the Lord.
R. Who made heaven and earth.

V. The Lord be with you.
R. And with your spirit.

Scripture Reading

It shall come to pass in the latter days
that the mountain of the house of the LORD
shall be established as the highest of the mountains,
and shall be raised above the hills;
and all the nations shall flow to it,
and many peoples shall come, and say:
"Come, let us go up to the mountain of the LORD,
to the house of the God of Jacob;
that he may teach us his ways
and that we may walk in his paths."
For out of Zion shall go forth the law,
and the word of the LORD from Jerusalem.
he shall judge between the nations,
and shall decide for many peoples;
and they shall beat their swords into plowshares,
and their spears into pruning hooks;
nation shall not lift up sword against nation,
neither shall they learn war any more.
O house of Jacob,
come, let us walk
in the light of the LORD.

—Isaiah 2:2-5

Prayer of Blessing

All-powerful God, you always show mercy toward those who love you and you are never far away for those who seek you. Remain with your servants on this holy pilgrimage and guide their way in accord with your will. Shelter them with your protection by day, give them the light of your grace by night, and, as their companion on the journey, bring them to their destination in safety. We ask this through Christ our Lord. Amen.

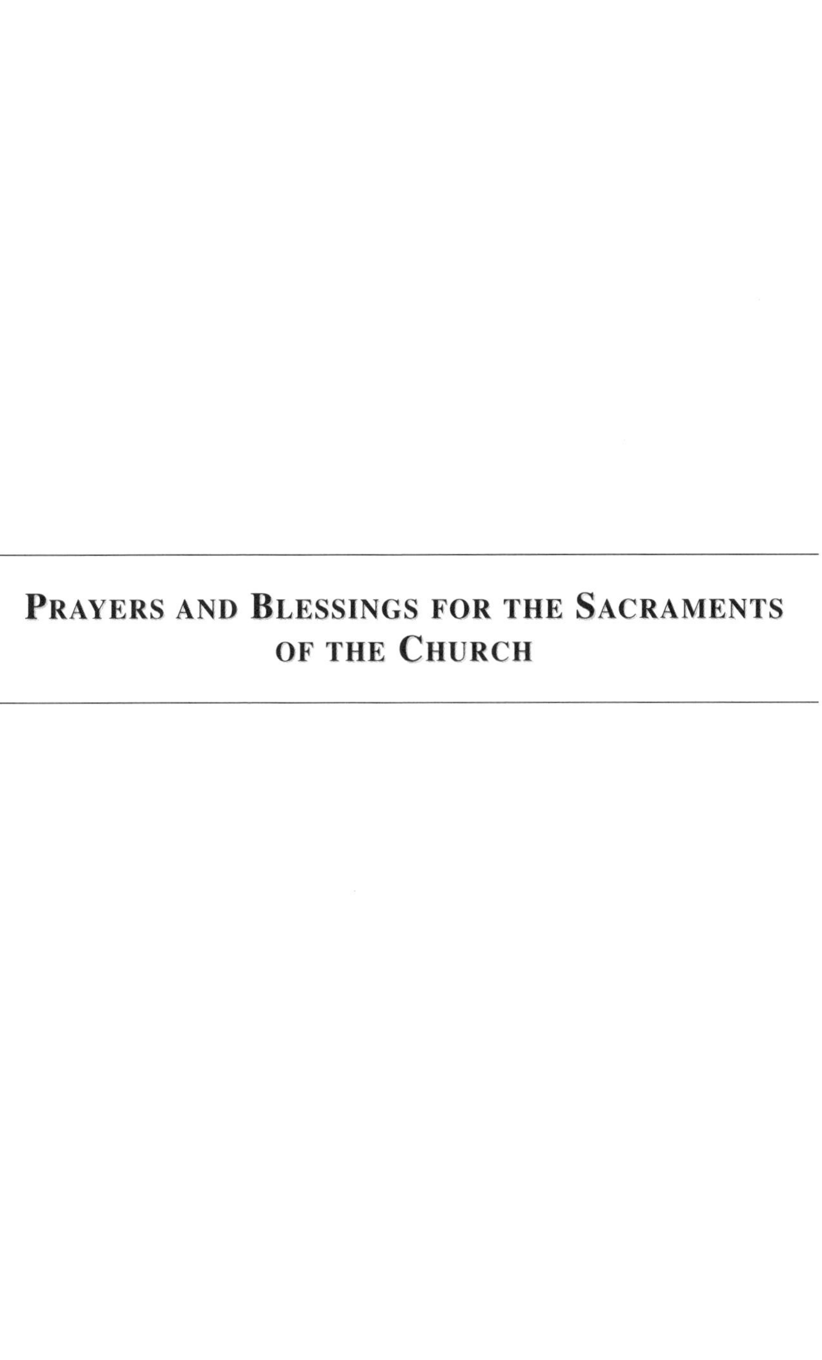

Prayers and Blessings for the Sacraments of the Church

Blessing of Ministers Before Mass

+In the name of the Father and of the Son and of the Holy Spirit. Amen.

V. Our help is in the name of the Lord.
R. Who made heaven and earth.

V. The Lord be with you.
R. And with your spirit.

Scripture Reading

Make a joyful noise to the LORD, all the lands!
Serve the LORD with gladness!
Come into his presence with singing!
Know that the LORD is God!
It is he that made us, and we are his;
we are his people, and the sheep of his pasture.
Enter his gates with thanksgiving,
and his courts with praise!
Give thanks to him, bless his name!
For the LORD is good;
his steadfast love endures for ever,
and his faithfulness to all generations.

—Psalm 100

Prayer of Blessing

Almighty God, you give us the privilege today of celebrating the Sacrifice of your Son in this Eucharist. Bless + these ministers who assist me today in offering this Mass. May we celebrate this liturgy with the dignity and recollection that it deserves. May the mysteries offered here draw us all into that Kingdom where you live and reign with the Son and Holy Spirit, one God forever and ever. Amen.

Blessing of Sacristans

+In the name of the Father and of the Son and of the Holy Spirit. Amen.

V. Our help is in the name of the Lord.
R. Who made heaven and earth.

V. The Lord be with you.
R. And with your spirit.

Scripture Reading

Jesus Christ is the same yesterday and today and for ever.
Do not be led away by diverse and strange teachings; for it is well that the heart be strengthened by grace, not by foods, which have not benefited their adherents.
We have an altar from which those who serve the tent have no right to eat.
For the bodies of those animals whose blood is brought into the sanctuary by the high priest as a sacrifice for sin are burned outside the camp.
So Jesus also suffered outside the gate in order to sanctify the people through his own blood.
Therefore let us go forth to him outside the camp and bear the abuse he endured.
For here we have no lasting city, but we seek the city which is to come.
Through him then let us continually offer up a sacrifice of praise to God, that is, the fruit of lips that acknowledge his name.
Do not neglect to do good and to share what you have, for such sacrifices are pleasing to God.

—Hebrews 13:8-16

Prayer of Blessing

Lord God, bless + these sacristans who work for the glory of the sacred liturgy. May their efforts bear blessings for eternal life for all who celebrate your mysteries in this church today. Grant this through Christ our Lord. Amen.

Blessing of Altar Servers' Robes

+In the name of the Father and of the Son and of the Holy Spirit. Amen.

V. Our help is in the name of the Lord.
R. Who made heaven and earth.

V. The Lord be with you.
R. And with your spirit.

Scripture Reading

I will greatly rejoice in the LORD, my soul shall be joyful in my God; for he hath clothed me with the garments of salvation, he hath covered me with the robe of righteousness, as a bridegroom decketh himself with ornaments, and as a bride adorneth herself with her jewels,

—Isaiah 61:10

Prayer of Blessing

Almighty everlasting God, giver of all good things and bountiful bestower of all graces, we humbly beg you to endow us with the power of your blessing. May it also please you to bless, + by the work of the Holy Spirit, these robes (cassocks and surplices) made ready for divine worship. Kindly let the grace of your holy mysteries descend on all who are to use it, so that they may appear holy, pure, and blameless in your presence, and may be aided by your mercy; through Christ our Lord. Amen.

The robes may be sprinkled with holy water.

Vesting Prayers

Roman Rite Vesting Prayers

When washing the hands:

Give virtue to my hands, O Lord, that being cleansed from all stain I might serve you with purity of mind and body.

With the amice:

Place upon me, O Lord, the helmet of salvation, that I may overcome the assaults of the devil.

With the alb:

Purify me, O Lord, and cleanse my heart; that, being made white in the Blood of the Lamb, I may come to eternal joy.

With the cincture:

Gird me, O Lord, with the girdle of purity, and extinguish in me all evil desires, that the virtue of chastity may abide in me.

With the maniple:

Grant, O Lord, that I may so bear the maniple of weeping and sorrow, that I may receive the reward for my labors with rejoicing.

With the stole:

Restore unto me, O Lord, the stole of immortality, which was lost through the guilt of our first parents; and, although I am unworthy to approach your sacred mysteries, nevertheless grant unto me eternal joy.

With the chasuble:

O Lord, who said: my yoke is easy and my burden light: grant that I may bear it well and follow after you with thanksgiving. Amen.

Eastern Rite Vesting Prayers

Sticharion:

"My soul shall rejoice in the Lord, for he has clothed me with the garment of righteousness and has covered me with a robe of gladness...." (Isaiah 61:10)

Epitrachelion:

"Blessed is God who pours out his grace upon his priests, as myrrh upon the head that ran down the beard of Aaron, which ran down to the collar of his garment." (Psalm 133:2)

Zone:

"Blessed is God who girds me with strength and makes my way blameless." (Psalm 18: 32-33)

Epimanikia:

(Right) "Your right hand, O Lord, is glorified in strength. Your right hand, has crushed the enemies. In the fullness of your glory you have shattered the adversaries." (Exodus 15: 6-7)

(Left) "Your hands have made me and have fashioned me. Grant me understanding and I shall learn from your commandments." (Psalm 119:73)

Phelonion:

"Your priests, O Lord, shall clothe themselves with righteousness, and your saints shall rejoice with joy...." (Psalm 132:9)

Priest's Prayers Before Mass

Prayer Before Mass by St. Ambrose

O gracious Lord Jesus Christ, though I, who am a sinner, in no way presume on any merits of my own, and put all my trust in your goodness and mercy, yet do I fear and tremble in drawing near to the Table on which is spread your banquet of all delights. Many a sin has sullied me in body and in soul because I did not restrain my thoughts nor guard my lips: nevertheless it is to you, O God of majesty and love, that I turn in my need, for you are the source of mercy; to you, as quickly as I may, I speed: for you alone can heal me; I take refuge under your protection. I dare not face you as my judge, but I cleave to you as my savior. Your mercy is above all your works. Though I fear, because of my sins, yet I trust in you on account of your mercy. Turn, then, your eyes upon me, O Jesus Christ, our everlasting king and Lord, who are God and man, and who for our sake was crucified. Have mercy upon me, full of misery and of sin though I be, upon me, whose only hope is in you, because of your loving-kindness. Hail! You saving victim, offered up for me and for all mankind upon the cross! Hail! You glorious and most Precious Blood, that flows from the wounds of Jesus Christ, my crucified Lord; to wash away the sins of all the world! Forget not, O Lord, that I am one of those whom you have created, and with your own blood have redeemed. I repent of my sins: I will strive to amend my ways. O most merciful Father, put far from me all my sins and all my offenses; so that, by you made whole in body and in soul, I may be accounted worthy to approach the Holy of holies. Grant that the holy foretaste of your Body and Blood, which you give to me, a poor sinner, may be a pledge of the full remission of my sins and of the washing away for evermore of all my guilt. From my mind may it chase away every sinful thought: in my will may it foster all holy desires: may it inspire me to do works pleasing to you; and may it be to me, of body and of soul, a very sure protection and defense against all evil. Amen.

Priest's Declaration of Intention

My purpose is to celebrate Mass and to make the Body and Blood of our Lord Jesus Christ according to the rite of the holy Roman Church, to the praise of almighty God and of the whole Church triumphant in heaven, for my own welfare and that of the whole Church militant on earth, for all who in general and in particular have commended themselves to my prayers, and for the well-being of the holy Roman Church. Amen.

May joy and peace, amendment of life, room for true penitence, the grace and comfort of the Holy Ghost, and steadfastness in good works be granted us by the almighty and merciful Lord. Amen.

God, who makest worthy of the unworthy, just and holy of sinners, and clean of the unclean, cleanse my heart and body from all taint and defilement of sin, and make me a worthy and strenuous minister at thy holy altars; and mercifully grant that on this altar, to which I unworthy make approach, I may offer a sacrifice acceptable and pleasing to thy loving-kindness, for my sins and offenses, and for my innumerable daily transgressions, and likewise for the washing away of the sins of all Christian people. And may my desire be acceptable to thee, through him who offered himself a sacrifice for us to thee his God and Father, who liveth and reigneth with thee and the Holy Ghost, one God, world without end. Amen.

Most merciful Father, you so loved the world that you sent your only Son to earth to redeem and save us. In obedience to your will He humbled Himself, even to death on a cross. He continues to offer Himself daily through the ministry of His priests for the living and the dead. We humbly pray, that motivated by a living faith, we may always assist with devotion and reverence at the oblation of his most precious Body and Blood which is made at Mass. In this way, we share in the supreme sacrifice which He accomplished on Cavalry; and His resurrection from the dead. In union with the whole Church, and in the company of the Blessed Virgin Mary and all the angels and saints, we now offer the adorable sacrifice of the Mass to your honor and glory. In it we acknowledge your infinite perfections, your supreme dominion over all creatures, our entire submission to you and our dependence on your gracious providence. We offer it in thanksgiving for your goodness to us and the forgiveness of our sins. We offer it also for the spread of the Catholic Church throughout the world and for our Pope, bishop and all the pastors that they may direct the faithful in the way of salvation. In this Mass, we pray for peace and goodwill among all peoples and for the needs of our world. May we, here present, receive grace to live a Christian life in this world in order to be with you in the world to come. We offer it for the eternal repose of the faithful departed. In this Mass, we remember, with gratitude, all that your Son Jesus Christ suffered for love of us as we commemorate His bitter passion and death and his glorious resurrection and ascension into heaven. We offer it for all the intentions agreeable to your Holy will through the same Jesus Christ, your Son, our Lord, who is both priest and victim. We make our prayer in the name of the most Holy Trinity, Father, Son and Holy Spirit to whom be honor, praise and glory for ever and ever. Amen.

Meditations on the Mass by Bl. John Henry Newman

---

(1) The Mass

1. I adore thee, O my Lord God, with the most profound awe for thy passion and crucifixion, in sacrifice for our sins thou didst' suffer incommu-

nicable sufferings in thy sinless soul. Thou wast exposed in thy innocent body to ignominious torments, to mingled pain and shame. Thou wast stripped and fiercely scourged, Thy sacred body vibrating under the heavy flail as trees under the blast. Thou wast, when thus mangled, hung up upon the Cross, naked, a spectacle for all to see thee quivering and dying. What does all this imply, O Mighty God! What a depth is here which we cannot fathom! My God, I know well, thou couldst have saved us at thy word, without thyself suffering; but thou didst choose to purchase us at the price of thy Blood. I look on thee, the victim lifted up on Calvary, and I know and protest that that death of thine was an expiation for the sins of the whole world. I believe and know, that thou alone couldst have offered a meritorious atonement; for it was thy divine nature which gave thy sufferings worth. Rather then that I should perish according to my deserts, thou wast nailed to the Tree and didst die.

2. Such a sacrifice was not to be forgotten. It was not to be—it could not be—a mere event in the world's history, which was to be done and over, and was to pass away except in its obscure, unrecognized effects. If that great deed was what we believe it to be, what we know it is, it must remain present, though past; it must be a standing fact for all times. Our own careful reflection upon it tells us this; and therefore, when we are told that thou, O Lord, though thou hast ascended to glory, hast renewed and perpetuated thy sacrifice to the end of all things, not only is the news most touching and joyful, as testifying to so tender a Lord and Savior, but it carries with it the full assent and sympathy of our reason. Though we neither could, nor would have dared, anticipate so wonderful a doctrine, yet we adore its very suitableness to thy perfections, as well as its infinite compassionateness for us, now that we are told of it. Yes, my Lord, though thou hast left the world, thou art daily offered up in the Mass; and, though thou canst not suffer pain and death, thou dost still subject thyself to indignity and restraint to carry out to the full thy mercies towards us. Thou dost humble thyself daily; for, being infinite, thou couldst not end thy humiliation while they existed for whom thou didst submit to it. So thou remainest a priest for ever.

3. My Lord, I offer thee myself in turn as a sacrifice of thanksgiving. Thou hast died for me, and I in turn make myself over to thee. I am not my own. Thou hast bought me; I will by my own act and deed complete the purchase. My wish is to be separated from everything of this world; to cleanse myself simply from sin; to put away from me even what is innocent, if used for its own sake, and not for thine. I put away reputation and honor, and influence,

and power, for my praise and strength shall be in thee. Enable me to carry out what I profess.

(2) Holy Communion

1. My God, who can be inhabited by thee, except the pure and holy? Sinners may come to thee, but to whom shouldst thou come except to the sanctified? My God, I adore thee as the holiest; and, when thou didst come upon earth, thou didst prepare a holy habitation for thyself in the most chaste womb of the Blessed Virgin. Thou didst make a dwelling place special for thyself. She did not receive thee without first being prepared for thee; for from the moment that she was at all, she was filled with thy grace, so that she never knew sin. And so she went on increasing in grace and merit year after year, till the time came, when thou didst send down the archangel to signify to her thy presence within her. So holy must be the dwelling place of the highest. I adore and glorify thee, O Lord my God, for thy great holiness.

2. O my God, holiness becometh thy house, and yet thou dost make thy abode in my breast. My Lord, my Savior, to me thou comest, hidden under the semblance of earthly things, yet in that very flesh and blood which thou didst take from Mary. Thou, who didst first inhabit Mary's breast, dost come to me. My God, thou seest me; I cannot see myself. Were I ever so good a judge about myself, ever so unbiased, and with ever so correct a rule of judging, still, from my very nature, I cannot look at myself, and view myself truly and wholly. But thou, as thou comest to me, contemplatest me. When I say, *Domine, non sum dignus*—"Lord, I am not worthy"—thou whom I am addressing, alone understandest in their fulness the words which I use. Thou seest how unworthy so great a sinner is to receive the One Holy God, whom the seraphim adore with trembling. Thou seest, not only the stains and scars of past sins, but the mutilations, the deep cavities, the chronic disorders which they have left in my soul. Thou seest the innumerable living sins, though they be not mortal, living in their power and presence, their guilt, and their penalties, which clothe me. Thou seest all my bad habits, all my mean principles, all wayward lawless thoughts, my multitude of infirmities and miseries, yet thou comest. Thou seest most perfectly how little I really feel what I am now saying, yet thou comest. O my God, left to myself should I not perish under the awful splendor and the consuming fire of thy Majesty. Enable me to bear thee, lest I have to say with Peter, "Depart from me, for I am a sinful man, O Lord!"

3. My God, enable me to bear thee, for thou alone canst. Cleanse my heart and mind from all that is past. Wipe out clean all my recollections of evil.

Rid me from all languor, sickliness, irritability, feebleness of soul. Give me a true perception of things unseen, and make me truly, practically, and in the details of life, prefer thee to anything on earth, and the future world to the present. Give me courage, a true instinct determining between right and wrong, humility in all things, and a tender longing love of thee.

(3) The Food of the Soul
Sitivit in Te anima mea
For Thee my soul hath thirsted

1. In thee, O Lord, all things live, and thou dost give them their food. *Oculi omnium in Te sperant*—"the eyes of all hope in thee." To the beasts of the field thou givest meat and drink. They live on day by day, because thou dost give them day by day to live. And, if thou givest not, they feel their misery at once. Nature witnesses to this great truth, for they are visited at once with great agony, and they cry out and wildly wander about, seeking what they need. But, as to us thy children, thou feedest us with another food. Thou knowest, O my God, who madest us, that nothing can satisfy us but thyself, and therefore thou hast caused thy own self to be meat and drink to us. O most adorable mystery! O most stupendous of mercies! Thou most glorious, and beautiful, and strong, and sweet, thou didst know well that nothing else would support our immortal natures, our frail hearts, but thyself; and so thou didst take a human flesh and blood, that they, as being the flesh and blood of God, might be our life.

2. O what an awful thought! Thou dealest otherwise with others, but, as to me, the flesh and blood of God is my sole life. I shall perish without it; yet shall I not perish with it and by it? How can I raise myself to such an act as to feed upon God? O my God, I am in a strait—shall I go forward, or shall I go back? I will go forward: I will go to meet thee. I will open my mouth, and receive thy gift. I do so with great awe and fear, but what else can I do? To whom should I go but to thee? Who can save me but thou? Who can cleanse me but thou? Who can make me overcome myself but thou? Who can raise my body from the grave but thou? Therefore I come to thee in all these my necessities, in fear, but in faith.

3. My God, thou art my life; if I leave thee, I cannot but thirst. Lost spirits thirst in hell, because they have not God. They thirst, though they fain would have it otherwise, from the necessity of their original nature. But I, my God, wish to thirst for thee with a better thirst. I wish to be clad in that new nature, which so longs for thee from loving thee, as to overcome in me the fear of

coming to thee. I come to thee, O Lord, not only because I am unhappy without thee, not only because I feel I need thee, but because thy grace draws me on to seek thee for thy own sake, because thou art so glorious and beautiful. I come in great fear, but in greater love. O may I never lose, as years pass away, and the heart shuts up, and all things are a burden, let me never lose this youthful, eager, elastic love of thee. Make thy grace supply the failure of nature. Do the more for me, the less I can do for myself. The more I refuse to open my heart to thee, so much the fuller and stronger be thy supernatural visitings, and the more urgent and efficacious thy presence in me.

Priest's Prayers Before Celebrating Baptism

Father of infinite love,
Your desire for our salvation was shown to us in the death and resurrection of Christ your Son, who won for you a chosen race, a royal priesthood, a holy nation, a people set apart. And through the sacrifice of your Son, I have been made worthy to assist him in his mission through the Sacrament of Baptism. Prepare the hearts and minds of all who are about to witness this amazing act of love. Grant each of us renewal in our own baptismal calling. Finally, protect and guard against the wickedness and snares of the devil those who are about to be baptized into your adopted family. I ask this through Christ our Lord. Amen.

Lord, Jesus Christ,
In perfect humility, you approached the Baptist on the bank of the Jordan River seeking to be baptized. You bowed low, so that each person might be raised up on high when your time came. Like the Baptist, never let me forget my unworthiness, but in that, may I always administer this sacrament boldly and without shame. Lord, through this sacrament, help me to decrease, so that I might be raised up on high in you, who live and reign with the Father and Holy Spirit, one God forever and ever. Amen.

Come Holy Spirit,
Descend upon those who are about to become adopted sons and daughters of you, the most high God. You were present at the Jordan in the form of a dove. Be present now and always to those about to receive Baptism. Enkindle in them and in all of us present a zeal to always deepen our faith in you. Amen.

Priest's Prayers After Celebrating Baptism

Father of all consolation,
Your plan for redemption that has existed for all eternity has once again been witnessed to and confirmed in history. Your most mysterious love and mercy have shone down upon your beloved children through the beautiful simplicity and the astounding power of water and words. I lift up my heart to you in gratitude for the gift of this extraordinary sacrament. I offer up to you, Father, those who have been baptized. Grant them the grace to faithfully endure this exile until they look upon your face in heaven. And Father, I thank you for counting me among those whom you have called to stand and preside over the Sacrament of Baptism. Continue to look down upon me with mercy and love, so that I will be strengthened by your grace to remain close to you always. I make this prayer through Christ our Lord. Amen.

⁕

Lord and Savior of all,
Our sin carried with it the penalty of death. Once banished from the Garden, we were destined for an eternity of suffering. Yet, our sin also won for us a great Redeemer, and you alone definitively effected the reconciliation between the Father and us. It is through the living waters of Baptism that we have been allowed to die with you, so that we can also rise to new life in you. My Lord, I direct all my praise and thanks to you for your gift of redemption that has been given to me and to all those who are baptized. Continue to guide me in my ministry. Let all that I do be for the salvation of souls and you, who live and reign with the Father and the Holy Spirit, one Lord forever and ever. Amen.

⁕

Creator Spirit,
You have been sent to aid all who have been received into the Father's e mbrace through the life-giving waters of Baptism. You are our constant and ever-faithful advocate. Grant that those who have just been baptized always experience your penetrating love and mystical guidance. May our hearts always be filled with gratitude for the labors of love you never cease to carry out on our behalf. Finally, may my love and devotion for you grow so that I become an overflowing vessel of your grace. Amen.

Blessing of Baptismal Garments

+In the name of the Father and of the Son and of the Holy Spirit. Amen.

V. Our help is in the name of the Lord.
R. Who made heaven and earth.

V. The Lord be with you.
R. And with your spirit.

Scripture Reading

Have mercy on me, God, in your goodness;
in your abundant compassion blot out my offense.
Wash away all my guilt; from my sin cleanse me.
Cleanse me with hyssop, that I may be pure;
wash me, make me whiter than snow.
Let me hear sounds of joy and gladness;
let the bones you have crushed rejoice.

—Psalm 51:3-4, 9-10

Prayer of Blessing

Father of Infinite Mercy, we were once a fallen race; a people without hope. We were exiled from the Garden and doomed to walk through this life crushed by the weight of our sins. All creation groaned as it awaited its redemption. Then you sent your Son, Jesus Christ, who stained our defiled world with his undefiled blood. In Baptism, the blood of the spotless lamb cleanses us of all our impurities. Through him our hope is restored and we are made into a new creation. And now I ask that you to bless this garment +. May it always remain spotless and unblemished, so that when your son (daughter) (N) approaches your heavenly throne, he (she) will be welcomed into your kingdom to dwell there for all of eternity. Amen.

Blessing of Baptismal Candles

+In the name of the Father and of the Son and of the Holy Spirit. Amen.

V. Our help is in the name of the Lord.
R. Who made heaven and earth.

V. The Lord be with you.
R. And with your spirit.

Scripture Reading

Jesus spoke to them again, saying, "I am the light of the world. Whoever follows me will not walk in darkness, but will have the light of life."

—John 8:12

Prayer of Blessing

Father in Heaven,
You sent your only begotten Son into a world glamorously darkened by the reality of sin. He was the one sent to redeem our gravely distorted nature. He came so that death could no longer lay hold of us, and we rejected him. Yet, it was in this world's darkest hour that your mercy for us pierced through our Lord most brightly as he hung upon the cross. He fulfilled your plan of salvation that has existed for all eternity, and through the waters of Baptism, we are able to participate in your plan for our salvation. Father, may this candle be for your son (daughter) (N) the light of Christ, the light of his (her) salvation in a world still darkened by sin. May its light always burn brightly within the heart of (N) so that others too might come to know the one true light of salvation. Amen.

Priest's Prayers Before Celebrating RCIA Rites

Heavenly Father,
After a period of silence,
Zechariah learned to trust in you.

Today we gather here,
as your Church,
ready to encourage, affirm, and recognize
the desire of these men and women,
to learn more about you.

Shower your grace upon them,
and enliven in their hearts,
a desire to learn more about you and your Church;
so that with greater zeal they may boldly proclaim,
"Let your mercy be on us,
as we place our trust in you."
We pray this through Christ our Lord. Amen.

⁕

Heavenly Father,
Like the Israelites who journeyed in the desert seeking the promised land,
we come here this day,
as an assembly of the Christian faithful.
We are here to affirm and encourage
these men and women,
on their faith journey.

As they prepare to receive the Rites of Christian Initiation,
open their hearts and give them peace and comfort;
let them know that they are not alone.
May they come to recognize the abundance of your grace in their lives;
and at the end of their journey,
let them rejoice in the one community of the Christian faithful.

We pray this all through our Lord Jesus Christ, your son,
who lives and reigns,
with you and the Holy Spirit,
one God, forever and ever. Amen.

✳

Merciful Father,
As I prepare to celebrate the rites of Christian Initiation,
enkindle in me the fire of your love,
and strengthen me with zeal for your Gospel,
through the witness of the profound love and faith,
alive in these men and women.
I ask this through Christ our Lord. Amen.

Priest's Prayers After Celebrating RCIA Rites

Lord Jesus,
Peter, your disciple, said:
"You have the words of eternal life."

Thank you for the gift of revealing your word to us.
We ask you to continue to strengthen our hearts,
as we continue our journey,
of growing in Christian holiness. Amen.

✳

Good and Gracious God,
you have been so generous to us,
thank you for the many blessings we have received.

As we continue studying your Word,
and the teaching of the Apostles,
handed down through the bishops,
continue to enlighten our minds,
and open out hearts,
so that we may better serve you by serving our community.

*

Bountiful God,
through the faith of your Church,
your love is realized in the world.

Thank you for revealing this gift.
As I feel more strongly called
to enter into the mystery of your Church,
open my ears,
so that I may hear your voice.

Through the anointing with the oil of Catechumens,
keep me mindful of your presence in my life.
Let me know that I am not alone on this journey,
through encouragement and prayers of your faithful.

I pray this all through Jesus Christ, your Son,
who lives and reigns with you and the Holy Spirit,
one God, forever and ever. Amen.

Meditation on Baptism by Pope Benedict XVI
Feast of the Baptism of the Lord 2006

On this Sunday following the solemnity of the Epiphany, we celebrate the feast of the Baptism of the Lord, which ends the liturgical time of Christmas. Today we contemplate Jesus who, at the age of about 30, had John baptize him in the Jordan River. It was a baptism of penance, which used the symbol of water to express the purification of heart and life.

John, called the "Baptist," that is, he who baptizes, preached this baptism to Israel to prepare for the imminent coming of the Messiah; and he told all that after him another would come, greater than he, who would not baptize with water but with the Holy Spirit (cf. Mark 1:7-8). When Jesus was baptized in the Jordan, the Holy Spirit descended, rested on him with the corporal appearance of a dove, and John the Baptist recognized that he was the Christ, the "Lamb of God," who came to take away the sins of the world (cf. John 1:29).

Therefore, the baptism in the Jordan is also an "epiphany," a manifestation of the messianic identity of the Lord and of his redeeming work, which will culminate with another "baptism," that of his death and resurrection, through which the whole world will be purified in the fire of divine mercy (cf. Luke 12:49-50).

On this feast, Pope John Paul II usually administered the sacrament of baptism to some children. For the first time, this morning, I also had the joy of baptizing 10 newborns in the Sistine Chapel. I renew with affection my greeting to these little ones, to their families, as well as to the godfathers and godmothers.

The baptism of children expresses and realizes the mystery of the new birth to divine life in Christ: Believing parents take their children to the baptismal font, representation of the "womb" of the Church, from whose blessed waters the children of God are begotten. The gift received by the newborns calls for its being accepted by them, once they become adults, in a free and responsible way: This process of maturation will lead them later to receive the sacrament of confirmation, which in fact will confirm their baptism and will confer on them the "seal" of the Holy Spirit.

Dear Brothers and Sisters, may today's solemnity be a propitious opportunity for all Christians to discover the joy and beauty of their baptism that, lived with faith, is an ever present reality: It continually renews us in the image of the new man, in holiness of thoughts and deeds. Baptism, moreover, unites Christians of all creeds. Insofar as we are baptized, we are all children of God in Christ Jesus, our master and Lord. May the Virgin Mary obtain for us the grace to understand ever more the value of our baptism and to witness to it with a worthy conduct of life.

Priest's Prayers Before Celebrating the Sacrament of Penance

Heavenly Father,
Through the gift of the Sacrament of Penance
the faithful are strengthened
to carry out the mission of the Gospel.

As an instrument of your reconciling love,
open my ears to hear the cry of the poor,
place on my tongue your words of good counsel,
and enliven my heart with your love and compassion.
I ask this not for my benefit,
but that I may celebrate this sacrament of penance
for the good of your Church and the reconciliation of sinners. Amen.

*

Lord Jesus,
You came not to call the righteous,

but to call the sinners.
I desire not my voice to be heard,
but your voice through me.

Send your Holy Spirit into my heart,
so that I may give comforting counsel to the afflicted;
as we, your children,
continue to make present the Kingdom of God in our world today. Amen.

⁕

Come Holy Spirit,
enliven my heart,
open my ears,
and place your wisdom on my tongue;

I ask this,
so that all whom I encounter,
through this sacrament;
may come to feel,
experience,
and know *your* love in their lives.

For it is through this sacrament that all seek reconciliation with you,
the veil of sin is removed,
and your Light of Life will shine ever more brightly in the world. Amen.

Blessing of Reconciliation Rooms and Confessionals

+In the name of the Father and of the Son and of the Holy Spirit. Amen.

V. Our help is in the name of the Lord.
R. Who made heaven and earth.

V. The Lord be with you.
R. And with your spirit.

Scripture Reading

And all this is from God, who has reconciled us to himself through Christ and given us the ministry of reconciliation, namely, God was reconciling the world to himself in Christ, not counting their trespasses against them and entrusting to us the message of reconciliation. So we are ambassadors for Christ, as if God were appealing through us. We implore you on behalf of Christ, be reconciled to God.

—2 Cor 5:18-20

Prayer of Blessing

Almighty God, Father of mercies, through your only Son, our Lord Jesus Christ, you have reconciled the world to yourself and entrusted the Church of Christ with the ministry of reconciliation. Grant your blessing to this place and to all who use it with trust in your great mercy. May sinners come to know the power of your forgiveness and all people come to know what you have done for us in Christ. Grant your people true conversion that they might live in union with you and with each other. We ask this through our Lord Jesus Christ, your Son, who lives and reigns with you and the Holy Spirit, one God, forever and ever. Amen.

Blessing of First Penitents

+In the name of the Father and of the Son and of the Holy Spirit. Amen.

V. Our help is in the name of the Lord.
R. Who made heaven and earth.

V. The Lord be with you.
R. And with your spirit.

Scripture Reading

See what love the Father has bestowed on us that we may be called the children of God. Yet so we are. The reason the world does not know us is that it did not know him. Beloved, we are God's children now; what we shall be has not yet been revealed. We do know that when it is revealed we shall be like him, for we shall see him as he is. Everyone who has this hope based on him makes himself pure, as he is pure.

—1 John 3:1-3

Prayer of Blessing

O Lord our God,
through your only Son, our Lord Jesus Christ,
you have given us the grace
of being able to be called your children.
In our struggle with sin, grant us your blessing.
Help us to live as your children,

confident to call you "Father."
Have mercy on your children gathered here.
Help them with your grace to make a good confession,
that they may always give you glory,
in all their words and all their deeds.

We ask this through our Lord Jesus Christ, your Son,
who lives and reigns with you and the Holy Spirit, one God, forever and ever.
Amen.

Blessing of Families Celebrating the Sacrament of Penance

+In the name of the Father and of the Son and of the Holy Spirit. Amen.

V. Our help is in the name of the Lord.
R. Who made heaven and earth.

V. The Lord be with you.
R. And with your spirit.

Scripture Reading

Put on then, as God's chosen ones, holy and beloved, heartfelt compassion, kindness, humility, gentleness, and patience, bearing with one another and forgiving one another, if one has a grievance against another; as the Lord has forgiven you, so must you also do. And over all these put on love, that is, the bond of perfection.

—Col 3:12-14

Prayer of Blessing

Almighty God, our Father, from whom every family in heaven and on earth is named, through the offering of your only Son, our Lord Jesus Christ, you have made possible the forgiveness of our sins and the growth of your people in grace. Grant your blessings to the family gathered here, in your name. Through the sincere confession of their sins, may they know your mercy and be led by your Spirit to grow in your grace and in a greater love for you and for each other. We ask this through our Lord Jesus Christ, your Son, who lives and reigns with you and the Holy Spirit, one God, forever and ever. Amen.

Meditations on Sin by Bl. John Henry Newman

(1) Against Thee Only Have I Sinned

1. Thou, O Lord, after living a whole eternity in ineffable bliss, because thou art the one and sole perfection, at length didst begin to create spirits to be with thee and to share thy blessedness according to their degree; and the return they made thee was at once to rebel against thee. First a great part of the angels, then mankind, have risen up against thee, and served others, not thee. Why didst thou create us, but to make us happy? Couldest thou be made more happy by creating us? And how could we be happy but in obeying thee? Yet we determined not to be happy as thou wouldst have us happy, but to find out a happiness of our own; and so we left thee. O my God, what a return is it that we—that I—make thee when we sin! What dreadful unthankfulness is it! And what will be my punishment for refusing to be happy, and for preferring hell to heaven! I know what the punishment will be; Thou wilt say, "Let him have it all his own way. He wishes to perish; let him perish. He despises the graces I give him; they shall turn to a curse."

2. Thou, O my God, hast a claim on me, and I am wholly thine! Thou art the Almighty Creator, and I am thy workmanship. I am the work of thy hands, and thou art my owner. As well might the axe or the hammer exalt itself against its framer, as I against thee. Thou owest me nothing; I have no rights in respect to thee, I have only duties. I depend on thee for life, and health, and every blessing every moment. I have no more power of exercising will as to my life than axe or hammer. I depend on thee far more entirely than anything here depends on its owner and master. The son does not depend on the father for the continuance of life—the matter out of which the axe is made existed first—but I depend wholly on thee—if thou withdraw thy breath from me for a moment, I die. I am wholly and entirely thy property and thy work, and my one duty is to serve thee.

3. O my God, I confess that before now I have utterly forgotten this, and that I am continually forgetting it! I have acted many a time as if I were my own master, and turned from thee rebelliously. I have acted according to my own pleasure, not according to thine. And so far have I hardened myself, as not to feel as I ought how evil this is. I do not understand how dreadful sin is—and I do not hate it, and fear it, as I ought. I have no horror of it, or loathing. I do not turn from it with indignation, as being an insult to thee, but I trifle with it, and, even if I do not commit great sins, I have no great reluctance to do small ones. O my God, what a great and awful difference is there between what I am and what I ought to be!

(2) Against Thee Only Have I Sinned

1. My God, I dare not offend any earthly superior; I am afraid—for I know I shall get into trouble—yet I dare offend thee. I know, O Lord, that, according to the greatness of the person offended against, the greater is the offense. Yet I do not fear to offend thee, whom to offend is to offend the infinite God. O my dear Lord, how should I myself feel, what should I say of myself, if I were to strike some revered superior on earth? if I were violently to deal a blow upon someone as revered as a father, or a priest; if I were to strike them on the face? I cannot bear even to think of such a thing—yet what is this compared with lifting up my hand against thee? And what is sin but this? To sin is to insult thee in the grossest of all conceivable ways. This then, O my soul is what the sinfulness of sin consists in. It is lifting up my hand against my Infinite Benefactor, against my Almighty Creator, Preserver and Judge—against Him in whom all majesty and glory and beauty and reverence and sanctity center; against the one only God.

2. O my God, I am utterly confounded to think of the state in which I lie! What will become of me if thou art severe? What is my life, O my dear and merciful Lord, but a series of offenses, little or great, against thee! O what great sins I have committed against thee before now—and how continually in lesser matters I am sinning! My God, what will become of me? What will be my position hereafter if I am left to myself! What can I do but come humbly to Him whom I have so heavily affronted and insulted, and beg Him to forgive the debt which lies against me? O my Lord Jesus, whose love for me has been so great as to bring thee down from heaven to save me, teach me, dear Lord, my sin—teach me its heinousness—teach me truly to repent of it—and pardon it in thy great mercy!

3. I beg thee, O my dear Savior, to recover me! Thy grace alone can do it. I cannot save myself. I cannot recover my lost ground. I cannot turn to thee, I cannot please thee, or save my soul without thee. I shall go from bad to worse, I shall fall from thee entirely, I shall quite harden myself against my neglect of duty, if I rely on my own strength. I shall make myself my center instead of making thee. I shall worship some idol of my own framing instead of thee, the only true God and my Maker, unless thou hinder it by thy grace. O my dear Lord, hear me! I have lived long enough in this undecided, wavering, unsatisfactory state. I wish to be thy good servant. I wish to sin no more. Be gracious to me, and enable me to be what I know I ought to be.

(3) The Effects of Sin

1. My Lord, thou art the infinitely merciful God. Thou lovest all things that thou hast created. Thou art the lover of souls. How then is it, O Lord, that

I am in a world so miserable as this is? Can this be the world which thou hast created, so full of pain and suffering? Who among the sons of Adam lives without suffering from his birth to his death? How many bad sicknesses and diseases are there! How many frightful accidents! How many great anxieties! How are men brought down and broken by grief, distress, the tumult of passions, and continual fear! What dreadful plagues are there ever on the earth: war, famine, and pestilence! Why is this, O my God? Why is this, O my soul? Dwell upon it, and ask thyself, Why is this? Has God changed His nature? Yet how evil has the earth become!

2. O my God, I know full well why all these evils are. Thou hast not changed thy nature, but man has ruined his own. We have sinned, O Lord, and therefore is this change. All these evils which I see and in which I partake are the fruit of sin. They would not have been, had we not sinned. They are but the first installment of the punishment of sin. They are an imperfect and dim image of what sin is. Sin is infinitely worse than famine, than war, than pestilence. Take the most hideous of diseases, under which the body wastes away and corrupts, the blood is infected; the head, the heart, the lungs, every organ disordered, the nerves unstrung and shattered; pain in every limb, thirst, restlessness, delirium—all is nothing compared with that dreadful sickness of the soul which we call sin. They all are the effects of it, they all are shadows of it, but nothing more. That cause itself is something different in kind, is of a malignity far other and greater than all these things. O my God, teach me this! Give me to understand the enormity of that evil under which I labor and know it not. Teach me what sin is.

3. All these dreadful pains of body and soul are the fruits of sin, but they are nothing to its punishment in the world to come. The keenest and fiercest of bodily pains is nothing to the fire of hell; the most dire horror or anxiety is nothing to the never-dying worm of conscience; the greatest bereavement, loss of substance, desertion of friends, and forlorn desolation is nothing compared to the loss of God's countenance. Eternal punishment is the only true measure of the guilt of sin. My God, teach me this. Open my eyes and heart, I earnestly pray thee, and make me understand how awful a body of death I bear about me. And, not only teach me about it, but in thy mercy and by thy grace, remove it.

(4) The Evil of Sin

1. My God, I know that thou didst create the whole universe very good; and if this was true of the material world which we see, much more true is it of the world of rational beings. The innumerable stars which fill the firmament, and the very elements out of which the earth is made, all are carried through their courses and their operations in perfect concord; but much higher was

the concord which reigned in heaven when the angels were first created. At that first moment of their existence the main orders of the angels were in the most excellent harmony, and beautiful to contemplate; and the creation of man was expected next, to continue that harmony in the instance of a different kind of being. Then it was that suddenly was discovered a flaw or a rent in one point of this most delicate and exquisite web—and it extended and unraveled the web, till a third part of it was spoilt; and then again a similar flaw was found in human kind, and it extended over the whole race. This dreadful evil, destroying so large a portion of all God's works, is sin.

2. My God, such is sin in thy judgment; what is it in the judgment of the world? A very small evil or none at all. In the judgment of the Creator it is that which has marred His spiritual work; it is a greater evil than though the stars got loose, and ran wild in heaven, and chaos came again. But man, who is the guilty one, calls it by soft names. He explains it away. The world laughs at it, and is indulgent to it; and, as to its deserving eternal punishment, it rises up indignant at the idea, and rather than admit it, would deny the God who has said it does. The world thinks sin the same sort of imperfection as an impropriety, or want of taste or infirmity. O my soul, consider carefully the great difference between the views of sin taken by Almighty God and the world! Which of the two views do you mean to believe?

3. O my soul, which of the two wilt thou believe—the word of God or the word of man? Is God right or is the creature right? Is sin the greatest of all possible evils or the least? My Lord and Savior, I have no hesitation which to believe. Thou art true, and every man a liar. I will believe thee, above the whole world. My God, imprint on my heart the infamous deformity of sin. Teach me to abhor it as a pestilence—as a fierce flame destroying on every side; as my death. Let me take up arms against it, and devote myself to fight under thy banner in overcoming it.

(5) The Heinousness of Sin

1. My Lord, I know well that thou art all perfect, and needest nothing. Yet I know that thou hast taken upon thyself the nature of man, and, not only so, but in that nature didst come upon earth, and suffer all manner of evil, and didst die. This is a history which has hung the heavens with sackcloth, and taken from this earth, beautiful as it is, its light and glory. thou didst come, O my dear Lord, and thou didst suffer in no ordinary way, but unheard of and extreme torments! The all-blessed Lord suffered the worst and most various of pains. This is the corner truth of the Gospel: it is the one foundation, Jesus Christ and He crucified. I know it, O Lord, I believe it, and I put it steadily before me.

2. Why is this strange anomaly in the face of nature? Does God do things for naught? No, my soul, it is sin; it is thy sin, which has brought the Everlasting down upon earth to suffer. Hence I learn how great an evil sin is. The death of the Infinite is its sole measure. All that slow distress of body and mind which He endured, from the time He shed blood at Gethsemani down to His death, all that pain came from sin. What sort of evil is that, which had to be so encountered by such a sacrifice, and to be reversed at such a price! Here then I understand best how horrible a thing sin is. It is horrible; because through it have come upon men all those evils whatever they are, with which the earth abounds. It is more horrible, in that it has nailed the Son of God to the accursed tree.

3. My dear Lord and Savior, how can I make light of that which has had such consequences! Henceforth I will, through thy grace, have deeper views of sin than before. Fools make jest of sin, but I will view things in their true light. My suffering Lord, I have made thee suffer. Thou art most beautiful in thy eternal nature, O my Lord; thou art most beautiful in thy sufferings! Thy adorable attributes are not dimmed, but increased to us as we gaze on thy humiliation. Thou art more beautiful to us than before. But still I will never forget that it was man's sin, my sin, which made that humiliation necessary. *Amor meus crucifixus est*—"my Love is crucified," but by none other than me. I have crucified thee, my sin has crucified thee. O my Savior, what a dreadful thought—but I cannot undo it; all I can do is to hate that which made thee suffer. Shall I not do that at least? Shall I not love my Lord just so much as to hate that which is so great an enemy of His, and break off all terms with it? Shall I not put off sin altogether? By thy great love of me, teach me and enable me to do this, O Lord. Give me a deep, rooted, intense hatred of sin.

(6) The Bondage of Sin

1. Thou, O my Lord and God, thou alone art strong, Thou alone holy! Thou art the *Sanctus Deus, Sanctus fortis*—"Holy God, holy and strong!" Thou art the sanctity and the strength of all things. No created nature has any stay or subsistence in itself, but crumbles and melts away, if thou art not with it, to sustain it. My God, thou art the strength of the angels, of the saints in glory—of holy men on earth. No being has any sanctity or any strength apart from thee. My God, I wish to adore thee as such. I wish with all my heart to understand and to confess this great truth, that not only thou art Almighty, but that there is no might at all, or power, or strength, anywhere but in thee.

2. My God, if thou art the strength of all spirits, O how pre-eminently art thou my strength! O how true it is, so that nothing is more so, that I have no strength but in thee! I feel intimately, O my God, that, whenever I am left to myself, I go wrong. As sure as a stone falls down to the earth if it be let go, so surely my heart and spirit fall down hopelessly if they are let go by thee. Thou must uphold me by thy right hand, or I cannot stand. How strange it is, but how true, that all my natural tendencies are towards sloth, towards excess, towards neglect of religion, towards neglect of prayer, towards love of the world, not towards love of thee, or love of sanctity, or love of self-governance. I approve and praise what I do not do. My heart runs after vanities, and I tend to death, I tend to corruption and dissolution, apart from thee, *Deus immortalis*.

3. My God, I have had experience enough what a dreadful bondage sin is. If thou art away, I find I cannot keep myself, however I wish it—and am in the hands of my own self-will, pride, sensuality, and selfishness. And they prevail with me more and more every day, till they are irresistible. In time the old Adam within me gets so strong, that I become a mere slave. I confess things to be wrong which nevertheless I do. I bitterly lament over my bondage, but I cannot undo it. O what a tyranny is sin! It is a heavy weight which cripples me—and what will be the end of it? By thy all-precious merits, by thy Almighty power, I entreat thee, O my Lord, to give me life and sanctity and strength! *Deus sanctus*, give me holiness; *Deus fortis*, give me strength; *Deus immortalis*, give me perseverance. *Sanctus Deus, Sanctus fortis, Sanctus immortalis, miserere nobis*.

(7) Every Sin Has Its Punishment

1. Thou art the all-seeing, all-knowing God. Thy eyes, O Lord, are in every place. Thou art a real spectator of everything which takes place anywhere. Thou art ever with me. Thou art present and conscious of all I think, say, or do. *Tu Deus qui vidisti me*—"Thou, God, who hast seen me." Every deed or act, however slight; every word, however quick and casual; every thought of my heart, however secret, however momentary, however forgotten, thou seest, O Lord, thou seest and thou notest down. Thou hast a book; Thou enterest in it every day of my life. I forget; Thou dost not forget. There is stored up the history of all my past years, and so it will be till I die—the leaves will be filled and turned over—and the book at length finished. *Quo ibo a Spiritu Tuo*—"whither shall I go from thy Spirit?" I am in thy hands, O Lord, absolutely.

2. My God, how often do I act wrongly, how seldom rightly! How dreary on the whole are the acts of any one day! All my sins, offenses, and negli-

gences, not of one day only, but of all days, are in thy book. And every sin, offense, negligence, has a separate definite punishment. That list of penalties increases, silently but surely, every day. As the spendthrift is overwhelmed by a continually greater weight of debt, so am I exposed continually to a greater and greater score of punishments catalogued against me. I *forget* the sins of my childhood, my boyhood, my adolescence, my youth. They are all noted down in that book. *There* is a complete history of all my life; and it will one day be brought up against me. Nothing is lost, all is remembered. O my soul, what hast thou to go through! What an examination that will be, and what a result! I shall have put upon me the punishment of ten thousand sins—I shall for this purpose be sent to Purgatory—how long will it last? when shall I ever get out? Not till I have paid the last farthing. When will this possibly be?

3. O my dear Lord, have mercy upon me! I trust thou hast forgiven me my sins—but the punishment remains. In the midst of thy love for me, and recognizing me as thine own, thou wilt consign me to Purgatory. There I shall go through my sins once more, in their punishment. There I shall suffer, but here is the time for a thorough repentance. Here is the time of good works, of obtaining indulgences, of wiping out the debt in every possible way. Thy saints, though to the eyes of man without sin, really had a vast account—and they settled it by continual trials here. I have neither their merit nor their sufferings. I cannot tell whether I can make such acts of love as will gain me an indulgence of my sins. The prospect before me is dark—I can only rely on thy infinite compassion. O my dear Lord, who hast in so many ways shown thy mercy towards me, pity me here! Be merciful in the midst of justice.

(8). The Power of the Cross

1. My God, who could have imagined, by any light of nature, that it was one of thy attributes to lower thyself, and to work out thy purposes by thy own humiliation and suffering? Thou hadst lived from eternity in ineffable blessedness. My God, I might have understood as much as this, viz. that, when thou didst begin to create and surround thyself with a world of creatures, that these attributes would show themselves in thee which before had no exercise. Thou couldest not show thy power when there was nothing whatever to exercise it. Then too, thou didst begin to show thy wonderful and tender providence, thy faithfulness, thy solicitous care for those whom thou hadst created. But who could have fancied that thy creation of the universe implied and involved in it thy humiliation? O my great God, thou hast humbled thyself, thou hast stooped to take our flesh and blood, and

hast been lifted up upon the tree! I praise and glorify thee tenfold the more, because thou hast shown thy power by means of thy suffering, than hadst thou carried on thy work without it. It is worthy of thy infinitude thus to surpass and transcend all our thoughts.

2. O my Lord Jesus, I believe, and by thy grace will ever believe and hold, and I know that it is true, and will be true to the end of the world, that nothing great is done without suffering, without humiliation, and that all things are possible by means of it. I believe, O my God, that poverty is better than riches, pain better than pleasure, obscurity and contempt than name, and ignominy and reproach than honor. My Lord, I do not ask thee to bring these trials on me, for I know not if I could face them; but at least, O Lord, whether I be in prosperity or adversity, I will believe that it is as I have said. I will never have faith in riches, rank, power, or reputation. I will never set my heart on worldly success or on worldly advantages. I will never wish for what men call the prizes of life. I will ever, with thy grace, make much of those who are despised or neglected, honor the poor, revere the suffering, and admire and venerate thy saints and confessors, and take my part with them in spite of the world.

3. And lastly, O my dear Lord, though I am so very weak that I am not fit to ask thee for suffering as a gift, and have not strength to do so, at least I will beg of thee grace to meet suffering well, when thou in thy love and wisdom dost bring it upon me. Let me bear pain, reproach, disappointment, slander, anxiety, suspense, as thou wouldest have me, O my Jesus, and as thou by thy own suffering hast taught me, when it comes. And I promise too, with thy grace, that I will never set myself up, never seek pre-eminence, never court any great thing of the world, never prefer myself to others. I wish to bear insult meekly, and to return good for evil. I wish to humble myself in all things, and to be silent when I am ill-used, and to be patient when sorrow or pain is prolonged, and all for the love of thee, and thy Cross, knowing that in this way I shall gain the promise both of this life and of the next.

Prayers Before Witnessing a Marriage

O God, source of all love, speak through me as I proclaim your truth through the homily. Help me to be sensitive to those who gather for this holy matrimony who are not Catholic or who rarely if ever take part in the Mass. Bless me with charity in my words as I explain the mystery of Christian marriage and the dignity of wedded love. Amen.

⁕

O God, fill me with your love, for without love, my lips will only speak half-heartedly of the truth which marriage signifies and shares: the mystery of the unity and fruitful love that exists between Christ and his Church. Amen.

⁕

O Lord, I pray that I have properly prepared this couple for the sacrament of marriage. Let me rest all my worries and concerns into your hands, and accept the support of the Holy Spirit during the rite of matrimony. Faith in you, O Lord, will guide me to be present to this couple as they join in this sacramental union of marriage. Amen.

Prayers After Witnessing a Marriage

O Lord, I give you thanks for the opportunity to share in the mystery of marriage. May the covenantal relationship I witnessed in the sacrament of marriage renew the promise I made to you, O Lord, in the sacrament of ordination. Thank you, O Lord, for the grace we receive through the sacraments and the unfailing love of Christ. Amen.

⁕

Holy Spirit, shower this newlywed couple with your loving grace and inspire them to live a life of holy unity. In times of trouble, bring them comfort. In times of joy, fill them with hope. Inspire this couple to always seek you in prayer as they have committed their lives to loving one another in a sacramental bond. Amen.

⁕

May the union of this couple signify and share in the unity of the community of faithful who are all part of the Church instituted by Jesus Christ. Open the hearts of other couples in this community to allow this newlywed couple to inspire them to renew their marriage vows and relationship with God. We ask this through Christ our Lord. Amen.

Meal Prayers for Wedding Dinners

Gracious and Loving God, we give thanks for your many blessings. Bring your blessings upon (N) and (N) as they join with their family and friends in celebrating this wonderful occasion of love. Gracious God, bless the food that has been prepared and the people who have prepared it. Loving

God, fill this splendid occasion with your love and happiness as we join together in this wedding celebration.

✳

We give thanks for the union of these two families in the marriage of (N) and (N). We ask of you, O God, to bless the food that has been prepared and open our hearts to join in fellowship during this time of celebration. May this food and celebration help unite the couples and their families in a bond of love and peace. We ask this through our Lord, Jesus Christ. Amen.

✳

We pray, Lord, that this meal we share will join us together in hope. Hope that you, O Lord, will sustain us with the nourishment we need and hope that there will be continued joys in the life of (N) and (N). Lord, bless this celebration and the meal prepared as we join together in this hopeful celebration of two joined in love. Amen.

Consecration of a Married Couple to the Precious Blood

Lord Jesus,
on this happy day
we thank you for the joy of (N) and (N).
Through all the years of their life
you have watched over them
to bring them together in holy Christian marriage.
Now Lord, bless them,
for they are united in love of you and of each other.
Redeemed by your Precious Blood
and strengthened by your grace,
may they live in kindness and fidelity,
in unfailing trust and love,
so that their whole life may be pleasing to you.

Mary, who with Joseph
made a happy home at Nazareth for Jesus,
take these dear friends into your motherly care.
You who showed concern for a newly married couple at Cana,
help and guide (N) and (N).
May their union on earth lead to that eternal union
in which all the blessed will be joined together,
praising the Redeeming Blood of Jesus, the Lord. Amen.

MEDITATION ON MARRIAGE BY ST. JOHN PAUL II

1. According to the Second Vatican Council, the Church is a "priestly community," whose, "sacred and organic nature" is realized through the sacraments, among which a special place must be given to the sacraments of Holy Orders and Matrimony.

Regarding Holy Orders, we read in the Constitution *Lumen gentium*: "Those among the faithful who have received Holy Orders are appointed to nourish the Church with the word and grace of God in the name of Christ"; regarding Matrimony we read: "In virtue of the sacrament of Matrimony by which they signify and share (cf. Eph 5:32) the mystery of the unity and faithful love between Christ and the Church, Christian married couples help one another to attain holiness" *(Lumen gentium, n. 11).*

We will devote today's catechesis exclusively to the sacrament of Matrimony and return to the ministerial priesthood at a later time.

2. In a previous catechesis we recalled that the first miracle Jesus worked took place in Cana during a wedding feast. Although the significance of this miracle, by which "Jesus revealed his glory" (Jn 2:11), goes far beyond the recorded event, nevertheless we can also discover the Lord's appreciation for married love and the institution of marriage, as well as his intention to bring salvation to this fundamental aspect of human life and society. He gives new wine, the symbol of new love. The episode in Cana shows us how marriage is threatened when love is in danger of running out. With this sacrament Jesus Christ reveals his own help in an effective way, in order to save and strengthen the couple's love through the gift of theological charity, and to give them the strength of fidelity. We can also say that the miracle worked by Jesus at the beginning of his public life is a sign of the importance marriage has in God's saving plan and the formation of the Church.

Finally, we can say that Mary's initiative in asking and obtaining the miracle foretells her future role in the divine plan for Christian marriage: a benevolent presence, an intercession and a help in overcoming the inevitable problems.

3. In light of Cana we now want to call attention to the aspect of marriage which concerns us in this cycle of ecclesiological catecheses. It is a fact that in Christian marriage the common priesthood of the faithful is exercised in a remarkable way, because the married couple themselves are the ministers of the sacrament.

The human act, "by which," as the Council says, "the partners mutually surrender themselves to each other," has been raised to the dignity of a sacrament. The couple administer the sacrament to one another by their mutual consent.

The sacrament shows the value of the man and woman's free consent, as a statement of their personality and an expression of mutual love.

4. The Council also said that through the sacrament Christian married couples "signify and share (cf. Eph 5:32) the mystery of the unity and faithful love between Christ and the Church" *(Lumen gentium, n. 11).*

"Authentic married love is caught up into divine love and is directed and enriched by the redemptive power of Christ and the salvific action of the Church, with the result that the spouses are effectively led to God and are helped and strengthened in their lofty role as fathers and mothers. Spouses, therefore, are fortified and, as it were, consecrated for the duties and dignity of their state by a special sacrament" (*Gaudium et spes,* n. 48).

This last assertion of *Gaudium et spes,* that spouses are "as it were, consecrated by a special sacrament," is very important. This shows precisely how they exercise their priesthood as those baptized and confirmed.

5. Through this special sharing in the common priesthood of the Church, couples can achieve holiness. Indeed, through the sacrament they receive the strength to fulfill their marital and family duties, and to advance in mutual holiness. "They help one another," the Council says, "to attain holiness in their married life and in the rearing of their children. Hence by reason of their state in life and of their position they have their own gifts in the People of God (cf. 1 Cor 7:7)" *(Lumen gentium, n. 11).*

6. The sacrament of Matrimony is oriented toward fruitfulness. It is an inclination which is inborn in human nature. "By its very nature," the Council says, "the institution of marriage and married love is ordered to the procreation and education of the offspring and it is in them that it finds its crowning glory" *(Gaudium et spes,* n. 48).

The sacrament provides the spiritual strength of faith, love and generosity for fulfilling the duty of procreating and rearing offspring. It is a resource of divine grace which confirms and perfects the right, natural inclination and marks the very psychology of the couple, who have been made conscious of their own mission as those who "cooperate with the love of God the Creator," as the Council says *(Gaudium et spes,* n. 50).

The realization that they are cooperating in the divine work of creation and the love which inspires it helps married couples better to understand the sacred character of procreation and procreative love, and strengthens the orientation of their love to transmitting life.

7. The Council also calls attention to the educational mission of the spouses. In fact, we read in *Gaudium et spes*: "As for the spouses, when they are given the dignity and role of fatherhood and motherhood, they will eagerly carry out their duties of education, especially religious education, which primarily devolves on them" *(Gaudium et spes,* n. 48). But light is shed on this exhortation by *Lumen gentium,* which says: "In what might be regarded as the domestic Church, the parents, by word and example, are the first heralds of the faith with regard to their children" (*Lumen gentium,* n. 11). The Council, then, casts an ecclesial light on the mission of married couples-parents, as members of the Church, the priestly and sacramental community.

Clearly, for believers Christian education is the most beautiful gift which parents can give their children, and it is the highest and truest sign of their love. It requires a sincere and consistent faith, and a life led in conformity with the faith.

8. The Council also says that the marital union, "as a mutual giving of two persons, and the good of the children demand total fidelity from the spouses and require an unbreakable unity between them" *(Gaudium et spes,* n. 48). Fidelity and unity come from the "special gifts of grace and love" *(Gaudium et spes,* n. 49) given by the sacrament. They ensure that, in imitation of Christ who loved the Church, "spouses, by their mutual self-giving, will love each other with enduring fidelity" *(Gaudium et spes,* n. 48). This, too, is a strength inherent in the grace of the sacrament.

9. Finally, we read in the Council that "the Christian family springs from marriage, which is an image and a sharing in the partnership of love between Christ and the Church; it will show forth to all men Christ's saving presence in the world and the authentic nature of the Church by the love and generous fruitfulness of the spouses, by their unity and fidelity, and by the loving way in which all members of the family cooperate with each other" *(Gaudium et spes,* n. 48).

Therefore, not only each Christian considered individually, but the whole family as such, consisting of Christian parents and children, is called to witness to the life, love and unity which the Church possesses as properties deriving from her nature as a sacred community, constituted and living in Christ's love.

—L'Osservatore Romano

BLESSING OF SICK PRIESTS

+In the name of the Father and of the Son and of the Holy Spirit. Amen.

V. Our help is in the name of the Lord.
R. Who made heaven and earth.

V. The Lord be with you.
R. And with your spirit.

Scripture Reading

"But he himself went a day's journey into the wilderness, and came and sat down under a solitary broom tree. He asked that he might die: "It is enough; now, O LORD, take away my life, for I am no better than my ancestors." Then he lay down under the broom tree and fell asleep. Suddenly an angel touched him and said to him, "Get up and eat." He looked, and there at his head was a cake baked on hot stones, and a jar of water. He ate and drank, and lay down again. The angel of the LORD came a second time, touched him, and said, "Get up and eat, otherwise the journey will be too much for you." He got up, and ate and drank; then he went by the strength of that food forty days and forty nights to Horeb the mount of God. At that place he came to a cave, and spent the night there."

—1 Kings 19:4-8

Prayer of Blessing

Strengthen and sustain your servants, God of Power and Might, like you strengthen and sustained your servant, Elijah. Elijah held a great love for you, Lord, but faced the apostasy of the Israelites and threat of death from Jezebel. Elijah fled into the wilderness, and being overwhelmed by the trials he faced, asked the Lord that he might die. On the strength of food sent by an angel, Elijah was able to travel forty days and forty nights to Horeb, the mount of God, where he received instructions from the Lord. So too, O Lord, send your angels to strengthen our brother priest with the spiritual food needed to battle this sickness. Overwhelming it can seem at times, but we know that you will be present to sustain your servant on the journey. Amen.

Blessing of a Pyx

+In the name of the Father and of the Son and of the Holy Spirit. Amen.

V. Our help is in the name of the Lord.
R. Who made heaven and earth.

V. The Lord be with you.
R. And with your spirit.

Prayer of Blessing

Almighty everlasting God, we humbly entreat your sovereignty to consecrate with your blessing + this pyx, made to contain the body of your Son, our Lord Jesus Christ. May those who receive Holy Communion through its use be strengthened and healed; through Christ our Lord. Amen.

It is sprinkled with holy water.

Blessing of Oil Stocks

+In the name of the Father and of the Son and of the Holy Spirit. Amen.

V. Our help is in the name of the Lord.
R. Who made heaven and earth.

V. The Lord be with you.
R. And with your spirit.

Prayer of Blessing

Most gracious Lord and Father, hear our prayers, and bless + this oil stock, used as a vessel prepared for the sacred ministry of your Church to those who are sick and dying; through Christ our Lord. Amen.

They are sprinkled with holy water.

Meditations on Sickness by Pope Benedict XVI

In this, my visit to San Giovanni Rotondo, I could not miss a stop at the Casa Sollievo della Sofferenza, designed and built by St. Pio of Pietrelcina as a "place of prayer and science where the human race finds itself again in Christ Crucified as a single flock with one shepherd." Precisely for this reason he wanted to entrust it to the material and spiritual support of the prayer groups, who here have the center of their mission to serve the Church. Padre Pio had the desire that in this well-equipped hospital the commitment of science in treating the patient never be separated from a filial trust in God, infinitely tender and merciful. Inaugurating it on May 5, 1956, he called it "a creature of Providence" and spoke of this institution as "a seed planted by God on earth, which he will warm with the rays of his love."

Here I am among you, therefore, to thank God for the good that, faithful to the directives of a humble Capuchin Friar for over fifty years, you do in this "Casa Sollievo della Sofferenza," with recognized scientific and medical results. It is not possible for me unfortunately, as I would like, to visit each hall and greet each patient one by one along with those who care for them. But I want to convey to everyone—patients, doctors, family members, health and pastoral workers—a word of paternal comfort and encouragement to continue together this evangelical work to relieve suffering, making the most of every resource for the human and spiritual good of the sick and their families.

With these sentiments, I cordially greet all of you, starting with you, brothers and sisters who are being tried by illness. I greet the doctors, nurses and medical staff and administration. I greet you, revered Capuchin Fathers, who, as chaplains, continue the apostolate of your holy confrere. I greet the prelates and, first of all, the Archbishop Domenico Umberto D'Ambrosio, former pastor of this diocese, and now called upon to lead the archdiocesan community of Lecce. I am grateful for the words that he addressed to me on your behalf. I next greet the director general of the hospital, Doctor Dominic Crupi, and the representative of the sick, and I am grateful for the kind and cordial words that they have just addressed to me, allowing me to better know what is being done here and the spirit with which you carry it out.

Each time one enters a place of care, one's thoughts turn naturally to the mystery of disease and pain, to the hope of healing and to the inestimable value of health, which is often only recognized when it is lost. In hospitals, one touches with one's hands the preciousness of our existence, but also its fragility. Following the example of Jesus, who traveled throughout Galilee, "healing every disease and every infirmity among the people" (Mt 4:23), the Church, from its very beginnings, moved by the Holy Spirit, has considered it her duty and privilege to stand beside those who suffer, cultivating a preferential attention for the sick.

Sickness, which manifests itself in many forms and strikes in different ways, raises disturbing questions: Why do we suffer? Can the experience of pain be considered positive? Who can liberate us from suffering and death? Existential questions, which remain often unanswered humanly, since suffering is an unfathomable mystery for our reason. Suffering is part of the very mystery of the human person. And that which I emphasized in the encyclical letter *Spe Salvi,* noting that "it follows, on the one hand, from our finitude, and on the other hand, from the mass of guilt that has accumulated throughout history and even at present continues its unstoppable growth." And I added that "certainly we must do everything we can to reduce suffering ... but to eliminate it completely from the world is not in our possibilities simply because ... none of us is able to eliminate the power of evil ... continually the source of suffering."

Only God can remove the power of evil. Precisely due to the fact that Jesus Christ came into the world to reveal the divine plan of our salvation, faith helps us to penetrate the meaning of all things human and therefore also of suffering. There is, therefore, an intimate relationship between the Cross of Jesus—the supreme symbol of the pain and the price of our freedom—and our pain, which is transformed and transcended when it is lived in the awareness of the closeness and solidarity of God. Padre Pio had understood this profound truth and, on the first anniversary of this work, said that in it "those who suffer must live the love of God through the wise acceptance of their pain, through serene meditation on their destiny to him" (Meeting of May 5, 1957). He noted further that in the Casa Sollievo "the recovering, doctors, priests will be reserves of love, which in as much as it abounds in one, the more it will be communicated to others" (ibid.).

Be "reserves of love": This, dear brothers and sisters, is the mission that this evening our saint refers you to, who each in his own way form the great family of this Casa Sollievo della Sofferenza. May the Lord help you bring to fruition the project initiated by Padre Pio with the support of all: doctors and scientific researchers, health care professionals and the employees of various departments, volunteers and benefactors, the Capuchin friars and other priests. Without forgetting the prayer groups that "attached to the house of relief, are the advanced positions of this citadel of charity, nurseries of faith, outbursts of love" (Padre Pio, Speech, May 5, 1966). On each and every one, I invoke the intercession of Padre Pio and the maternal protection of Mary, Health of the Sick. Thank you again for your welcome and, while I assure you of my prayers for each of you, I cordially bless you all.

The Death of a Priest and General Prayers

Prayers for a Dying Priest

Heavenly Father, we pray for the soul of this man, (N), your servant. Remember the good work he has done for you while on earth, forgive him of his sins, and grant him eternal happiness. We ask this through the great, high priest your Son, who lives, and reigns with you and the Holy Spirit, one God, forever and ever. Amen.

✳

Almighty Father, we humbly ask for the repose of your priest, (N). He gave his life in service to you, your Church, and your people. Remember his successes and forget his defeats. Look with mercy and compassion and grant him the joy of eternal peace. We ask this through our Divine Savior, your Son, Jesus Christ, who lives and reigns with you and the Holy Spirit, forever and ever. Amen.

✳

Almighty God and Father, we pray for the soul of this dying priest. This man has given his life to bring the love of your Son to the world. Look kindly on him and give him the share of your eternal glory in heaven. We ask this in the name of your Son the high priest, Jesus Christ. Amen.

Blessing of a Dying Priest

+In the name of the Father and of the Son and of the Holy Spirit. Amen.

V. Our help is in the name of the Lord.
R. Who made heaven and earth.

V. The Lord be with you.
R. And with your spirit.

Scripture Reading

For I am already being poured out like a libation, and the time of my departure is at hand. I have competed well; I have finished the race; I have kept the faith. From now on the crown of righteousness awaits me, which the Lord, the just judge, will award to me on that day, and not only to me, but to all who have longed for his appearance.

—2 Timothy 4:6-8

Prayer of Blessing

Heavenly Father, giver of every good gift. You award those who fulfill your will and work for peace in the world. Bless your servant, (N), and grant him his crown of righteousness. We ask this through Christ our Lord. Amen.

Blessing of the Body of the Priest After Death

+In the name of the Father and of the Son and of the Holy Spirit. Amen.

V. Our help is in the name of the Lord.
R. Who made heaven and earth.

V. The Lord be with you.
R. And with your spirit.

Scripture Reading

Precious in the sight of the Lord is the death of his saints. O Lord, truly I am your servant; I am your servant, the son of your maidservant; you have freed me from my chains.

—Psalm 116:15-16

Prayer of Blessing

Almighty God, free this servant of yours from his sins. Grant him your Divine Mercy and may your holy angels take his soul to eternal peace. We ask this in the name of our Blessed Lord, your Son, Jesus Christ. Amen.

Prayers for Vesting a Priest After Death

With the amice:

Place upon him, O Lord, the helmet of salvation, that he may overcome the assaults of the devil.

With the alb:

Purify him, O Lord, and cleanse his heart; that, being made white in the Blood of the Lamb, he may come to eternal joy.

With the cincture:

Gird him, O Lord, with the reward of purity, and remember not any evil desires, that the virtue of chastity may abide in him.

With the stole:

Give unto him, O Lord, the stole of immortality, which was lost through the guilt of our first parents: and, although he was unworthy to approach your sacred Mysteries, nevertheless grant unto him eternal joy.

With the chasuble:

O Lord, who said: My yoke is easy and my burden light: grant that he may bear his last burden well and follow after you with thanksgiving. Amen.

General Prayers

A Priest's Devotions to Our Lord

Sweetest Jesus, who, being subject as a child to Mary and Joseph at Nazareth, didst leave to children an excellent pattern of affection and obedience to parents, and of wondrous reverence for all men, grant, I most earnestly beseech thee, that I may strive to see thee always and in all things, so that as my years increase, I too may increase in thy grace and love: Who livest and reignest world without end. Amen.

⁂

Lord Jesus Christ, in union with that divine intention wherewith on earth thou didst offer to God thy praises through thy Most Sacred Heart, and dost now offer them in the Sacrament of the Eucharist everywhere on earth even to the end of time, I most gladly offer thee throughout this entire day, all my thoughts and intentions, all my affections and desires, all my words and deeds, in imitation of the most Sacred Heart of the blessed and ever Virgin Mary Immaculate. Amen.

⁂

Grant me thy grace, most merciful Jesus, that it may be with me and work with me and persevere with me even to the end.
Grant that I may always desire and will that which is to thee most acceptable and most dear.
Let thy will be mine, and let my will ever follow thine and agree perfectly with it.
Let my willing and not-willing be all one with thine, and let me not be able to will or not will anything else but what thou willest or not. Amen.

⁂

Jesus Christ my God, I adore thee and thank thee for all the graces thou hast given me this day. I offer thee my sleep and all the moments of this night, and I beseech thee to keep me without sin. Wherefore I put myself within thy sacred side and under the mantle of our Lady, my Mother. Let thy holy angels stand about me and keep me in peace; and let thy blessing be upon me. Amen.

⁂

O Jesus, my Savior and Redeemer, Son of the living god, behold we kneel before thee and offer thee our reparation; we would make amends for all the blasphemies uttered against thy holy Name, for all the injuries done to thee in the Blessed Sacrament, for all the irreverence shown toward thine

Immaculate Virgin Mother, for all the calumnies and slanders spoken against thy spouse, the holy Catholic and Roman Church. O Jesus, who hast said: "If you ask the Father anything in my name, he will give it you," we pray and beseech thee for all our brethren who are in danger of sin; shield them from every temptation to fall away from the true faith; save those who are even now standing on the brink of the abyss; to all of them give light and knowledge of the truth, courage, and strength for the conflict with evil, perseverance in faith, and active charity! For this do we pray, most merciful Jesus, in thy Name, unto God the Father, with whom thou livest and reignest in the unity of the Holy Ghost, world without end. Amen.

⁜

Our sins, O Lord, darken our understanding and hide from us the blessing of loving thee as thou dost merit. Enlighten our minds with a ray of thy divine light. Thou art the Friend, the Redeemer, and the Father of him who turns penitent to thy Sacred Heart; we, too, turn penitent to thee, Jesus, we hope in thee, for we know that our salvation cost thee thy death upon the Cross and moved thee to remain continually in the Blessed Sacrament, in order to unite thyself with us as often as we desire. We, O Lord, to give thee thanks for the great love thou bearest toward us, promise thee, by the help of thy grace, to receive thee in thy Sacrament as often as we can, and to sing thy praises in church and in every place, without human respect. Lord, we beseech thee, trusting in thy Most Sacred Heart, that thou wouldst call all men to receive thee daily at the altar, according to thy burning desire. Amen.

⁜

O Jesus, Son of the glorious Virgin Mary, and only Son of the living God, I adore thee and acknowledge thee as my God, the only true God, unique and infinitely perfect, who hast made out of nothing all things that are outside of thee, and dost preserve and govern them with infinite wisdom, sovereign goodness, and supreme power; I beg of thee, by the mysteries that were fulfilled in thy sacred humanity, to cleanse me in thy Blood from all my past sins; pour forth abundantly upon me thy Holy Spirit, together with his grace, his virtues, and his gifts; make me believe in thee, hope in thee, love thee, and labor to merit thee in each of my actions; give thyself to me one day, in the brightness of thy glory, in the midst of the assembly of all thy saints. Amen.

⁜

Our Lord Jesus Christ, we have recourse to thee, Holy God, Mighty God, Immortal God, have mercy on us and on all mankind. Cleanse us in thy

Precious Blood from all our sins and infirmities. My Jesus, I believe in thee, I hope in thee, I love thee, I give myself to thee. Amen.

✳

Lord Jesus, I unite myself to thy perpetual, unceasing, universal sacrifice. I offer myself to thee every day of my life and every moment of every day, according to thy most holy and adorable will. Thou hast been the victim of my salvation, I wish to be the victim of thy love. Accept my desire, take my offering, graciously hear my prayer. Let me live for love of thee, let me die for love of thee; let my last heartbeat be an act of perfect love! Amen.

✳

O Jesus! I come to thee! Thou art the Way that I would follow in obedience to thy commandments, thy counsels, and thine example; let me walk after thee in the way of obedience, of self-denial, and of sacrifice, which leads to heaven and thee! O Jesus, thou art the Truth; thou art "the true Light which enlighteneth every man coming into this world." I believe in thee! I believe in thy Gospel; I would know thee in order to love thee; I would make thee known in order to make thee loved. O Jesus! Thou art the Life, through thy sanctifying grace which is the life of our souls; through thy words which are "the words of everlasting life"; through thy Eucharist which is "the living bread come down from heaven"; through thy heart which is the fountain of life for individual souls and for society. I cling to thy Word with all my heart; I hunger for the living Bread of thy Eucharist; I open my heart without reserve to the life-giving streams from thy Sacred Heart; I unite myself inwardly to all its intentions. Ah, may this divine heart reign universally over the children of the Church and over all humanity. Amen.

✳

My Lord Jesus Christ, Son of the living God, I humbly beseech thee to scatter the darkness of my mind, and to give me lively faith, firm hope, and burning love. Grant, O my God, that I may know thee well and may do all things in thy light and in conformity to thy holy will. Amen.

✳

O Jesus our Savior, give us thy blessing, deliver us from everlasting death, assist thy holy Church, give peace to all nations, deliver the holy souls suffering in purgatory. Amen.

✳

O Lord God, King of heaven and earth, may it please thee this day to order and to hallow, to rule and to govern our hearts and our bodies, our thoughts, our words, and our works, according to thy law and in the doing of thy commandments, that we, being helped by thee, may here and hereafter worthily be saved and delivered by thee, O Savior of the world, who livest and reignest for ever and ever. Amen.

Deliver me, Lord Jesus Christ, from all my iniquities and from every evil, make me ever hold fast to thy commandments and never allow me to be separated from thee. Amen.

We offer thee, Lord Jesus Christ, the merits of Mary, thy mother and ours, as she stood beneath the Cross, in order that, by her tender intercession, we may obtain the happy fruits of thy passion and death. Amen.

O dearly beloved Word of God, teach me to be generous, to serve thee as thou dost deserve, to give without counting the cost, to fight without fretting at my wounds, to labor without seeking repose, to be prodigal of myself without looking for any other reward save that of knowing that I do thy holy will. Amen.

Change my heart, O Jesus, thou who didst empty thyself for love of me! Make known to my spirit how excellent were thy sacred humiliations. Let me begin this day, illumined by thy divine light, to do away with that portion of the natural man, that still lives undiminished in me. This is the chief source of my misery, this the barrier that I constantly oppose to thy love. Amen.

O Lord Jesus Christ, who hast said: Ask and ye shall receive, seek and ye shall find, knock and it shall be opened unto you; mercifully attend to our supplications, and grant us the gift of thy divine charity, that we may ever love thee with our whole heart and with all our words and deeds, and may never cease from praising thee.

Make us, O Lord, to have a perpetual fear and love of thy holy Name, for thou never failest to help and govern those whom thou dost bring up in thy steadfast fear and love: who livest and reignest for ever and ever. Amen.

O good Jesus, according to thy great mercy, have mercy on me. O most merciful Jesus, by that Precious Blood which thou didst will to shed for sinners, I beseech thee to wash away all mine iniquities and to look graciously upon me, a poor and unworthy sinner, as I call upon thy holy Name. Therefore, O Jesus, do thou save me for thy holy Name's sake. Amen.

⁕

O God, who didst appoint thine only begotten Son to be the Savior of mankind and didst command his name to be called Jesus; mercifully grant that we may enjoy the vision of him in heaven, whose holy Name we venerate on earth. Through the same Christ our Lord. Amen.

⁕

O God, whose only-begotten Son hath appeared in the substance of our flesh; grant, we beseech thee, that through him, whom we acknowledge to have been outwardly like unto us, we may deserve to be renewed in our inward selves. Who liveth and reigneth with thee forever and ever. Amen.

⁕

I. Jesus, sweetest Child, who didst come down from the bosom of the Father for our salvation, who wast conceived by the Holy Ghost, who didst not abhor the Virgin's womb, and who, being the Word made flesh, didst take upon thee the form of a servant, have mercy on us.

II. Jesus, sweetest Child, who by means of thy Virgin Mother didst visit Saint Elizabeth, who didst fill thy forerunner, John the Baptist, with thy Holy Spirit and didst sanctify him in his mother's womb, have mercy on us.

III. Jesus, sweetest Child, who, enclosed for nine months in thy Mother's womb, wast looked for with eager expectation by the Virgin Mary and Saint Joseph, and wast offered by God the Father for the salvation of the world, have mercy on us.

IV. Jesus, sweetest Child, born in Bethlehem of the Virgin Mary, wrapped in swaddling clothes and laid in a manger, announced by angels and visited by shepherds, have mercy on us.

V. Jesus, sweetest Child, in thy circumcision, called by the glorious Name of Jesus, and at once by thy Name and by thy Blood foreshown as the Savior of the world, have mercy on us.

VI. Jesus, sweetest Child, manifested by the leading of a star to the three wise men, worshiped in the arms of thy Mother, presented with the mystic gifts of gold, frankincense, and myrrh, have mercy on us.

VII. Jesus, sweetest Child, presented in the temple by thy Virgin Mother, taken up in Simeon's arms, and revealed to Israel by Anna, a prophetess, have mercy on us.

VIII. Jesus, sweetest Child, sought by wicked Herod to be slain, carried with thy Mother into Egypt by Saint Joseph, rescued from the cruel slaughter, and glorified by the praises of the martyred innocents, have mercy on us.

IX. Jesus, sweetest Child, who didst dwell in Egypt with most holy Mary and the Patriarch Saint Joseph until the death of Herod, have mercy on us.

X. Jesus, sweetest Child, who didst return from Egypt to the land of Israel with thy parents, suffering many hardships on the way, and didst enter into the city of Nazareth, have mercy on us.

XI. Jesus, sweetest Child, who didst dwell most holily in the holy house at Nazareth, in subjection to thy parents, wearied by poverty and toil, and didst increase in wisdom, age, and grace, have mercy on us.

XII. Jesus, sweetest Child, brought to Jerusalem at twelve years of age, sought by thy parents sorrowing and found with joy after three days in the midst of the doctors, have mercy on us. Amen.

Almighty and everlasting God, Lord of heaven and earth, who dost reveal thyself to little ones; grant, we beseech thee that we, venerating with due honor the sacred mysteries of thy Son, the Child Jesus, and copying them with due imitation, may be enabled to enter the kingdom of heaven which thou hast promised to little children. Through the same Christ our Lord. Amen.

Most dear Lord Jesus Christ, who, being made a Child for us, didst will to be born in a cave to free us from the darkness of sin, to draw us unto thee, and to set us on fire with thy holy love; we adore thee as our Creator and Redeemer, we acknowledge thee and choose thee for our King and Lord, and for tribute we offer thee all the affection of our poor hearts. Dear Jesus, our Lord and God, graciously accept this offering, and that it may be worthy of thine acceptance, forgive us our sins, enlighten us, and inflame us with that sacred fire which thou camest to bring upon the earth and to enkindle in our hearts. May our souls thus become an altar, on which we may offer thee the sacrifice of our mortifications; grant that we may ever seek thy greater glory here on earth, so that one day we may come to enjoy thine infinite loveliness in heaven. Amen.

⁕

At thy birth, O Jesus, a star of wondrous splendor shone forth in the Eastern skies, and led to Bethlehem the Magi, those envoys of far-distant, pagan peoples, even as the angel, bathed in heavenly light, was summoning to thy manger the shepherds, as representatives of the chosen people. For all must recognize in thee, a poor and helpless infant, the almighty King of Ages, the Savior of mankind. Neither scepter nor diadem disclosed thy kingly state; no sweet harmonies, no hosts of angels mustering round thy crib revealed thy divine nature; but the star, shining above thy wretched stable, pointed to the heavens, the earth, and the entire universe as thine absolute possessions; even as the Magi, who at the inspiration of thy grace, coming promptly from afar, caring naught for dangers, overcoming every difficulty, and embracing every sacrifice, reached thy feet and kneeling down in reverence offered thee their gifts of gold, frankincense, and myrrh. Thirsting for God, they had gone eagerly in search of thee, and thou didst reveal thyself to them in a wonderful manner while still in thy crib, filling them with ineffable joys and transforming them into the first messengers of thy glories to the peoples of the Orient. After the appearance of the star, which sufficed to render the magi thy ardent followers, with what marvels, O Jesus, didst thou demonstrate thy divinity! Yet what darkness still overshadows our poor minds! How reluctantly our will gives way to the loving impulses of thy grace, even when they do not openly resist thee! Give us, therefore, O Jesus, the strength to reply ever promptly and generously to thy call, and grant that the divine light of faith, which was enkindled by thee within us while still in our cradles, may ever accompany us on the road of life, until, blessed at last in heaven, we shall be able to fix our eyes upon thee in the light of glory. Amen.

A Priest's Devotions to the Holy Spirit

General Prayers and Invocations to the Holy Spirit

O Holy Spirit, Spirit of Truth, come into our hearts; shed the brightness of thy light upon the nations, that they may please thee in unity of faith.

O Holy Spirit, sweet guest of my soul, abide in me and grant that I may ever abide in thee.

God the Holy Ghost, have mercy on us.

May the grace of the Holy Spirit enlighten our senses and our hearts.

May our hearts be cleansed, O Lord, by the inpouring of the Holy Spirit, and may he render them fruitful by watering them with his heavenly dew.

Hymn to the Holy Spirit (Sequence)

Come, thou Holy Paraclete,
And from thy celestial seat
Send thy light and brilliancy.

Father of the poor, draw near,
Giver of all gifts, be here,
Come, the soul's true radiancy.

Come, of comforters the best,
Of the soul the sweetest guest,
Come in toil refreshingly.

Thou in labor rest most sweet,
Thou art shadow from the heat,
Comfort in adversity.

O thou light, most pure and blest,
Shine within the inmost breast
Of thy faithful company.

Where thou art not, man hath naught;
Ev'ry holy deed and thought
Comes from thy divinity.

What is soiled, make thou pure;
What is wounded, work its cure;
What is parched, fructify.

What is rigid, gently bend;
What is frozen, warmly tend;
Strengthen what goes erringly.

Fill thy faithful, who confide
In thy power to guard and guide,
With thy sevenfold mystery.

Here thy grace and mercy send;
Grant salvation in the end,
And in heaven felicity. Amen.

Come, Holy Ghost, Creator blest,
And in our souls take up thy rest,
Come with thy grace and heavenly aid,
And fill the hearts which thou hast made.

To thee, the Comforter, we cry,
To thee, the gift of God most high,
The font of life, the fire of love,
The soul's anointing from above.

The sevenfold gifts of grace are thine,
O Finger of the hand Divine;
True promise of the Father thou,
Who dost the tongue with speech endow.

Thy light to every thought impart,
And shed thy love in every heart;
Our body's poor infirmity
With strength perpetual fortify.

Our mortal foe afar repel,
Grant us henceforth in peace to dwell;
If thou be our preventing guide,
No evil can our steps betide.

Make thou to us the Father known;
Teach us th' Eternal Son to own,
And thee, whose name we ever bless,
Of both the Spirit to confess.

All glory while the ages run
Be to the Father and the Son,
Who rose from death; the name to thee,
O Holy Ghost, eternally. Amen.

V. Send forth thy Spirit and they shall be created;
R. And thou shalt renew the face of the earth.

Let us pray.
O God, who didst teach the hearts of thy faithful people by sending them the light of thy Holy Spirit, grant us by the same Spirit to have a right judgment in all things, and evermore to rejoice in his holy comfort. Through Christ our Lord. Amen.

Chaplet of the Holy Spirit

In the name of the Father, and of the Son, and of the Holy Spirit. Amen.

I—FIRST MYSTERY
Jesus is conceived by the Holy Ghost of the Virgin Mary

Meditation. The Holy Spirit shall come upon thee, and the power of the Most High shall overshadow thee. Therefore also the Holy One which shall be born of thee shall be called the Son of God (Luke 1:35).

Application. Pray earnestly for the assistance of the Spirit of God and the intercession of Mary to imitate the virtues of Jesus Christ who is the pattern of every virtue, in order that you may be conformed to the image of the Son of God.

Our Father and *Hail Mary* once; *Glory Be* seven times.

II—SECOND MYSTERY
The Spirit of the Lord rests upon Jesus

Meditation. Now Jesus being baptized went up immediately from the water; and behold, the heavens were opened unto him; and he saw the Spirit of God descending like a dove and coming upon him (Matt. 3:16).

Application. Hold in the highest esteem the precious gift of sanctifying grace which was infused into your heart in baptism by the Holy Spirit. Keep the promises to whose observance you then bound yourself. By continual exercise, increase your faith, your hope, and your charity. Ever live as becomes a child of God and a member of the Church, so that after this life, you may receive heaven as your inheritance.

Our Father and *Hail Mary* once; *Glory Be* seven times.

III—THIRD MYSTERY
Jesus is led by the Spirit into the desert

Meditation. And Jesus being full of the Holy ghost returned from the Jordan: and was led by the Spirit into the desert for the space of forty days, and was tempted by the devil (Luke 4: 1, 2).

Application. Be ever thankful for the sevenfold gifts of the Holy Spirit given to you in Confirmation, for the Spirit of wisdom and understanding, of counsel and fortitude, of knowledge and piety, and of the fear of the Lord. Faithfully obey your divine Guide, so that you may act with courage in all the perils of this life and in all temptations, as becomes a perfect Christian and a strong athlete of Jesus Christ.

Our Father and *Hail Mary* once; *Glory Be* seven times.

IV—FOURTH MYSTERY
The Holy Spirit in the Church

Meditation. And suddenly there came from heaven a sound as of a mighty wind coming, where they were sitting; and they were all filled with the Holy Ghost, speaking the wonderful works of God (Acts 2:2, 4, 11).

Application. Give thanks to God that he has made you a child of his Church which is always quickened and governed by his divine Spirit, who was sent into the world on the day of Pentecost. Hear and follow the sovereign Pontiff who teaches infallibly through the Holy Spirit, and the Church which is the pillar and ground of truth. Hold fast her doctrines, maintain her cause, defend her rights.

Our Father and *Hail Mary* once; *Glory Be* seven times.

V—FIFTH MYSTERY
The Holy Spirit in the souls of the righteous

Meditation. Know ye not that your members are the temple of the Holy Ghost who is in you? (1 Cor. 6:19).

Extinguish not the Spirit (1 Thess. 5:19).

And grieve not the Holy Spirit of God, in whom ye are sealed unto the day of redemption (Eph. 4:30).

Application. Be ever mindful of the Holy Spirit who is in you, and make every effort to be pure in mind and body. Faithfully obey his divine inspirations, that you may bring forth the fruits of the Spirit: which are charity, joy, peace, patience, kindness, goodness, long-suffering, meekness, faith, moderation, continence, and chastity.

Our Father and *Hail Mary* once; *Glory Be* seven times.

Come, Holy Ghost, fill the hearts of thy faithful and kindle in them the fire of thy love.

V. Send forth thy Spirit, and they shall be created
R. And thou shalt renew the face of the earth.

Let us pray.

O God, who didst teach the hearts of thy faithful people by sending them the light of thy Holy Spirit, grant us by the same Spirit to have a right judgment in all things, and evermore to rejoice in his holy comfort. Through Christ our Lord. Amen.

Prayers for Priests

O Holy Spirit, Creator, mercifully assist thy Catholic Church and her priests, and by thy heavenly power strengthen and establish her against the assaults of all her enemies; and by thy love and grace renew the spirit of thy servants whom thou hast anointed, that in thee they may glorify the Father and his only-begotten Son, Jesus Christ our Lord. Amen.

O Holy Spirit, divine Spirit of light and love, as a faithful priest, I consecrate to thee my understanding, my heart, and my will, my whole being for time and for eternity. May my understanding be always submissive to thy heavenly inspirations and to the teachings of the holy Catholic Church, of which thou art the infallible Guide; may my heart be ever inflamed with love of God and of my neighbor; may my will be ever conformed to the divine will, and may my whole life be a faithful imitation of the life and virtues of Our Lord and Savior Jesus Christ, to whom with the Father and thee be honor and glory forever. Amen.

Come, Holy Ghost, Sanctifier all powerful, God of love, thou who didst fill the Virgin Mary with grace, thou who didst wonderfully transform the hearts of the apostles, thou who didst endow all thy martyrs with a miraculous heroism, come and sanctify us. Illumine the minds, strengthen the wills, purify the consciences, rectify the judgments, set the hearts of priests on fire, and preserve us from the misfortune of resisting thine inspirations. Amen.

A Priest's Devotions to Our Lady

V. Angelus Domini nuntiavit Mariæ.
R. Et concepit de Spiritu Sancto.

Ave Maria, gratia plena, Dominus tecum. Benedicta tu in mulieribus, et benedictus fructus ventris tui, Iesus.
Sancta Maria, Mater Dei, ora pro nobis peccatoribus, nunc et in hora mortis nostræ. Amen.

V. Ecce Ancilla Domini.
R. Fiat mihi secundum Verbum tuum.

Ave Maria...

V. Et Verbum caro factum est.
R. Et habitavit in nobis.

Ave Maria...

V. Ora pro nobis, Sancta Dei Genetrix.
R. Ut digni efficiamur promissionibus Christi.

Oremus: Gratiam tuam quæsumus, Domine, mentibus nostris infunde; ut qui, angelo nuntiante, Christi Filii tui Incarnationem cognovimus, per passionem eius et crucem, ad resurrectionis gloriam perducamur.
Per eumdem Christum Dominum nostrum. Amen.

V. The angel of the Lord announced unto Mary.
R. And she conceived by the Holy Spirit.

Hail Mary, full of grace, the Lord is with you. Blessed are you among women, and blessed is the fruit of your womb, Jesus.
Holy Mary, Mother of God, pray for us sinners, now and at the hour of our death. Amen.

V. Behold the handmaid of the Lord.
R. Be it unto me according to your Word.

Hail Mary...

V. And the Word was made flesh.
R. And dwelt among us.

Hail Mary...

V. Pray for us, O Holy Mother of God.
R. That we may be made worthy of the promises of Christ.

Let us pray: We beseech you, O Lord, pour your grace into our hearts, that as we have known the incarnation of your Son Jesus Christ by the message of an angel, so by his cross and passion we may be brought to the glory of his resurrection; through the same Christ our Lord. Amen.

Litany of Loreto

V. Lord, have mercy.
R. Christ have mercy.
V. Lord have mercy. Christ hear us.
R. Christ graciously hear us.
God the Father of heaven, *have mercy on us.*
God the Son, Redeemer of the world, *have mercy on us.*
God the Holy Spirit, *have mercy on us.*
Holy Trinity, one God, *have mercy on us.*

Holy Mary, *pray for us.*
Holy Mother of God, "
Holy Virgin of Virgins,
Mother of Christ,
Mother of divine grace,
Mother most pure,
Mother most chaste,
Mother inviolate,
Mother undefiled,
Mother most amiable,
Mother most admirable,
Mother of good Counsel,
Mother of our Creator,
Mother of our Savior,
Virgin most prudent,
Virgin most venerable,
Virgin most renowned,
Virgin most powerful,
Virgin most merciful,
Virgin most faithful,
Mirror of justice,
Seat of wisdom,
Cause of our joy,
Spiritual vessel,
Vessel of honor,
Singular vessel of devotion,
Mystical rose,
Tower of David,
Tower of ivory,
House of gold,
Ark of the covenant,
Gate of heaven,
Morning star,
Health of the sick,
Refuge of sinners,
Comforter of the afflicted,
Help of Christians,
Queen of Angels,
Queen of Patriarchs,
Queen of Prophets,
Queen of Apostles,

Queen of Martyrs, *pray for us.*
Queen of Confessors, "
Queen of Virgins,
Queen of all Saints,
Queen conceived without original sin,
Queen assumed into heaven,
Queen of the most holy Rosary,
Queen of peace,

V. Lamb of God, who takest away the sins of the world,
R. Spare us, O Lord.
V. Lamb of God, who takest away the sins of the world,
R. Graciously hear us, O Lord.
V. Lamb of God, who takest away the sins of the world,
Have mercy on us.

V. Pray for us, O holy Mother of God.
R. That we may be made worthy of the promises of Christ.

Let us pray. Grant, we beseech thee, O Lord God, that we thy servants may enjoy perpetual health of mind and body, and by the glorious intercession of blessed Mary, ever Virgin, may we be freed from present sorrow, and rejoice in eternal happiness. Through Christ our Lord.

R. Amen.

The versicle and prayer after the litany may be varied by season. Thus, during Advent (from the fourth Sunday before Christmas to Christmas Eve):

V. The Angel of the Lord declared unto Mary.
R. And she conceived by the Holy Spirit.

Let us pray. O God, who hast willed that by the message of an angel, thy Word should receive flesh from the womb of the Virgin Mary: grant unto thy suppliants, that we who believe that she is truly the Mother of God, may be assisted by her intercession before thee. Through the same Christ our Lord.

R. Amen.

From Christmas to Candlemas (the Feast of the Presentation), that is, through February 1:

V. Thou gavest birth without loss of thy virginity.
R. Intercede for us, O holy Mother of God.

Let us pray. O God, who by the fruitful virginity of blessed Mary hast offered unto the human race the rewards of eternal salvation, grant, we beseech thee, that we may know the effects of her intercession, through whom we have deserved to receive the author of life, our Lord Jesus Christ, thy Son.

R. Amen.

From Candlemas to Easter (through Holy Week), AND from the day after Pentecost (or from Trinity Sunday, if Pentecost is celebrated with octave) to the beginning of Advent:

V. "Pray for us" and prayer "Grant unto thy servants," as above:

During Eastertide (from Easter day through Pentecost, and throughout the octave of Pentecost if it is celebrated):

V. Rejoice and be glad, O Virgin Mary, alleluia.
R. For the Lord is truly risen, alleluia.

Let us pray. O God, who by the resurrection of thy Son, our Lord Jesus Christ, hast vouchsafed to make glad the whole world, grant, we beseech thee, that through the intercession of the Virgin Mary, his mother, we may attain the joys of eternal life, through the same Christ our Lord.

R. Amen.

Litany of Our Lady of Seven Sorrows by Pope Pius VII

V. Lord, have mercy on us.
R. Christ, have mercy on us.
V. Lord, have mercy on us. Christ, hear us.
R. Christ, graciously hear us.
God, the Father of heaven, *have mercy on us.*
God the Son, Redeemer of the world, *have mercy on us.*
God the Holy Spirit, *have mercy on us.*

Holy Mary, Mother of God, *pray for us.*
Holy Virgin of virgins, "
Mother of the Crucified,
Sorrowful Mother,
Mournful Mother,
Sighing Mother,

Afflicted Mother, *pray for us.*
Foresaken Mother, "
Desolate Mother,
Mother most sad,
Mother set around with anguish,
Mother overwhelmed by grief,
Mother transfixed by a sword,
Mother crucified in thy heart,
Mother bereaved of thy Son,
Sighing Dove,
Mother of Dolors,
Fount of tears,
Sea of bitterness,
Field of tribulation,
Mass of suffering,
Mirror of patience,
Rock of constancy,
Remedy in perplexity,
Joy of the afflicted,
Ark of the desolate,
Refuge of the abandoned,
Shield of the oppressed,
Conqueror of the incredulous,
Solace of the wretched,
Medicine of the sick,
Help of the faint,
Strength of the weak,
Protectress of those who fight,
Haven of the shipwrecked,
Calmer of tempests,
Companion of the sorrowful,
Retreat of those who groan,
Terror of the treacherous,
Standard-bearer of the Martyrs,
Treasure of the Faithful,
Light of Confessors,
Pearl of Virgins,
Comfort of Widows,
Joy of all Saints,
Queen of thy Servants,
Holy Mary, who alone art unexampled,

V. Pray for us, most Sorrowful Virgin,
R. That we may be made worthy of the promises of Christ.

Let us pray.

O God, in whose Passion, according to the prophecy of Simeon, a sword of grief pierced through the most sweet soul of thy glorious Blessed Virgin Mother Mary: grant that we, who celebrate the memory of her Seven Sorrows, may obtain the happy effect of thy Passion, who lives and reigns world without end. Amen.

The Seven Sorrows of Our Lady

1. The Prophecy of Simeon
2. The Flight into Egypt
3. The Loss of Jesus in the Temple
4. Mary Meets Jesus Carrying the Cross
5. The Crucifixion
6. Mary Receives the Dead Body of Her Son
7. The Burial of Her Son and Closing of the Tomb

Alma Redemptoris Mater

O Loving Mother of Our Redeemer

O loving Mother of our Redeemer, gate of heaven, star of the sea,
Hasten to aid thy fallen people who strive to rise once more.
Thou who brought forth thy holy Creator, all creation wond'ring,
Yet remainest ever Virgin, taking from Gabriel's lips
That joyful "Hail!": be merciful to us sinners.

Up through the day before Christmas Eve:

V. The Angel of the Lord declared unto Mary.
R. And she conceived by the Holy Spirit.

Let us pray. Pour forth, we beseech thee, O Lord, thy grace into our hearts, that we, to whom the incarnation of Christ, thy Son, was made known by the message of an angel, may by his passion and cross be brought to the glory of his resurrection, through the same Christ our Lord. Amen.

From Christmas Eve on:

V. Thou gavest birth without loss of thy virginity:
R. Intercede for us, O holy Mother of God.

Let us pray. O God, who by the fruitful virginity of blessed Mary hast offered unto the human race the rewards of eternal salvation, grant, we beseech thee, that we may know the effects of her intercession, through whom we have deserved to receive the author of life, our Lord Jesus Christ, thy Son. Amen.

Alma Redemptoris Mater

Alma Redemptoris Mater, quae pervia caeli
Porta manes, et stella maris, sucurre cadenti,
Surgere qui curat populo: tu quae genuisti,
Natura mirante, tuum sanctum Genitorem,
Virgo prius ac posterius, Gabrielis ab ore
Sumens illud Ave, peccatorum miserere.

Usque ad diem 23 decembris:

V. Angelus Domini nuntiavit Mariae.
R. Et concepit de Spiritu Sancto.

Oremus. Gratiam tuam, quaesumus, Domine, mentibus nostris infunde; ut, qui, angelo nuntiante, Christi Filii tui incarnationem cognovimus, per passionem ejus et crucem, ad resurrectionis gloriam perducamur. Per eumdem Christum Dominum nostrum. Amen.

A die 24 decembris:

V. Post partum, Virgo, inviolata permansisti.
R. Dei Genitrix, intercede pro nobis.

Oremus. Deus, qui salutis aeternae, beatae Mariae virginitate fecunda, humano generi praemia praestitisti: tribue, quaesumus, ut ipsam pro nobis intercedere sentiamus, per quam meruimus auctorem vitae suscipere, Dominum nostrum Iesum Christum, Filium tuum. Amen.

Ave, Regina Caelorum

This is one of four Marian antiphons, with following versicles and prayers, traditionally said or sung after night prayer, immediately before going to sleep. It is said from Candlemas Day (the Feast of the Presentation, February 2) through Wednesday of Holy Week.

Hail, O Queen of Heaven

Welcome, O Queen of Heaven,
Welcome, O Lady of Angels,

Hail! Thou root, hail! Thou gate
from whom unto the world, a light has arisen:

Rejoice, O glorious Virgin,
Lovely beyond all others,
Farewell, most beautiful maiden,
And pray for us to Christ.

V. Allow me to praise thee, O sacred Virgin.
R. Against thy enemies give me strength.

Grant unto us, O merciful God, a defense against our weakness, that we who remember the holy Mother of God, by the help of her intercession, may rise from our iniquities, through the same Christ our Lord. Amen.

Ave, Regina Caelorum

Ave, Regina caelorum,
Ave, Domina Angelorum:
Salve, radix, salve, porta
Ex qua mundo lux est orta:

Gaude, Virgo gloriosa,
Super omnes speciosa,
Vale, o valde decora,
Et pro nobis Christum exora.

V. Dignare me laudare te, Virgo sacrata.
R. Da mihi virtutem contra hostes tuos.

Oremus. Concede, misericors Deus, fragilitati nostrae praesidium: ut, qui sanctae Dei Genitricis memoriam agimus; intercessionis eius auxilio, a nostris iniquitatibus resurgamus. Per eundem Christum Dominum nostrum. Amen.

Regina Caeli

This is one of four Marian antiphons, with following versicles and prayers, traditionally said or sung after night prayer, immediately before going to sleep. It is said throughout Eastertide. (That is, from Easter Day through Pentecost, the seventh Sunday after Easter.)

The Regina caeli *is also said in place of the Angelus during Eastertide.*

Queen of Heaven

V. Queen of Heaven, rejoice, alleluia.
R. For he whom you did merit to bear, alleluia.
V. Has risen, as he said, alleluia.
R. Pray for us to God, alleluia.
V. Rejoice and be glad, O Virgin Mary, alleluia.
R. For the Lord has truly risen, alleluia.

Let us pray. O God, who gave joy to the world through the resurrection of thy Son, our Lord Jesus Christ, grant we beseech thee, that through the intercession of the Virgin Mary, his Mother, we may obtain the joys of everlasting life. Through the same Christ our Lord. Amen.

Regina caeli

V. Regina caeli, laetare, alleluia.
R. Quia quem meruisti portare, alleluia.
V. Resurrexit, sicut dixit, alleluia.
R. Ora pro nobis Deum, alleluia.
V. Gaude et laetare, Virgo Maria, alleluia.
R. Quia surrexit Dominus vere, alleluia.

Oremus. Deus, qui per resurrectionem Filii tui, Domini nostri Iesu Christi, mundum laetificare dignatus es: praesta, quaesumus; ut per eius Genetricem Virginem Mariam, perpetuae capiamus gaudia vitae. Per eundem Christum Dominum nostrum. Amen.

Salve, Regina

This is one of four Marian antiphons, with following versicles and prayers, traditionally said or sung after night prayer, immediately before going to sleep. It is said from the end of Eastertide until the beginning of Advent. (That is, from the day after Pentecost, the seventh Sunday after Easter—or from the following Sunday, if Pentecost is celebrated with octave—through the Friday before the fourth Sunday before Christmas).

Hail, Holy Queen

Hail, holy Queen, Mother of mercy, our life, our sweetness and our hope. To thee do we cry, poor banished children of Eve. To thee do we send up our sighs, mourning, and weeping in this valley of tears. Turn, then, most gracious advocate, thine eyes of mercy toward us, and after this, our exile, show unto us the blessed fruit of thy womb, Jesus. O clement, O loving, O sweet Virgin Mary.

V. Pray for us, O holy Mother of God.
R. That we may be made worthy of the promises of Christ.

Let us pray. Almighty and everlasting God, who by the working of the Holy Spirit didst prepare both body and soul of the glorious Virgin Mother, Mary, that she might deserve to be made a worthy dwelling for thy Son, grant that we who rejoice in her memory, may, by her loving intercession, be delivered from present evils and from lasting death, through the same Christ our Lord. Amen.

Salve, Regina

Salve, Regina, mater misericordiae;
vita, dulcedo et spes nostra, salve.
Ad te clamamus exsules filii Hevae.
Ad te suspiramus gementes et flentes
in hac lacrimarum valle.
Eia ergo, advocata nostra,
illos tuos misericordes oculos ad nos converte.
Et Iesum, benedictum fructum ventris tui,
nobis post hoc exsilium ostende.
O clemens, o pia, o dulcis Virgo Maria.

V. Ora pro nobis, sancta Dei Genitrix.
R. Ut digni efficamur promissionibus Christi.

Oremus. Omnipotens sempiterne Deus, qui gloriosae Virginis Matris Mariae corpus et animam, ut dignum Filii tui habitaculum effici mereretur, Spiritu Sancto cooperante, praeparasti, da, ut cuius commemoratione laetamur; eius pia intercessione, ab instantibus malis et a morte perpetua liberemur. Per eundem Christum Dominum nostrum. Amen.

Prayers in the Life of the Priest

Prayers of Thanksgiving

Jesus Christ, Only True and Eternal
High Priest; you have graciously bestowed
the gift of the priesthood on your Church,
most graciously on me; the most unworthy of all your servants.

Please, grant us grace to faithfully serve you
in all your children.

You who live and reign in union with the Father and the Holy Spirit, one God forever and ever. Amen.

✳

Heavenly Father, through your grace, you have invested your Church with the Priesthood that belongs to Jesus Christ,
your only and begotten Son.

Help us to be the servants of all your children,
and to faithfully give witness of the great gift, that
in a loving and gracious manner you have conferred on us,
through the imposition of the bishop's hands.

We ask you this in the name of Jesus Christ our Lord,
who lives and reigns with you and the Holy Spirit,
one God forever and ever. Amen.

✳

Father, through the Holy Spirit, the Giver of all gifts,
you have bestowed on us the gift of the priesthood.
Through your breath we, your people set apart, the priestly
and kingly nation, are sanctified.

We beseech you the grace to live according to the name
we bear, and to faithfully remain true to the teachings
of Jesus Christ and His Church.

We ask you this in the name of Jesus Christ our Lord,
who lives and reigns in union with you and the Holy Spirit,
one God forever and ever. Amen.

✳

The People of God, Prayer of Thanksgiving for the Priesthood

Heavenly Father, through Jesus, your only-begotten Son;
you have given us the gift of priesthood. We in return give you
thanks because you continue sending laborers into your vineyard.

We, your children, receive the graces you conferred in the sacraments
dispensed through your ministers. Help us to give you thanks unceasingly,
to support and pray for our priests.

We ask you this in the name of Jesus Christ your Son, who lives
and reigns with you and the Holy Spirit,
one God forever and ever. Amen

✳

Prayers in Times of Trial

Heavenly Father, our refuge, our strength and consolation;
Help us to endure these moments of trial.

Grant us the grace and patience to be purified by the fire of the difficulties, to remain firm in hope and to completely trust in your loving care and providence.

We ask you this in the name of our Lord Jesus Christ your Son, who lives and reigns with you and the Holy Spirit, one God forever and ever. Amen.

⁕

Almighty Father, Jesus your Son endured trial and suffering. You know our human weaknesses.

We ask you to be with us and to help us to firmly believe that sin and death were defeated by your love. Help us to remain hopeful as we await the glorious coming of Jesus Christ; then all of us will be transformed and will see the glory of your kingdom, the kingdom where you live in union with Jesus Christ our Lord and the Holy Spirit, one God forever and ever. Amen.

⁕

Almighty and ever living God, help us to be always hopeful and to know that your promise stands unshaken.

Grant us this grace during moments of trial, when our sight is obscured by suffering and our faith is shaken.

We ask you this in the name of Jesus Christ your Son, who lives and reigns with you and the Holy Spirit, one God forever and ever. Amen.

⁕

Prayers in Times of Loneliness

All powerful and loving God,
You are a community of persons and have created man not to be alone but to be in communion with you and with your creation.

Help us in these moments of loneliness; do not let us be overwhelmed by sin, because it will separate us from you and from our brethren.

We ask this in the name of Jesus Christ your Son, who lives and reigns with you and the Holy Spirit, one God forever and ever. Amen.

✳

Lord Jesus Christ, when you decided to become flesh you also decided to endure loneliness. While you were on the cross, betrayed by a friend, you felt the sadness of being alone and forgotten; With all your strength you cried out to the Father.

Help us to cry out to our heavenly Father, especially during the moments when we face loneliness and tribulation. Do not permit temptation and desperation to destroy our faith and hope in you.

We ask this of you, who live and reign in union with the Father and the Holy Spirit, one God forever and ever. Amen.

✳

Heavenly and Almighty Father,
Hear our cries and lamentations; the sighs of desperation which we send up to you, our only hope.

Help us to overcome loneliness and to know that in your loving care you are always attentive to our prayers.

We ask you this in the name of our Lord Jesus Christ your Son, who lives and reigns with you, in union with the Holy Spirit, one God forever and ever. Amen.

✳

God of mercy and love,
you chose Mary to be the mother of your only begotten Son and granted her the grace and courage to remain standing at the foot of the cross.

Through her intercession grant us the grace of remaining hopeful while we endure loneliness and trial.

We ask this in the name of Jesus Christ our Lord,
who lives and reigns with you and the Holy Spirit,
one God forever and ever. Amen.

✳

Prayers for Priests in Trouble

God, heed our prayer for your priests who are in trouble.
Help them to remain in grace.
Make them aware that you're with them

in every Mass they celebrate,
in every wedding that they witnessed,
in every funeral that they served,
in every absolution they perform in your Name,
and in every baptism they celebrated.

Console them when they are distressed,
strengthen their faith in every doubt in their faith,
help them to trust you more,
for you are the one who called them to the priesthood,
you are the one who inspired them to be selfless.
With the intercession of the Blessed Mother, may you grant our petition as we say: Glory to the Father and to the Son and to the Holy Spirit, as it was in the beginning is now and will be forever. Amen.

✻

Gracious God, source of all compassion and strength.
Give your guiding hand to your priest who is experiencing problems.
Make his mind clear, his heart pure, and his soul sanctified.
Let him be inspired that you are his hope and his love.
Let him remember the day of his ordination when you
confirmed in his soul your Son's priestly character.

Help him grow in his vows of obedience and celibacy.
May his vows be his way to love you more through serving your people.
May his faithfulness to you through his vows be ways to understand
the privilege to participate in the salvific action of your Son.
Grant this through Our Lord Jesus Christ who lives and reigns with you
and the Holy Spirit, one God forever and ever. Amen.

Prayers for Priests on Leave from Active Ministry

Lord, grant your priests on leave from active ministry
to see beyond the situation they are in.
Help them to reflect on the things that they have done,
so as to understand what it is.
Help them renew their fidelity to you
and let them hear what you want them to do
as they rejuvenate in the goodness that comes from you.

Give them the strength to trust you.
Help them accept the things that were,
and accept the things that will be.

Make them and us see that your spouse the Church
remains holy because of you, and our call
is to be one with you.

O Lord, grant that after being on leave,
they may seek to be closer to you,
and have a deeper understanding about you,
who is united with the Father and the Holy Spirit. Amen.

❋

Lord, for your priests on leave from active ministry,
give them the grace to know and to finish what must they do.
Keep them in the state of grace.
Give them peace of mind and heart
so that they can clearly discern your will.
Keep them from the temptation of breaking
the vows of obedience and celibacy.

Lord, forgive them every transgression.
Free them from all worries and doubts,
and grant them the grace to trust to you more. Amen.

❋

God our Father, with a contrite heart
we pray for your priest who is on leave of absence.
Be gracious to him and forgive him his sins.
Grant that in his present ordeal, may he find strength in you.
May he remember his vows to you when you ordained him,
so that he may remember how your love overflows for him.

We pray for his wellbeing, for his peace of mind and heart,
so that he may discern well your divine will for him.
We ask you to keep him from harm and keep him safe wherever he goes.

Let all his encounters with your people be a sign of your loving presence.
Grant that through this encounter with your Divine Presence, he may
love you more.

If it be your will to place him back in active ministry, grant him the wisdom to listen and to look for you in each day. We ask this through our Lord Jesus Christ, who lives and reigns with you and the Holy Spirit, one God forever and ever. Amen.

❋

Additional Prayers for Priests

O good Jesus, grant that I may become a priest after thine own heart.

Put upon me, O Lord, the new man who is created according to God in justice and the holiness of truth. Amen.

⁜

Heart of Jesus, victim of love, make me a living victim for thee, holy and pleasing unto God.

⁜

Saint Aloysius, exemplar of clerics and their protector, pray for me.

⁜

Dearest Jesus, who of thy great goodness hast called me to be thy follower in preference to countless others and hast raised me to the high dignity of thy priesthood, bestow upon me abundantly, I pray, thy divine help in fulfilling my duties in a right spirit. I beseech thee, Lord Jesus, to stir up in me thy grace both today and always, that grace which is in me by reason of the laying on of hands of the bishop. O mighty physician of souls, heal me in such ways that I may never be entangled in sinful habits, but that I may renounce them all and be enabled to please thee even to the day of my death. Amen.

⁜

Lord Jesus Christ, bridegroom of my soul, the beloved of my heart, nay, my very heart and soul, I throw myself upon my knees in thy sight, and most earnestly implore thee to give me grace to keep the faith I solemnly gave unto thee. Wherefore, O sweetest Jesus, let me deny all ungodliness; let me ever be a stranger to carnal desires and earthly lusts which war against the soul, and, with thy help, let me preserve my chastity unspotted.

O Mary most holy and immaculate, the Virgin of virgins, and our loving Mother, make clean my heart and my soul ever more and more; obtain for me the fear of the Lord and a great distrust of myself.

Saint Joseph, guardian of Mary's virginity, keep my soul free from every sin.

All ye holy virgins who follow the Lamb whithersoever he goeth, be ever watchful over me, a sinner, lest at any time I go astray from the most pure heart of Jesus and transgress by thought, word, or deed. Amen.

⁜

Give me, O Lord, a mild and judicious eloquence which shall keep me from being puffed up and exalted above my brethren by reason of thy gifts. Put into my mouth, I beseech thee, words of consolation and edification and exhortation through thy Holy Spirit, that I may be enabled to exhort the good to better things, and, by word and example, to recall to the straight way of thy righteousness those who walk perversely. Let the words which thou shalt give thy servant, be like to sharp javelins and burning arrows that shall pierce and enkindle unto thy fear and holy love the minds of all them that hear me. Amen.

✳

O good Jesus, grant that I may be a priest after thine own Heart.

Almighty and merciful God, graciously attend to my humble prayers; and make me, thy servant, whom thou hast appointed to dispense thy heavenly mysteries, through no merits of mine own, but only of the infinite bounty of thy mercy, a worthy minister at thy sacred altar, that what is set forth by my voice may be confirmed by thy hallowing grace. Through Christ our Lord. Amen.

✳

O Almighty God, let thy grace assist us, that we who have undertaken the office of priesthood, may be able to wait upon thee worthily and devoutly, in all purity, and with a good conscience. And if we cannot live in so great innocence of life as we ought to do, grant to us at the least worthily to lament the sins that we have committed; and in the spirit of humility, and with the full purpose of a good will, to serve thee more earnestly for the time to come. Through Christ our Lord. Amen.

✳

Accept my confession, O most tender and merciful Lord Jesus Christ, my soul's only hope of salvation; and give me, thy priest, I pray, true contrition and tears to mine eyes, that I may weep night and day for all my shortcomings in humility and cleanness of heart. My Lord and God, accept my prayers. Savior of the world, good Jesus, who gavest thyself to the death of the Cross to save sinners, look upon me, a miserable sinner, calling upon thy holy Name, and regard not my wickedness in such wise as to forget thy goodness; and if I have done that which deserves thy condemnation, thou hast not lost that whereby thou art wont to save. Spare me, therefore, thou who art my Savior, and have pity on my sinful soul. Loose its bonds, heal its wounds. O most gracious Lord, by the merits of thy pure and inviolate Mother Mary ever Virgin, whom thou hast bequeathed especially unto thy priests to be their Mother, and by the merits of all thy saints, send out thy light and thy truth into my soul, and show me all my shortcomings in truth which I am bound to confess, and assist and teach me to unfold them fully and with a contrite heart: Who livest and reignest God, forever and ever. Amen.

✳

Let this my confession, I beseech thee, O Lord, be pleasing and acceptable in thy sight, by the merits of thy blessed and ever Virgin Mother Mary and of all thy saints; and whatsoever is wanting, now or at any other time, in sufficient contrition, or in sincerity and integrity of confession, do thou, of thy loving kindness and mercy, supply and deign thereby to hold me more fully and perfectly absolved in heaven: Who livest and reignest God, world without end. Amen.

⁂

Lord Jesus, who art our most loving Redeemer and a Priest forever, look mercifully on us, thy humble suppliants, whom thou hast been pleased to call thy friends and partakers of thy priesthood. We are thine; we wish to be thine forever: therefore to thy Most Sacred Heart which thou hast shown to oppressed humanity as their only safe refuge, we dedicate and devote ourselves wholly this day. Thou who hast promised plenteous fruit in the divine ministry to those priests who are devoted to thy Sacred Heart. Make us, we beseech thee, fit workmen in thy vineyard, truly meek and humble, filled with the spirit of devotion and patience, so fired with love of thee that we shall never cease to enkindle and quicken the same fire of love in the hearts of the faithful. Renew our hearts, therefore, in the fire of thy Heart, so that henceforth we shall desire nothing save to promote thy glory and win for thee the souls whom thou didst redeem by thy Precious Blood. Show thy mercy, good Shepherd, chiefly to those priests, our brethren, if there be any such, who, walking in the vanity of sense, have saddened thee and thy beloved spouse, Holy Church, by their lamentable falling away from thee. Grant us grace to bring them back to thine embrace, or, at least, to atone for their crimes, to repair the harm they have done, and to lessen the sorrow they have caused thee, by the consolation of our love. Allow each one of us, finally, to pray to thee in the words of Saint Augustine:
"O sweet Jesus, live thou in me, and let the living coal of thy love burn brightly in my spirit, and grow into a perfect conflagration; let it burn perpetually on the altar of my heart, let it glow in my marrow, let it blaze up in the most secret places of my soul; in the day of my consummation let me be found totally consumed thereby in thy presence, who with the Father and the Holy Ghost livest and reignest one God, forever and ever." Amen.

⁂

Let us rejoice with thee, blessed John, who, by a privilege of special love, wast honored by Christ Jesus above all the other disciples: being held worthy to recline upon his bosom at the Last Supper, and to be entrusted with his holy Mother at the hour of his death. We know that thou didst deserve this on account of thy special gift of chastity; because, being chosen as a virgin by our Lord, thou didst remain a virgin for ever. Accordingly, since thou didst imbibe the living streams of the Gospel from its very source, the bosom of our Lord, thou didst speak more fully and more sublimely of the divinity of Christ; and since thou didst catch thy flame of love from the fire burning in his Sacred Heart, we do not wonder that thou wast the only disciple to accompany Jesus in his Passion, and thereafter didst write such burning words that thou art rightly called "the Apostle of Love." Moreover, it behooves us, who are the ministers of Christ and stewards of the mysteries of God, by the gift of his goodness, to lift our eyes to thee, who hast been set before us as an example for our imitation: it is likewise meet, and we ask it of thee in great humility, that thou wouldst assist us as our own special patron before Jesus and Mary. Grant us, therefore, to walk worthy of the vocation wherewith we are called; in particular that we may perform our priestly tasks with due purity of mind and body; fired with zeal for the glory of God, may we attain to intimate fellowship with the heart of Jesus, and console the most holy Virgin, who was given from the Cross to be a Mother to all of us after thee, by the kindly offices of our ardent affection, even as thou didst do. Finally grant, that after this mortal life we may be numbered with the elders, whom thou didst see clothed in white raiment and sitting round the throne of the spotless Lamb, who is worthy to receive honor, blessing, and glory for endless ages. Amen.

⁂

Most lovable Jesus, today, the anniversary of the day on which, in spite of my misery, thou didst deign to raise me to the dignity of the priesthood by an impulse of thy goodness, and to make me thy minister and messenger as well as the dispense of thy sublime mysteries of wisdom and grace, my heart is filled with joy and grateful memories towards thee because of this singular favor conferred upon me. But it is afflicted with sadness and grief, inasmuch as I have not corresponded with this great gift in the manner or to the extent I should have done. To my mind, as it reviews the past, there comes a brilliant light, even though it is somewhat obscured by the darkness: Thou, indeed, O Jesus, both in thy light and in my darkness, dost shine by reason of thy mercy, and from my heart bursts forth an exultant hymn of glory.

O Lord, while I acknowledge and deplore in all humility my unworthiness I earnestly beseech the continual help of thy infinite goodness, assisted by which I may be able to conform my life to the high office committed to me, enlightened thereby may I be enabled to impart daily to my fellowmen richer fruits of thy Redemption, finally strengthened thereby may I be strong enough to continue on this mortal journey in a worthy manner, until my last day shall dawn, when, having finished my earthly pilgrimage, I may lay my weary head upon thy bosom, and enjoy for ever thy light and peace.

Most holy Virgin, thou who didst receive on Calvary at the foot of the Cross in the person of the beloved disciple all priests under they maternal protection, pray for me.

I wish to celebrate Mass and consecrate the Body and Blood of our Lord Jesus Christ after the use of the Holy Roman Church to the praise of Almighty God and of all the court of heaven, to my own benefit and that of all the Church militant: for all who have commended themselves to my prayers, in general and in particular, and for the happy estate of the holy Roman Church. Amen.

A Rosary for Priests

The Joyful Mysteries

The First Joyful Mystery—The Incarnation

Scripture

The Angel Gabriel was sent from God... to a virgin betrothed to a man, named Joseph, of the House of David. The virgin's name was Mary. (Luke 1:26)

Meditation

The youth of the Virgin.
The surprise of the angel's appearance.
The sound of his words like a trumpet.
The smallness of her room and the greatness of her heart.
The relief of her yes.

Priest's Meditation:

As we meditate on the origins of our salvation, as priests we might also contemplate the beginnings of our vocations. Do we remember the surprise we experienced at hearing God's call for the first time in our lives? Do we recall the moment when we experienced the clarion sound of that invitation that brought us eventually to the priesthood? Can we remember the relief of our own yes as we answered that call?

Prayer

O God, you prepared Mary to trust your word. Help me as a priest to be worthy to bear your Son into the world. We ask this through Christ our Lord. Amen.

The Second Joyful Mystery—The Visitation

Scripture

Mary set out, proceeding in haste into the hill country to a town of Judah, where she entered Zechariah's house and greeted Elizabeth (Luke 1:39-40).

Meditation

The hardship of her journey.
The baby leaping in Elizabeth's womb.
The joy of the embrace.
The calm of being together.
The reflection on God's goodness.

Priest's Meditation

The priesthood brings both sorrows and joys, hardships and great rewards. We might do well to contemplate Our Lady's unhesitating answer to the call to serve, the call to be of service to those in need. The joy of St. John the Baptist, anonymous as it is, hidden and not yet public, may, in many ways mirror the unseen benefits of our work, our service, and our sacrifices.

Prayer

Loving God, you gave Mary the courage to live the Gospel by her journey of faith. Keep our minds faithful to your Word, and our feet firmly in your path as we seek to do your will as priests. Give us faith in times of trial and open hearts in moments of joy. We ask this through Christ our Lord. Amen.

The Third Joyful Mystery—The Nativity

Scripture

I come to proclaim good news to you, tidings of great joy. This day in David's city a savior has been born to you, the Messiah and Lord (Luke 2:10-11).

Meditation

The weariness of the journey to Bethlehem.
The rejection at the inn.

The exhilaration of birth.
The warmth of the animals.
The wonder of the shepherds.

Priest's Meditation

How often as priests have we felt that we just could not go on? Perhaps it comes from a lack of energy, too much work, too many problems. Sometimes it comes from too little prayer, too little faith. The weariness of the journey to Bethlehem, the rejection from the inn, might be mirrored in our lives as priests. We know, however, that God always provides a haven, a place where his love can be experienced. God was manifested to the world at the end of Mary and Joseph's hardships. Is it not often true for us that after great trials, grace rushes in?

Prayer

Gracious Father, you give us joy at the birth of your Son made flesh for our salvation. Help us as priests of your Church to be true disciples of the promise you give us in this child. Sustain us in times of weakness. Flood our hearts with your grace in times of joy. We ask this through Christ our Lord. Amen.

The Fourth Joyful Mystery—The Presentation in the Temple

Scripture

Simeon blessed them and said to Mary his Mother; This child is destined to be the downfall and the rise of many in Israel, a sign that will be opposed (Luke 2:34).

Meditation

The crowds in the temple.
The sounds of the sacrifices.
The worn faces of Simeon and Anna.
The sword in Mary's heart.
The wonder of future.

Priest's Meditation

Who speaks to us in our work as priests? What are the voices that get heard? Simeon and Anna were like countless, sometimes forgotten, faces of faithful men and women who serve the Church. Sometimes we might overlook them or fail to hear their voices speaking wisdom to us. Often it is in the old and occasionally overlooked that we find our greatest inspiration for holiness.

Prayer

O God, through Simeon and Anna you have taught us to wait patiently for your promises to be fulfilled. Fill our priestly hearts with the spirit of humility, that we may recognize the presence of your Word among us. We ask this through Christ our Lord. Amen.

The Fifth Joyful Mystery—The Finding of Jesus in the Temple

Scripture

On the third day they came upon him in the temple sitting in the midst of the teachers.... All who heard him were amazed at his intelligence and his answers (Luke 2:46-47).

Meditation

The confusion of the temple.
The panic of the parents.
The wonder of the elders.
The eloquence of Jesus.
The relief of the journey home.

Priest's Meditation:

Sometimes our lives as priests can seem out of control. There is confusion in the temple of our lives, panic and distress. That is when we must remember that Jesus is in control and not us. Jesus was found in the temple, not running around and not causing a stir, but meditating with the elders, calmly and patiently, although his wisdom was so superior to theirs. Can we find the calm center of our lives in times of turmoil where Jesus teaches us?

Prayer

Almighty God, when your Son conversed with the elders in the temple, he confounded the expectations of worldly wisdom. Help us to be truly wise priests by listening intently to the Word made flesh. We ask this through Christ our Lord. Amen.

The Luminous Mysteries

The First Luminous Mystery—The Baptism of Jesus

Scripture

After Jesus was baptized, he came out of the water and, behold, the heavens were opened unto him (Matthew 3:16).

Meditation

The humility of John.
The rush of the water.
The stirring of the clouds.
The wonder of the crowd.
The voice from the heavens.

Priest's Meditation

John's humility in baptizing Jesus must have been profound. Perhaps it is the same humility we need as we realize the awesome call we have received to be custodians of Christ's mysteries. As priests, we are certainly called to hear in our lives the voice from heaven, "Here is my beloved Son." We are also called to speak that Good News to those we baptize. They are now beloved sons and daughters of God.

Prayer

Lord God, your Son Jesus was baptized in the Jordan by John as a sign of his humility. Help us to recall our baptism by which we were freed from sin and made your sons and daughters. Help us as priests to welcome others in the sacrament of baptism. We ask this through Christ our Lord. Amen.

The Second Luminous Mystery—The Sign at Cana

Scripture

Jesus did this as the beginning of his signs in Cana of Galilee, and so revealed his glory; and his disciples believed in Him (John 2:11).

Meditation

The joy of the wedding.
The certitude of Mary.
The embarrassment of the host.

The amazement of the steward.
The joy of the guests.

Priest's Meditation

As priests we have the opportunity to witness many marriages. At each one we are caught up in the joy of new beginnings and new relationships. As priests, we speak the words of Our Lady to newly married couples: "Do whatever Jesus tells you." The luminous mystery of the wedding allows us to express our amazement at the miracle of the way God touches lives in every vocation.

Prayer

Loving Father, your Son performed his first miracle at the wedding feast of Cana. Help your priests to realize the power of his presence and to drink the cup of his graciousness. We ask this through Christ our Lord. Amen.

The Third Luminous Mystery—Proclamation of the Kingdom of God

Scripture

"The kingdom of God is at hand" (Mark 1:15).

Meditation

The power of Jesus' preaching.
The amazement of the crowds.
The joy of the promise.
The hope for fulfillment.
The goodness of the savior.

Priest's Meditation

In the person of Christ, priests are called to proclaim the reality of the Kingdom of God. The power of Jesus' preaching must be echoed in our willingness to take up his mantle for the life of the world. Timidity and half-heartedness have no place in the preaching of the priest. The stakes are too high for us to give anything less than our full measure.

Prayer

Lord God of power and might, your Son came to proclaim the advent of your kingdom. May the priests of your Church be true ambassadors of that kingdom in a world that needs to hear Good News. We ask this through Christ our Lord. Amen.

The Fourth Luminous Mystery—The Transfiguration

Scripture

While he prayed, his face changed and his clothing became dazzling white (Luke 9:29).

Meditation

The journey up the mountain.
The blinding light.
The voice from heaven.
The confusion of Peter.
The promise of the future.

Priest's Meditation

The mystery of the transfiguration is a promise of the future, the fulfillment of our priestly lives in the realization of the heavenly banquet. Likewise, our priestly ministry offers us those moments of blinding light, moments of truly understanding what we do and who we are. They are enough to sustain us for the road.

Prayer

Lord God, you gave the apostles a sign of the future glory of your Son to sustain them on their journey. Help your priests to follow Jesus, encouraged by the promise of eternal life. We ask this through Christ our Lord. Amen.

The Fifth Luminous Mystery—The Institution of the Eucharist

Scripture

And as they were eating, Jesus took bread, blessed it, broke it, and gave it to his disciples and said, "Take and eat; this is My body" (Matthew 26:26).

Meditation

The fellowship of the table.
The savoring of the bread.
The taste of the wine.
The generosity of the Host.
The memory of the evening.

Priest's Meditation

What is this but the very heart and soul of our existence as priests? We live for the Eucharist. As we stand in the person of Christ we become what we celebrate. We become what we eat and are thus bread and life for the world. The priesthood exists to make Christ present in this most extraordinary way. How can I keep the Eucharist as the center of my life?

Prayer

God our Father, your Son Jesus gave us his most wondrous gift when he gave us his body and blood in the Eucharist. Sustain the holy priesthood by his Body and Blood and help us to do everything we do in memory of him. We ask this through Christ our Lord. Amen.

The Sorrowful Mysteries

The First Sorrowful Mystery—The Agony in the Garden

Scripture

Jesus went with them to a place called Gethsemane; and He began to experience sorrow and distress (Matthew 26:36-37).

Meditation

The tears of Jesus.
The disappointment with the disciples.
The darkness of the night.
The heartbroken savior.
The distant soldiers.

Priest's Meditation

Jesus' suffering and pain is our suffering and pain. Jesus' acceptance of the Father's will in his life must be our acceptance as well. Is there any other prayer that we can pray as priests other than, "Thy will be done"? This prayer carries with it the power to turn suffering and pain into joy, the joy we experience in our priesthood, the ultimate joy of the resurrection.

Prayer

Lord God, your Son fulfilled his destiny by doing your will. Help us to know your will for us and put it into action in our lives. We ask this through Christ our Lord. Amen.

The Second Sorrowful Mystery—The Scourging at the Pillar

Scripture

Jesus answered, "My Kingdom does not belong to this world." At this, Pilate said to Him, "So then you are a King?" Jesus replied, "It is you who say I am a King. The reason I was born, the reason why I came into the world is to testify to the truth. Anyone committed to the truth, hears my voice" (John 18:36-37).

Meditation

The shame of his nakedness.
The crack of the whip.
The sting of the wounds.
The jeering of the soldiers.
The indifference of Pilate.

Priest's Meditation

Where is our vulnerability as priests? St. Paul encourages us to embrace our weakness as our source of strength. Sometimes this need to be truly vulnerable can fly in the face of cultural expectations about masculinity, etc. May we learn as priests to embrace our weakness and live the strength of Jesus.

Prayer

God our Father, Jesus endured the agony and humiliation of torture for our sake. Help us to learn to love his sacrifice and despise our sins. We ask this through Christ our Lord. Amen.

The Third Sorrowful Mystery—The Crowning with Thorns

Scripture

They dressed Him in royal purple, then wove a crown of thorns and put it on Him (Mark 15:17).

Meditation

The bite of the thorns.
The trickle of blood.
The blinding of his eyes.
The jeers of the spectators.
The purple of the cloak.

Prayer

Almighty God, although he was a king, your Son became sin for us. Make him the king of our lives. We ask this through Christ our Lord. Amen.

The Fourth Sorrowful Mystery—The Carrying of the Cross

Scripture

When they had finished making a fool of him, they stripped Jesus of the cloak, dressed him in his own clothes, and led him off to the crucifixion (Matthew 27:31).

Meditation

The press of the wood.
The stumbling of his feet.
The reluctance of Simon.
The lamenting of the women.
The hardness of the road.

Prayer

Great and Loving God, Jesus took up his cross for our salvation; give us the courage to embrace the sign of his suffering, for it is our salvation. We ask this through Christ our Lord. Amen.

The Fifth Sorrowful Mystery—The Crucifixion

Scripture

When they had crucified him, they divided his clothes among them by casting lots; then they sat down and kept watch over him (Matthew 27:35-36).

Meditation

The ring of the hammer.
The piercing of his flesh.
The weight of his tired body.
The cries of the thieves.
The ridicule of the crowd.

Prayer

Lord God, we look upon him who was punished for our sins. May he remember us in his Kingdom. We ask this through Christ our Lord. Amen.

The Glorious Mysteries

The First Glorious Mystery—The Resurrection

Scripture

I am the resurrection and the life; whoever believes in Me, though he should die, will come to life (John 11:25-26).

Meditation

The stillness of the garden.
The empty tomb.
The dazzling vision of the angel.
The thrill of the women.
The amazement of the disciples.

Prayer

Almighty Father, you give us joy in the resurrection of your Son. Like the women at the tomb, make us joyful heralds of the Good News we have witnessed. We ask this through Christ our Lord. Amen.

The Second Glorious Mystery—The Ascension

Scripture

He was lifted up before their eyes in a cloud which took him from their sight (Acts 1:9).

Meditation

The sadness of parting.
The rush of his ascent.
The brilliance of the cloud.
The promise of the Spirit.
The return of the disciples to Jerusalem.

Prayer

Heavenly Father, Jesus has ascended to your right hand. Lift our hearts and minds to heaven even as we celebrate his presence with us on earth. We ask this through Christ our Lord. Amen.

The Third Glorious Mystery—The Descent of the Holy Spirit

Scripture

When the day of Pentecost came, it found them gathered in one place. Suddenly from up in the sky there came a noise like a strong driving wind, which was heard all through the house (Acts 2:1-2).

Meditation

The closeness of the room.
The anticipation of the disciples and Mary.
The rush of the wind.
The heat of the fire.
The music of their speech.

Prayer

Loving God, you sent the Holy Spirit as comforter and fire of hope to the disciples on the day of Pentecost. May that same Spirit brighten our hearts and fire our wills to boldly proclaim his truth. We ask this through Christ our Lord. Amen.

The Fourth Glorious Mystery—The Assumption of Mary

Scripture

For He has looked upon his servant in her lowliness (Luke 1:48).

Meditation

The sorrow of her friends.
The miracle of her rising.
The greatness of her memory.
The goodness of her life.
The faithfulness of God's promise.

Prayer

God of power and might, the lowliness of your servant, the Virgin Mary, was the glory of her life. Help us to follow her example of lowliness and come to share in the promise of eternal life. We ask this through Christ our Lord. Amen.

The Fifth Glorious Mystery—The Crowning of Mary as Queen of Heaven and Earth

Scripture

A great sign appeared in the sky, a woman clothed with the sun, with the moon under her feet, and on her head a crown of twelve stars (Revelations 12:1).

Meditation

The joy of the heavenly host.
The glimmer of the crown.
The stateliness of her throne.
The bow of her head.
The whisper of promise to us.

Prayer

All loving God, you crowned the life of Mary with eternal glory. Place us one day in her company. May our meditation on the mysteries of the rosary, draw us closer to your divine life. We ask this through Christ our Lord. Amen.

Little Office of the Blessed Virgin Mary for Saturday Devotions

---

Morning

God, come to my assistance. Lord, make haste to help me. Glory to the Father, and to the Son, and to the Holy Spirit: as it was in the beginning, is now, and will be for ever. Amen.

To the souls of your servants, O Christ, grant rest among the saints, where there is no pain, no sorrow, no mourning, but only life without end.

✳

O Lord, Maker of nature, the world offers you the godly martyrs as the first-fruits of nature. By their supplications, through the Mother of God, preserve your Church and your people in profound peace, O most Merciful One.

✳

Have mercy on me, O God, according to thy great mercy. And according to the multitude of thy tender mercies blot out my iniquity. Wash me yet more from my iniquity, and cleanse me from my sin. For I know my iniquity, and my sin is always before me. To thee only have I sinned, and have done evil before thee: that thou mayst be justified in thy words, and mayst overcome when thou art judged. For behold I was conceived in iniquities; and in sins did my mother conceive me. For behold thou hast loved truth: the uncertain and hidden things of thy wisdom thou hast made manifest to me. Thou shalt sprinkle me with hyssop, and I shall be cleansed: thou shalt wash me, and I shall be made whiter than snow. To my hearing thou shalt give joy and gladness: and the bones that have been humbled shall rejoice. Turn away thy face from my sins, and blot out all my iniquities. Create a clean heart in me, O God: and renew a right spirit within me. Cast me not away from thy face; and take not thy holy spirit from me. Restore unto me the joy of thy salvation, and strengthen me with a perfect spirit. I will teach the unjust thy ways: and the wicked shall be converted to thee. Deliver me from blood, O God, thou God of my salvation: and my tongue shall extol thy justice. O Lord, thou wilt open my lips: and my mouth shall declare thy praise. For if thou hadst desired sacrifice, I would indeed have given it: with burnt offerings thou wilt not be delighted. A sacrifice to God is an afflicted spirit: a contrite and humbled heart, O God, thou wilt not despise. Deal favorably, O Lord, in thy good will with Sion; that the walls of Jerusalem may be built up. Then shalt thou accept the sacrifice of justice, oblations and whole burnt offerings: then shall they lay calves upon thy altar.

✳

Holy God, Holy and Mighty, Holy and Immortal, have mercy on us. Holy God, Holy and Mighty, Holy and Immortal, have mercy on us. Holy God, Holy and Mighty, Holy and Immortal, have mercy on us.

✳

Glory to the Father, and to the Son, and to the Holy Spirit: as it was in the beginning, is now, and will be for ever. Amen.

✳

It is truly right to bless you, O God-bearing One, as the ever-blessed and Immaculate Mother of our God. More honorable than the cherubim and by far more glorious than the seraphim; ever a virgin, you gave birth to God the Word, O true Mother of God, we magnify you.

⁂

God, be merciful to me, a sinner.

God, cleanse me of my sins and have mercy on me.

I have sinned without number, forgive me, O Lord.

⁂

Hail, holy Queen of the Heavens. Hail, holy Queen of the Angels. Hail, Root of Jesse. Hail, Gate of Heaven. By you the Light has entered the world. Rejoice, glorious Virgin, Beautiful among all women. Hail, radiant Splendor, intercede with Christ for us.

⁂

Holy Mary, my Queen and sovereign Lady, I give you myself, trusting in your fidelity and your protection. I surrender myself entirely to your motherly tenderness, my body, my soul, all that I am, all that I possess, for the whole of this day, for every moment of my life, and especially at the hour of my death. I entrust to you once more all my hopes, all my consolations, all my anxieties, all my troubles, my life, my dying breath, so that by your prayers and merits, I may have, in all I do, one only goal, your good pleasure and the holy will of your Son.

⁂

Blessed are you, O Mary, for the world's salvation come forth through you; now in glory, you rejoice for ever with the Lord.

⁂

It is good to give praise to the Lord: and sing to thy name, O most High. To show forth thy mercy in the morning, and thy truth in the night: Upon an instrument of ten strings, upon the psaltery: with a canticle upon the harp. For thou hast given me, O Lord, a delight in thy doings: and in the works of thy hands I shall rejoice. O Lord, how great are thy works! Thy thoughts are exceeding deep. The senseless man shall not know: nor will the fool understand these things. When the wicked shall spring up as grass: and all the workers of iniquity shall appear: That they may perish for ever and ever: but thou, O Lord, art most high for evermore. For behold thy enemies, O Lord, for behold thy enemies shall perish: and all the workers of iniquity shall be scattered. But my horn shall be exalted like that of the unicorn: and my old age in plentiful mercy. My eye also hath looked down upon my enemies: and my ear shall hear of the downfall of the malignant that rise up against me. The just shall flourish like the palm tree: he shall grow up like the cedar of Libanus. They that are planted in the house of the Lord shall flourish in the courts of the house of our God. They shall still increase in a fruitful old age: and shall be well treated, that they may show, that the Lord our God is righteous, and there is no iniquity in him.

⁕

The Virgin Mary is exalted above the choirs of angels; let all believers rejoice and bless the Lord.

⁕

For I will take you from among the Gentiles, and will gather you together out of all the countries, and will bring you into your own land. And I will pour upon you clean water, and you shall be cleansed from all your filthiness, and I will cleanse you from all your idols. And I will give you a new heart, and put a new spirit within you: and I will take away the stony heart out of your flesh, and will give you a heart of flesh. And I will put my spirit in the midst of you: and I will cause you to walk in my commandments, and to keep my judgments, and do them. And you shall dwell in the land which I gave to your fathers, and you shall be my people, and I will be your God.

⁕

The Lord has made you so glorious that your praise will never cease to resound among men.

⁕

O Lord our Lord, how admirable is thy name in the whole earth! For thy magnificence is elevated above the heavens. Out of the mouth of infants and of sucklings thou hast perfected praise, because of thy enemies, that thou mayst destroy the enemy and the avenger. For I will behold thy heavens, the works of thy fingers: the moon and the stars which thou hast founded. What is man that thou art mindful of him? or the son of man that thou visitest him? Thou hast made him a little less than the angels, thou hast crowned him with glory and honor: and hast set him over the works of thy hands. Thou hast subjected all things under his feet, all sheep and oxen: moreover the beasts also of the fields. The birds of the air, and the fishes of the sea, that pass through the paths of the sea. O Lord our Lord, how admirable is thy name in all the earth!

⁕

I will greatly rejoice in the Lord, and my soul shall be joyful in my God: for he hath clothed me with the garments of salvation: and with the robe of justice he hath covered me, as a bridegroom decked with a crown, and as a bride adorned with her jewels.

⁕

And a great sign appeared in heaven: A woman clothed with the sun, and the moon under her feet, and on her head a crown of twelve stars.

⁕

And they all adored the Lord, and said to her: The Lord hath blessed thee by his power, because by thee he hath brought our enemies to nought.

⁂

And Ozias the prince of the people of Israel, said to her: Blessed art thou, O Daughter, by the Lord the most high God, above all women upon the earth. Blessed be the Lord who made heaven and earth, who hath directed thee to the cutting off the head of the prince of our enemies. Because he hath so magnified thy name this day, that thy praise shall not depart out of the mouth of men who shall be mindful of the power of the Lord for ever, for that thou hast not spared thy life, by reason of the distress and tribulation of thy people, but hast prevented our ruin in the presence of our God. And all the people said: So be it, so be it.

⁂

Today the glorious, ever-virgin Mary ascends to heaven. I urge you to rejoice, for, if I may so put it, she has been raised up in an ineffable way to be with Christ who reigns for ever. The Queen of the world is today taken from the earth and from this present evil time. I say again: rejoice, because she who is sure of her imperishable glory has reached the palace of heaven. Exalt, I say, and rejoice, and let the whole world rejoice, because this day Salvation has drawn nearer for us all... "Hail, Mary, full of grace; the Lord is with you; blessed are you among women." It was fitting that the Virgin should be given such gifts and be full of grace, since she has bestowed glory on heaven and has brought God and peace to the earth, faith to pagans, an end to vice, order to life, and discipline to morals. And it was right that an angel be sent to the Virgin, because virginity always means kinship with the angels... "Rejoice," the angel says, "for you are full of grace." Yes, full! for while a share of grace was given to others, the undiminished fullness of grace was poured into Mary.

⁂

The Virgin Mary was taken up to heaven. For all eternity she shares the victory of Christ. The Virgin Mary was taken up to heaven. Glory to the Father, and to the Son, and to the Holy Spirit: as it was in the beginning, is now, and will be for ever. The Virgin Mary was taken up to heaven. This daughter of Jerusalem is lovely and beautiful as she ascends to heaven like the rising sun at daybreak.

⁂

Drop down dew, ye heavens, from above, and let the clouds rain the just: let the earth be opened and bud forth a Savior. Lord, thou hast blessed thy land: thou hast turned away the captivity of Jacob.

⁂

Blessed be the Lord God of Israel; because he hath visited and wrought the redemption of his people: And hath raised up a horn of salvation to us, in the house of David his servant: As he spoke by the mouth of his holy prophets, who are from the beginning: Salvation from our enemies, and from the hand of all that hate us: To perform mercy to our fathers, and to remember his holy testament, the oath, which he swore to Abraham our father, that he would grant to us, that being delivered from the hand of our enemies, we may serve him without fear, in holiness and justice before him, all our days. And thou, child, shalt be called the prophet of the Highest: for thou shalt go before the face of the Lord to prepare his ways: To give knowledge of salvation to his people, unto the remission of their sins: through the mercy of our God, in which the Orient from on high hath visited us: To enlighten them that sit in darkness, and in the shadow of death: to direct our feet into the way of peace.

❊

Glory to the Father, and to the Son, and to the Holy Spirit: as it was in the beginning, is now, and will be for ever. Amen.

❊

All-powerful and ever-living God, you raised the sinless Virgin Mary, mother of your Son, body and soul to the glory of heaven. May we see heaven as our final goal and come to share her glory. We ask this through our Lord Jesus Christ, your Son, who lives and reigns with you and the Holy Spirit, one God, for ever and ever. Amen.

❊

May the Lord bless us, protect us from all evil and bring us to everlasting life. Amen.

❊

Evening

God, come to my assistance. Lord, make haste to help me. Glory to the Father, and to the Son, and to the Holy Spirit: as it was in the beginning, is now, and will be for ever. Amen.

❊

The Lord is reigning, He is clothed with beauty. The Lord is clothed with power, and has girded Himself. For He has so firmly established the earth that it will not be overthrown. Holiness becomes thy house, O Lord, forever.

❊

My Lady, my refuge, life and help, my armor and my boast, my hope and my strength, grant that I may enjoy the ineffable, inconceivable gifts of your Son, your God and our God, in the heavenly kingdom. For I know surely that you have power to do as you will, since you are Mother of the Most High. Therefore, Lady Most Pure, I beg you that I may not be disappointed in my expectations but may obtain them, O spouse of God, who bore him who is the expectation of all: Our Lord Jesus Christ, true God and Master of all things, visible and invisible, to whom belongs all glory, honor, and respect, now and always and through endless ages. Amen.

✳

Mary has been taken up to heaven; the angels rejoice. They bless the Lord and sing his praises.

✳

I rejoiced at the things that were said to me: We shall go into the house of the Lord. Our feet were standing in thy courts, O Jerusalem. Jerusalem, which is built as a city, which is compact together. For thither did the tribes go up, the tribes of the Lord: the testimony of Israel, to praise the name of the Lord. Because their seats have sat in judgment, seats upon the house of David. Pray ye for the things that are for the peace of Jerusalem: and abundance for them that love thee. Let peace be in thy strength: and abundance in thy towers. For the sake of my brethren, and of my neighbors, I spoke peace of thee. Because of the house of the Lord our God, I have sought good things for thee.

✳

Through Eve the gates of heaven were closed to all mankind: through the Virgin Mother they were opened wide again.

✳

Out of the depths I have cried to thee, O Lord: Lord hear my voice. Let thy ears be attentive to the voice of my supplication. If thou, O Lord, wilt mark iniquities: Lord, who shall stand it? For with thee is merciful forgiveness: and by reason of thy law, I have waited for thee, O Lord. My soul hath relied on his word: my soul hath hoped in the Lord. From the morning watch even until night, let Israel hope in the Lord. Because with the Lord there is mercy: and with him plentiful redemption. And he shall redeem Israel from all his iniquities.

✳

The Virgin Mary has been exalted above all the heavens; come, let all men glorify Christ the King, whose kingdom will endure for ever.

✳

For let this mind be in you, which was also in Christ Jesus: Who being in the form of God, thought it not robbery to be equal with God: But emptied himself, taking the form of a servant, being made in the likeness of men, and in the habit found as a man. He humbled himself, becoming obedient unto death, even to the death of the cross. For which cause God also hath exalted him, and hath given him a name which is above all names: That in the name of Jesus every knee should bow, of those that are in heaven, on earth, and under the earth: and that every tongue should confess that the Lord Jesus Christ is in the glory of God the Father.

✳

Wherefore as by one man, sin entered into this world, and by sin, death; and so death passed upon all men, in whom all have sinned. For until the law, sin was in the world; but sin was not imputed, when the law was not. But death reigned from Adam unto Moses, even over them also who have not sinned after the similitude of the transgression of Adam, who is a figure of him who was to come. But not as the offense, so also the gift. For if by the offense of one, many died; much more the grace of God, and the gift, by the grace of one man, Jesus Christ, hath abounded unto many. And not as it was by one sin, so also is the gift. For judgment indeed was by one unto condemnation; but grace is of many offenses, unto justification. For if by one man's offense death reigned through one; much more they who receive abundance of grace, and of the gift, and of justice, shall reign in life through one, Jesus Christ. Therefore, as by the offense of one, unto all men to condemnation; so also by the justice of one, unto all men to justification of life. For as by the disobedience of one man, many were made sinners; so also by the obedience of one, many shall be just. Now the law entered in, that sin might abound. And where sin abounded, grace did more abound. That as sin hath reigned to death; so also grace might reign by justice unto life everlasting, through Jesus Christ our Lord.

⁂

Truly, yes truly, and again I shall say in thanksgiving: even though you have left us, you have not deserted the Christian race. You who are like incorruptible life have not abandoned our mortal world, but on the contrary you draw near to those who call upon your name. You are found by those who faithfully seek you. And these visions indicate a living and continually active spirit and an everlasting body. For how could dissolution of the body return you to dust and ashes, you who delivered the human race from the destruction of death through the incarnation of your Son?

⁂

Indeed you left our earth to prove that the mystery of the awe- inspiring incarnation was really fulfilled. The fact that you waited for the natural end of human life would convince the world that the God who was born of you came into being also as perfect man, the Son of a true Mother, who was subject to the laws and constraints of nature, by divine decree and the requirement of an earthly lifetime. As one who possessed a human body you could not escape death, the common fate of humanity.

⁂

Thus even your Son, though God of all things, even he, through sharing, so to speak, the mortality of all our race, TASTED a similar bodily DEATH. It was clearly in the same way as he made his own life-giving tomb that he made your sepulchre wonderful also, as the tomb of your falling asleep, a tomb which received life; therefore both tombs really received your bodies, but could in no way affect them with corruption. For nor could you, as the vessel which contained God, waste away to dust in the destruction of death.

⁕

For since he who humbled himself in you was God from beginning and eternal life, so the Mother of Life was to share the dwelling of Life, to accept her death like a sleep and consent to her translation like a waking, as the Mother of Life. For just as a child seeks and longs for its own mother, and the mother loves to spend her time with her child, so it was right that you, with your maternal love for your Son and God, should return to him. And it was right too that God, preserving a Son's love for you, should make his companionship with you into a perpetual association.

In this way, then, you suffered the death of finite beings and the translation to the immortal way of life of eternal beings where God dwells; and because you are his companion, Mother of God, you do not abandon your life with him.

⁕

The august Mother of God was mysteriously united from all eternity with Jesus Christ in one and the same decree of predestination, immaculate in her conception, a virgin inviolate in her divine motherhood, the whole-hearted companion of the divine Redeemer who won complete victory over sin and its consequences.

Thus, she gained at last the supreme crown of her privileges—to be preserved immune from the corruption of the tomb, and like her Son, when death had been conquered, to be carried up body and soul to the exalted glory of heaven, there to sit in splendor at the right hand of her Son, the immortal King of the ages.

⁕

The Virgin Mary is exalted above the choirs of angels. Blessed is the Lord who has raised her up. Above the choirs of the angels. Glory to the Father, and to the Son, and to the Holy Spirit: as it was in the beginning, is now, and will be for ever. The Virgin Mary is exalted above the choirs of angels.

⁕

As Mary is taken up to heaven, the angels of God rejoice. They worship the Lord and sing his praises. The angels of God rejoice. Glory to the Father, and to the Son, and to the Holy Spirit: as it was in the beginning, is now, and will be for ever. As Mary is taken up to heaven, the angels of God rejoice.

⁕

Today the Virgin Mary was taken up to heaven; rejoice, for she reigns with Christ for ever.

⁕

O my most holy Mother, I see the graces which thou hast obtained for me; and I see the ingratitude of which I have been guilty towards thee. An ungrateful soul is no longer worthy of favors; but I will not on this account distrust thy mercy, which is greater than my ingratitude. O my great advocate, pity me. Thou dispensest all the graces which God grants to us miserable creatures, and for this purpose he has made thee so powerful, so rich, and so benign. He hath done so, that thou mightest succor us in our miseries. Ah, Mother of mercy, leave me not in my poverty. Thou art the advocate of the most miserable and guilty criminals who have recourse to thee; defend me also, who recommend myself to thee. Say not that my cause is too difficult to be gained; for all causes, however desperate, when defended by thee are gained. In thy hands, then, do I place my eternal salvation; to thee do I entrust my soul: it was lost; thou, then, by thy intercession hast to save it. I wish to be inscribed amongst thy most devoted servants; reject me not. Thou seekest the miserable to relieve them; abandon me not, who am a wretched sinner, and who have recourse to thee. Speak for me; thy Son does all that thou askest him. Take me under thy protection; that is all that I ask. Yes; for if thou protectest me, I fear nothing. I do not fear my sins; for thou wilt obtain me a remedy for the evil they have done me. I do not fear the devils; for thou art more powerful than all hell. I do not even fear Jesus my Judge himself; for by a single prayer of thine he is appeased. I only fear that by my negligence I may cease to recommend myself to thee, and thus be lost. It is true that these graces are too great for me, who have not deserved them; but they are not too great for thee, who art so much loved by God. Hence he grants thee all that thou askest. Thou hast only to speak, and he denies thee nothing. Pray, then, to Jesus for me; tell him that thou protectest me; and then he is sure to pity me. My Mother, in thee too I do trust; in this hope I shall live in peace, and in it I wish to die.

⁕

Live Jesus our love, and Mary our hope!

⁕

My soul doth magnify the Lord. And my spirit hath rejoiced in God my Savior. Because he hath regarded the humility of his handmaid; for behold from henceforth all generations shall call me blessed. Because he that is mighty, hath done great things to me; and holy is his name. And his mercy is from generation unto generations, to them that fear him. He hath showed might in his arm: he hath scattered the proud in the conceit of their heart. He hath put down the mighty from their seat, and hath exalted the humble. He hath filled the hungry with good things; and the rich he hath sent empty away. He hath received Israel his servant, being mindful of his mercy: As he spoke to our fathers, to Abraham and to his seed for ever.

Glory to the Father, and to the Son, and to the Holy Spirit: as it was in the beginning, is now, and will be for ever. Amen.

❊

Mary, full of grace, intercede for us.

All-powerful and ever-living God, you raised the sinless Virgin Mary, mother of your Son, body and soul to the glory of heaven. May we see heaven as our final goal and come to share her glory. We ask this through our Lord Jesus Christ, your Son, who lives and reigns with you and the Holy Spirit, one God, for ever and ever.

❊

Eternal and incarnate Wisdom, most lovable and adorable Jesus, true God and true man, only Son of the eternal Father and of Mary always Virgin, I adore you profoundly, dwelling in the splendor of our Father from all eternity and in the virginal womb of Mary, your most worthy Mother, at the time of your Incarnation.

I thank you for having emptied yourself in assuming the condition of a slave to set me free from the cruel slavery of the Evil One.

I praise and glorify you for having willingly chosen to obey Mary, your holy Mother, in all things, so that through her I may be your faithful slave of love.

But I must confess that I have not kept the vows and promises which I made to you so solemnly at my baptism. I have not fulfilled my obligations, and I do not deserve to be called a child or even your slave.

Since I cannot lay claim to anything except what merits your rejection and displeasure, I dare no longer approach the holiness of your majesty on my own. That is why I turn to the intercession and the mercy of your holy Mother, whom you yourself have given me to mediate with you. Through her I hope to obtain from you contrition and pardon for my sins, and that Wisdom whom I desire to dwell in me always.

I turn to you, then, Mary immaculate, living tabernacle of God, in whom Eternal Wisdom willed to receive the adoration of both men and angels. I greet you as Queen of heaven and earth, for all that is under God has been made subject to your sovereignty.

I call upon you, the unfailing refuge of sinners, confident in your mercy that has never forsaken anyone.

Grant my desire for divine Wisdom and, in support of my petition, accept the promises and the offering of myself which I now make, conscious of my unworthiness.

I, an unfaithful sinner, renew and ratify today through you my baptismal promises. I renounce forever Satan, his empty promises, and his evil designs, and I give myself completely to Jesus Christ, the incarnate Wisdom, to carry my cross after him for the rest of my life, and to be more faithful to him than I have been till now.

This day, with the whole court of heaven as witness, I choose you, Mary, as my Mother and Queen. I surrender and consecrate myself to you, body and soul, as your slave, with all that I possess, both spiritual and material, even including the value of all my good actions, past, present and to come. I give you the full right to dispose of me and all that belongs to me, without any reservations, in whatever way you please, for the greater glory of God in time and throughout eternity.

Accept, gracious Virgin, this little offering to honor and imitate the obedience which Eternal Wisdom willingly chose to have towards you, his Mother. I wish to acknowledge the authority which both of you have over this pitiful sinner. By it I wish also to thank God for the privileges bestowed on you by the Blessed Trinity. I declare that for the future I will try to honor and obey you in all things as your true servant of love.

O admirable Mother, present me to your dear Son as his servant now and for always, so that he who redeemed me thorough you, will now receive me through you.

Mother of mercy, grant me the favor of obtaining the true Wisdom of God, and so make me one of those whom you love, teach and guide, whom you nourish and protect as your children and servants.

Virgin most faithful, make me in everything so committed a disciple, imitator, and servant of Jesus, your Son, incarnate Wisdom, that I may become, through your intercession and example, fully mature with the fullness which Jesus possessed on earth, and with the fullness of his glory in heaven.

May the Lord bless us, protect us from all evil and bring us to everlasting life. Amen.

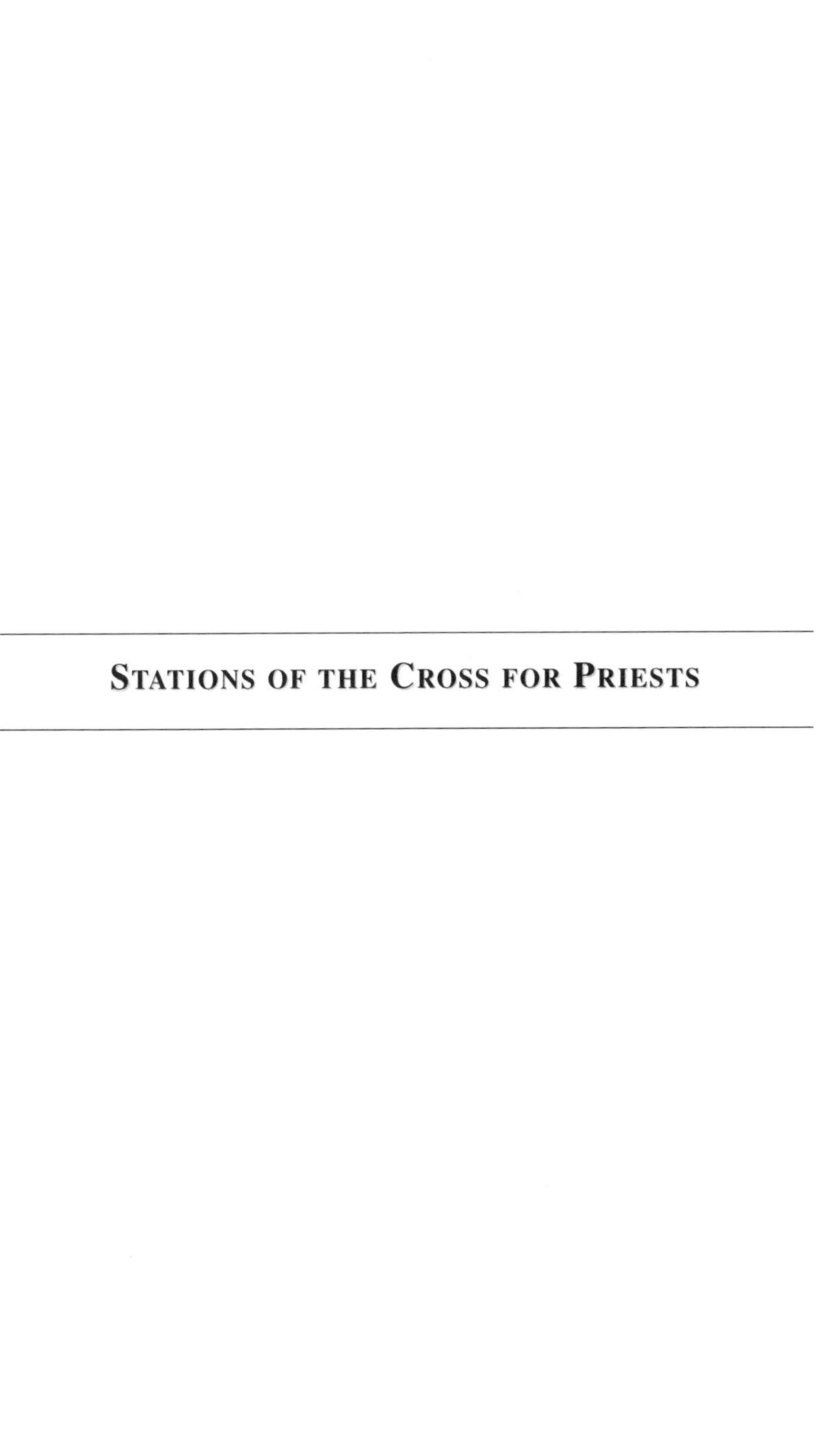

Stations of the Cross for Priests

Stations of the Cross for Priests Based on the Writings of St. Alphonsus Liguori

Opening Prayer:

Lord God, open my heart and my mind as I meditate on the suffering and death of your Son. May Jesus' sacrifice strengthen my life as a priest. Through Christ our Lord. Amen.

Station One: Jesus Is Condemned to Death

V. We adore thee, O Christ, and bless thee.
R. Because by thy holy cross thou hast redeemed the world.

Consider that Jesus, after having been scourged and crowned with thorns, was unjustly condemned by Pilate to die on the cross. My adorable Jesus, it was not Pilate, no, it was my sins, that condemned thee to die. I beseech thee, by the merits of this sorrowful journey, to assist my soul in its journey toward eternity.

I love thee, my beloved Jesus; I love thee more than myself; I repent with my whole heart of having offended thee. Never permit me to separate myself from thee again. Grant that I may love thee always; and then do with me what thou wilt.

Priest's Meditation

How often do we as priests find ourselves the subject of false judgment, of misunderstandings? Sometimes these judgments can be the result of real malice; often they are merely the result of living lives in the public eye. As priests, we can never lose sight of our very public relationships and, occasionally, hardships. When we are the subject of rumors and false accusations, can we follow the example of Jesus?

Our Father, Hail Mary, Glory Be…

Station Two: Jesus Is Given the Cross

V. We adore thee, O Christ, and bless thee.
R. Because by thy holy cross thou hast redeemed the world.

Consider that Jesus, in making this journey with the cross on his shoulders, thought of us, and offered for us, to his Father, the death that he was about to undergo. My most beloved Jesus, I embrace all the tribulations that thou hast destined for me until death. I beseech thee, by the merits of the pain thou didst suffer in carrying thy cross, to give me the necessary help to carry mine with perfect patience and resignation. I love thee, Jesus, my love, I repent of having offended thee. Never permit me to separate myself from thee again. Grant that I may love thee always, and then do with me what thou wilt.

Priest's Meditation

What crosses have we been asked to bear? As priests, we must consider our own crosses, but often we have the crosses of others, our parishioners, our brother priests, our relatives to bear as well. God never gives us a vocation that he does not give us the grace and courage to live. He never gives us a cross too heavy for us to bear. Can we unite our crosses to his and find in this unity the gentleness of the burden?

Our Father, Hail Mary, Glory Be...

Station Three: Jesus Falls the First Time

V. We adore thee, O Christ, and bless thee.
R. Because by thy holy cross thou hast redeemed the world.

Consider this first fall of Jesus under His cross. His flesh was torn by the scourges, His head crowned with thorns, and he had lost a great quantity of blood. He was so weakened that he could scarcely walk, and yet he had to carry this great load upon his shoulders. The soldiers struck him rudely, and thus he fell several times in his journey.

My beloved Jesus, it is not the weight of the cross, but of my sins, which has made thee suffer so much pain. Ah, by the merits of this first fall, deliver me from the misfortune of falling into mortal sin. I love thee, O my Jesus, with my whole heart; I repent of having offended thee. Never permit me to offend thee again. Grant that I may love thee always; and then do with me what thou wilt.

Priest's Meditation

Where do we fall? How do we experience weakness in our lives as priests? St. Paul writes: "When I am weak, then I am strong." Occasionally our sense of pride or accomplishment can hinder us from embracing an appropriate vulnerability, an openness that conforms our priestly hearts to the heart of the suffering Jesus.

Our Father, Hail Mary, Glory Be...

Station Four: Jesus Meets His Mother

V. We adore thee, O Christ, and bless thee.
R. Because by thy holy cross thou hast redeemed the world.

Consider the meeting of the Son and the Mother, which took place on this journey. Jesus and Mary looked at each other, and their looks became as so many arrows to wound those hearts which loved each other so tenderly.

My most loving Jesus, by the sorrow thou didst experience in this meeting, grant me the grace of a truly devoted love for thy most holy Mother. And thou, my Queen, who wast overwhelmed with sorrow, obtain for me by thy intercession a continual and tender remembrance of the Passion of thy Son. I love thee, Jesus, my love; I repent of ever having offended thee. Never permit me to offend thee again. Grant that I may love thee always, and then do with me what thou wilt.

Priest's Meditation

As priests, we sometimes experience mixed relationships with our family members. They know us in many ways and they have been with us through many of life's transitions. What a meeting this must have been between Jesus and his mother. In spite of his ministry and his service, he could still respond to his mother's care, the most intimate human relationship we have. What is our relationship with our parents? How do we experience our priesthood in light of the many other roles we must play in our lives?

Our Father, Hail Mary, Glory Be…

Station Five: Simon Carries the Cross of Jesus

V. We adore thee, O Christ, and bless thee.
R. Because by thy holy cross thou hast redeemed the world.

Consider that at each step Jesus, from weakness, was on the point of expiring, and fearing that He would die on the way when they wished him to die the ignominious death of the cross, they constrained Simon the Cyrenian to carry the cross behind Our Lord.

My most sweet Jesus, I will not refuse the cross as the Cyrenian did; I accept it, I embrace it. I accept in particular the death that thou hast destined for me with all the pains which may accompany it; I unite it to thy death, I offer it to thee. Thou has died for love of me, I will die for love of thee, and to please thee. Help me by thy grace. I love thee, Jesus, my love; I repent of having offended thee. Never permit me to offend thee again. Grant that I may love thee always, and then do with me what thou wilt.

Priest's Meditation

Who are our helpers? So often in our priestly ministry we need to call upon others to help us with burdens that we cannot continue to carry ourselves. Sometimes we do not really care to have others help us. We think that it implies weakness on our part or an inability to get the job done. This kind of pride might even be the cross we carry. Can we let others help us with our cross?

Our Father, Hail Mary, Glory Be…

Station Six: Veronica Wipes the Face of Jesus

V. We adore thee, O Christ, and bless thee.
R. Because by thy holy cross thou hast redeemed the world.

Consider that the holy woman named Veronica, seeing Jesus so afflicted, and his face bathed in sweat and blood, presented him with a towel with which he wiped his adorable face, leaving on it the impression of his holy countenance.

My most beloved Jesus, thy face was beautiful before, but in this journey it has lost all its beauty, and wounds and blood have disfigured it. Alas! my soul also was once beautiful, when it received thy grace in Baptism; but I have disfigured it since by my sins. Thou alone, my Redeemer, canst restore it to its former beauty. Do this by thy Passion, O Jesus. I repent of having offended thee. Never permit me to offend thee again. Grant that I may love thee always, and then do with me what thou wilt.

Priest's Meditation

Do I believe in my own worth? Veronica wiped the face of Jesus to reveal his beauty, his goodness. There may be times in the life of the priest where he feels a lack of self-worth, even a sense that he is unloved or abandoned by God. Sometimes this comes from overwork, or perhaps we use work to hide our lack of self-esteem. The passion of Christ reveals the worth of all of those who have been redeemed by his blood. Can we uncover that sense of beauty and goodness in ourselves?

Our Father, Hail Mary, Glory Be…

Station Seven: Jesus Falls the Second Time

V. We adore thee, O Christ, and bless thee.
R. Because by thy holy cross thou hast redeemed the world.

Consider the second fall of Jesus under the cross—a fall which renews the pain of all the wounds of the head and members of our afflicted Lord.

My most gentle Jesus, how many times thou hast pardoned me, and how many times have I fallen again, and begun again to offend thee! Oh, by the merits of this new fall, give me the necessary helps to persevere in thy grace until death. Grant that in all temptations which assail me I may always commend myself to thee. I love thee, Jesus, my love, with my whole heart; I repent of having offended thee. Never permit me to offend thee again. Grant that I may love thee always; and then do with me what thou wilt.

Priest's Meditation

How many times can I pick myself up as a priest? How often will my human frailty be revealed? When we sin as priests, when we make mistakes, we are called to announce the Good News of perseverance to ourselves first, or our ability to be credible in the announcement of that news to others is at risk.

Our Father, Hail Mary, Glory Be…

Station Eight: Jesus Meets the Women of Jerusalem

V. We adore thee, O Christ, and bless thee.
R. Because by thy holy cross thou hast redeemed the world.

Consider that those women wept with compassion at seeing Jesus in so pitiable a state, streaming with blood, as he walked along. But Jesus said to them, "Weep not for Me but for your children."

My Jesus, laden with sorrows, I weep for the offenses that I have committed against thee, because of the pains which they have deserved, and still more because of the displeasure which they have caused thee, who hast loved me so much. It is thy love, more than the fear of hell, which causes me to weep for my sins. My Jesus, I love thee more than myself; I repent of having offended thee. Never permit me to offend thee again. Grant that I may love thee always; and then do with me what thou wilt.

Priest's Meditation

As priests we know the truly faithful disciples among those we serve. Often these are the stalwart women who come to daily Mass, who clean the church building, and are there whenever we need them. We encounter many such people along the way of our priestly life. Do we give thanks for the silent support they give us or do we occasionally take them for granted?

Our Father, Hail Mary, Glory Be…

Station Nine: Jesus Falls the Third Time

V. We adore thee, O Christ, and bless thee.
R. Because by thy holy cross thou hast redeemed the world.

Consider the third fall of Jesus Christ. His weakness was extreme, and the cruelty of his executioners excessive, who tried to hasten His steps when he had scarcely strength to move. Ah, my outraged Jesus, by the merits of the weakness thou didst suffer in going to Calvary, give me strength sufficient to conquer all human respect and all my wicked passions, which have led me to despise thy friendship. I love thee, Jesus, my love, with my whole heart; I repent of having offended thee. Never permit me to offend thee again. Grant that I may love thee always; and then do with me what thou wilt.

Priest's Meditation

Sometimes the priest finds himself at the end of his strength. Where does he turn? All too often we attempt to work our solutions for real crises in our lives that are not healthy and will certainly not satisfy. In our concentration on our hardships we may forget the crowd standing by, or the Father who is as near as our ability to call upon his name. We are never truly alone. Our strength will always return through prayer.

Our Father, Hail Mary, Glory Be…

Station Ten: Jesus Is Stripped of His Garments

V. We adore thee, O Christ, and bless thee.
R. Because by thy holy cross thou hast redeemed the world.

Consider the violence with which the executioners stripped Jesus. His inner garments adhered to his torn flesh and they dragged them off so roughly that the skin came with them.

My innocent Jesus, by the merits of the torment which thou hast felt, help me to strip myself of all affection to things of earth, in order that I may place all my love in thee, who art so worthy of my love. I love thee, O Jesus, with my whole heart: I repent of having offended thee. Never permit me to offend thee again. Grant that I may love thee always; and then do with me what thou wilt.

Priest's Meditation

The magnitude of the sacrifice of Jesus must overwhelm us as priests. Yet it is a sacrifice that we renew each day in our celebration of the Holy Mass. We are called not only to speak the words of Jesus but to offer ourselves as Jesus did for the life of the world.

Our Father, Hail Mary, Glory Be…

Station Eleven: Jesus Is Nailed to the Cross

V. We adore thee, O Christ, and bless thee.
R. Because by thy holy cross thou hast redeemed the world.

Consider that Jesus, after being thrown on the cross, extended his hands, and offered to his eternal Father the sacrifice of his life for our salvation. These barbarians fastened him with nails; and then, raising the cross, left him to die with anguish on this infamous gibbet.

My Jesus, loaded with contempt, nail my heart to thy feet, that it may ever remain there to love thee, and never quit thee again. I love thee more than myself; I repent of having offended thee. Never permit me to offend thee again. Grant that I may love thee always; and then do with me what thou wilt.

Priest's Meditation

"Do with me what you wish, Lord." It is the ultimate self-giving that the priest must offer. What would our priesthood look like if we were completely consumed in Christ? It would look like a kind of death, a crucifixion. What is in our lives as priests that is extraneous? What do I need to have nailed to the cross today?

Our Father, Hail Mary, Glory Be…

Station Twelve: Jesus Dies on the Cross

V. We adore thee, O Christ, and bless thee.
R. Because by thy holy cross thou hast redeemed the world.

Consider how thy Jesus, after three hours of agony on the cross, consumed at length with anguish, abandons himself to the weight of his body, bows his head, and dies.

O my dying Jesus, I kiss devoutly the cross on which thou didst die for love of me. I have merited by my sins to die a miserable death, but thy death is my hope. Ah, by the merits of thy death, give me grace to die, embracing thy feet and burning with love of thee. I commit my soul into thy hands. I love thee with my whole heart; I repent of ever having offended thee. Never permit me to offend thee again. Grant that I may love thee always; and then do with me what thou wilt.

Priest's Meditation

One of the challenges we often face as priests is in giving the final measure. There is a tendency in all human beings to want to hold something in reserve, to care for the self, to protect the self. Jesus in the sacrifice of the cross is calling priests to offer everything on behalf of the world. Can we say with Jesus: "This is my body. This is my blood"?

Our Father, Hail Mary, Glory Be…

Station Thirteen: Jesus Is Taken Down from the Cross

V. We adore thee, O Christ, and bless thee.
R. Because by thy holy cross thou hast redeemed the world.

Consider that, our Lord having expired, two of His disciples, Joseph and Nicodemus, took him down from the cross, and placed him in the arms of his afflicted Mother, who received him with unutterable tenderness, and pressed him to her bosom.

O Mother of Sorrow, for the love of this Son, accept me for thy servant and pray to him for me. And thou, my Redeemer, since thou hast died for me, permit me to love thee; for I wish but thee, my Jesus, and I repent of ever having offended thee. Never permit me to offend thee again. Grant that I may love thee always; and then do with me what thou wilt.

Priest's Meditation

Jesus places himself in the hands of others. In his death he allows others to take charge. The deposition of the cross is the ultimate loss of control. How do we respond to our own loss of control?

Our Father, Hail Mary, Glory Be…

Station Fourteen: Jesus Is Placed in the Tomb

V. We adore thee, O Christ, and bless thee.
R. Because by thy holy cross thou hast redeemed the world.

Consider that the disciples carried the body of Jesus to bury it, accompanied by his holy Mother, who arranged it in the sepulcher with her own hands. They then closed the tomb and all withdrew.

Oh, my buried Jesus, I kiss the stone that encloses thee. But thou didst rise again the third day. I beseech thee, by thy resurrection, make me rise glorious with thee at the last day, to be always united with thee in heaven, to praise thee and love thee forever. I love thee, and I repent of ever having offended thee. Never permit me to offend thee again. Grant that I may love thee; and then do with me what thou wilt.

Priest's Meditation

Our desire as disciples and our desire as priests is to be caught up in the mystery of Christ's resurrection. First we must endure the wait of the tomb. How can my priesthood be seen as a time of transition to the final expression of the truth of the Resurrection?

Our Father, Hail Mary, Glory Be…

Closing Prayer

God our Father, give me the courage and the will to unite my priesthood to the passion and death of your son. May I truly follow the path laid down for the Church and its priests in Jesus' way of the cross.

Through the passion of Jesus, may my sins be forgiven and my vocation be strengthened.

Through the same Jesus Christ, our Lord. Amen.

Short Meditations on the Stations of the Cross by Bl. John Henry Newman

---

First Station
Jesus Condemned to Death

V. *Adoramus te, Christe, et benedicimus tibi.*
R. *Quia per sanctam Crucem tuam redemisti mundum.*

The Holy, Just, and True was judged by sinners, and put to death. Yet, while they judged, they were compelled to acquit Him. Judas, who betrayed Him, said, "I have sinned in that I have betrayed the innocent blood." Pilate, who sentenced Him, said, "I am innocent of the blood of this just person." The Centurion who saw Him crucified said, "Indeed this *was* a just man." Thus ever, O Lord, thou art justified in thy words, and dost overcome when thou art judged. And so, much more, at the last day "they shall *look* on Him whom they pierced"; and He who was condemned in weakness shall judge the world in power, and even those who are condemned will confess their judgment is just.

Pater, Ave, Gloria ...

V. *Miserere nostri, Domine.*
R. *Miserere nostri.*
Fidelium animæ, etc.

The Second Station
Jesus Receives His Cross

V. *Adoramus te, Christe, et benedicimus tibi.*
R. *Quia per sanctam Crucem tuam redemisti mundum.*

Jesus supports the whole world by His divine power, for He is God; but the weight was less heavy than was the Cross which our sins hewed out for Him. Our sins cost Him this humiliation. He had to take on Him our nature, and to appear among us as a man, and to offer up for us a great sacrifice. He had to pass a life in penance, and to endure His passion and death at the end of it. O Lord God Almighty, who dost bear the weight of the whole world without weariness, who bore the weight of all our sins, though they wearied thee, as thou art the Preserver of our bodies by thy providence, so be thou the Savior of our souls by thy precious blood.

Pater, Ave, Gloria ...

The Third Station
Jesus Falls Under the Weight of the Cross the First Time

V. *Adoramus te, Christe, et benedicimus tibi.*
R. *Quia per sanctam Crucem tuam redemisti mundum.*

Satan fell from heaven in the beginning; by the just sentence of his Creator he fell, against whom he had rebelled. And when he had succeeded in gaining man to join him in his rebellion, and his Maker came to save him, then his brief hour of triumph came, and he made the most of it. When the Holiest had taken flesh, and was in his power, then in his revenge and malice he determined, as he himself had been struck down by the Almighty arm, to strike in turn a heavy blow at Him who struck him. Therefore it was that Jesus fell down so suddenly. O dear Lord, by this thy first fall raise us all out of sin, who have so miserably fallen under its power.

Pater, Ave, Gloria ...

The Fourth Station
Jesus Meets His Mother

V. *Adoramus te, Christe, et benedicimus tibi.*
R. *Quia per sanctam Crucem tuam redemisti mundum.*

There is no part of the history of Jesus but Mary has her part in it. There are those who profess to be His servants, who think that her work was ended when she bore Him, and after that she had nothing to do but disappear and be forgotten. But we, O Lord, thy children of the Catholic Church, do not so think of thy Mother. She brought the tender infant into the temple, she lifted Him up in her arms when the wise men came to adore Him. She fled with Him to Egypt, she took Him up to Jerusalem when He was twelve years old. He lived with her at Nazareth for thirty years. She was with Him at the marriage-feast. Even when He had left her to preach, she hovered about Him. And now she shows herself as He toils along the sacred way with His cross on His shoulders. Sweet Mother, let us ever think of thee when we think of Jesus, and when we pray to Him, ever aid us by thy powerful intercession.

Pater, Ave, Gloria ...

The Fifth Station
Simon of Cyrene Helps Jesus to Carry the Cross

V. *Adoramus te, Christe, et benedicimus tibi.*
R. *Quia per sanctam Crucem tuam redemisti mundum.*

Jesus could bear His Cross alone, did He so will; but He permits Simon to help Him, in order to remind us that we must take part in His sufferings, and have a fellowship in His work. His merit is infinite, yet He condescends to let His people add their merit to it. The sanctity of the Blessed Virgin, the blood of the martyrs, the prayers and penances of the saints, the good deeds of all the faithful, take part in that work which, nevertheless, is perfect without them. He saves us by His blood, but it is through and with ourselves that He saves us. Dear Lord, teach us to suffer with thee, make it pleasant to us to suffer for thy sake, and sanctify all our sufferings by the merits of thy own.

Pater, Ave, Gloria ...

The Sixth Station
The Face of Jesus Is Wiped by Veronica

V. *Adoramus te, Christe, et benedicimus tibi.*
R. *Quia per sanctam Crucem tuam redemisti mundum.*

Jesus let the pious woman carry off an impression of His sacred countenance, which was to last to future ages. He did this to remind us all, that His image must ever be impressed on all our hearts. Whoever we are, in whatever part of the earth, in whatever age of the world, Jesus must live in our hearts. We may differ from each other in many things, but in this we must all agree, if we are His true children. We must bear about with us the napkin of St. Veronica; we must ever meditate upon His death and resurrection, we must ever imitate His divine excellence, according to our measure. Lord, let our countenances be ever pleasing in thy sight, not defiled with sin, but bathed and washed white in thy precious blood.

Pater, Ave, Gloria ...

The Seventh Station
Jesus Falls a Second Time

V. *Adoramus te, Christe, et benedicimus tibi.*
R. *Quia per sanctam Crucem tuam redemisti mundum.*

Satan had a second fall, when our Lord came upon earth. By that time he had usurped the dominion of the whole world—and he called himself its king. And he dared to take up the Holy Savior in his arms, and show Him all kingdoms, and blasphemously promise to give them to Him, His Maker, if He would adore him. Jesus answered, "Begone, Satan!"—and Satan fell down from the high mountain. And Jesus bears witness to it when He said, "I saw Satan, as lightning, falling from heaven." The Evil One remembered this second defeat, and so now he smote down the innocent Lord a second time, now that he had Him in his power. O dear Lord, teach us to suffer with thee, and not be afraid of Satan's buffetings, when they come on us from resisting him.

Pater, Ave, Gloria ...

The Eighth Station
The Women of Jerusalem Mourn for Our Lord

V. *Adoramus te, Christe, et benedicimus tibi.*
R. *Quia per sanctam Crucem tuam redemisti mundum.*

Ever since the prophecy of old time, that the Savior of man was to be born of a woman of the stock of Abraham, the Jewish women had desired to bear Him. Yet, now that He was really come, how different, as the Gospel tells us, was the event from what they had expected. He said to them "that the days were coming when they should say, blessed are the barren, and the wombs that have not borne, and the breasts which have not given suck." Ah, Lord, we know not what is good for us, and what is bad. We cannot foretell the future, nor do we know, when thou comest to visit us, in what form thou wilt come. And therefore we leave it all to thee. Do thou thy good pleasure to us and in us. Let us ever look at thee, and do thou look upon us, and give us the grace of thy bitter Cross and Passion, and console us in thy own way and at thy own time.

Pater, Ave, Gloria …

The Ninth Station
Jesus Falls the Third Time

V. *Adoramus te, Christe, et benedicimus tibi.*
R. *Quia per sanctam Crucem tuam redemisti mundum.*

Satan will have a third and final fall at the end of the world, when he will be shut up for good in the everlasting fiery prison. He knew this was to be his end—he has no hope, but despair only. He knew that no suffering which he could at that moment inflict upon the Savior of men would avail to rescue himself from that inevitable doom. But, in horrible rage and hatred, he determined to insult and torture while he could the great King whose throne is everlasting. Therefore a third time he smote Him down fiercely to the earth. O Jesus, only-begotten Son of God, the Word Incarnate, we adore with fear and trembling and deep thankfulness thy awful humiliation, that thou who art the highest, should have permitted thyself, even for one hour, to be the sport and prey of the Evil One.

Pater, Ave, Gloria …

The Tenth Station
Jesus Is Stripped of His Garments

V. *Adoramus te, Christe, et benedicimus tibi.*
R. *Quia per sanctam Crucem tuam redemisti mundum.*

Jesus would give up everything of this world, before He left it. He exercised the most perfect poverty. When He left the holy house of Nazareth, and went out to preach, He had not where to lay His head. He lived on the poorest food, and on what was given to Him by those who loved and served Him. And therefore He chose a death in which not even His clothes were left to Him. He parted with what seemed most necessary, and even a part of Him, by the law of human nature since the fall. Grant us in like manner, O dear Lord, to care nothing for anything on earth, and to bear the loss of all things, and to endure even shame, reproach, contempt, and mockery, rather than that thou shalt be ashamed of us at the last day.

Pater, Ave, Gloria ...

The Eleventh Station
Jesus Is Nailed to the Cross

V. *Adoramus te, Christe, et benedicimus tibi.*
R. *Quia per sanctam Crucem tuam redemisti mundum.*

Jesus is pierced through each hand and each foot with a sharp nail. His eyes are dimmed with blood, and are closed by the swollen lids and livid brows which the blows of His executioners have caused. His mouth is filled with vinegar and gall. His head is encircled by the sharp thorns. His heart is pierced with the spear. Thus, all His senses are mortified and crucified, that He may make atonement for every kind of human sin. O Jesus, mortify and crucify us with thee. Let us never sin by hand or foot, by eyes or mouth, or by head or heart. Let all our senses be a sacrifice to thee; let every member sing thy praise. Let the sacred blood which flowed from thy five wounds anoint us with such sanctifying grace that we may die to the world, and live only to thee.

Pater, Ave, Gloria ...

The Twelfth Station
Jesus Dies Upon the Cross

V. *Adoramus te, Christe, et benedicimus tibi.*
R. *Quia per sanctam Crucem tuam redemisti mundum.*

"Consummatum est." It is completed—it has come to a full end. The mystery of God's love towards us is accomplished. The price is paid, and we are redeemed. The Eternal Father determined not to pardon us without a price, in order to show us especial favor. He condescended to make us valuable to Him. What we buy we put a value on. He might have saved us without a price—by the mere fiat of His will. But to show His love for us He took a price, which, if there was to be a price set upon us at all, if there was any ransom at all to be taken for the guilt of our sins, could be nothing short of the death of His Son in our nature. O my God and Father, thou hast valued us so much as to pay the highest of all possible prices for our sinful souls—and shall we not love and choose thee above all things as the one necessary and one only good?

Pater, Ave, Gloria …

The Thirteenth Station
Jesus Is Laid in the Arms of His Blessed Mother

V. *Adoramus te, Christe, et benedicimus tibi.*
R. *Quia per sanctam Crucem tuam redemisti mundum.*

He is thy property now, O Virgin Mother, once again, for He and the world have met and parted. He went out from thee to do His Father's work—and He has done and suffered it. Satan and bad men have now no longer any claim upon Him—too long has He been in their arms. Satan took Him up aloft to the high mountain; evil men lifted Him up upon the Cross. He has not been in thy arms, O Mother of God, since He was a child—but now thou hast a claim upon Him, when the world has done its worst. For thou art the all-favored, all-blessed, all-gracious Mother of the Highest. We rejoice in this great mystery. He has been hidden in thy womb, He has lain in thy bosom, He has been suckled at thy breasts, He has been carried in thy arms—and now that He is dead, He is placed upon thy lap. Virgin Mother of God, pray for us.

Pater, Ave, Gloria …

The Fourteenth Station
Jesus Is Laid in the Sepulchre

V. *Adoramus te, Christe, et benedicimus tibi.*
R. *Quia per sanctam Crucem tuam redemisti mundum.*

Jesus, when He was nearest to His everlasting triumph, seemed to be farthest from triumphing. When He was nearest upon entering upon His kingdom, and exercising all power in heaven and earth, He was lying dead in a cave of the rock. He was wrapped round in burying-clothes, and confined within a sepulchre of stone, where He was soon to have a glorified spiritual body, which could penetrate all substances, go to and fro quicker than thought, and was about to ascend on high. Make us to trust in thee, O Jesus, that thou wilt display in us a similar providence. Make us sure, O Lord, that the greater is our distress, the nearer we are to thee. The more men scorn us, the more thou dost honor us. The more men insult over us, the higher thou wilt exalt us. The more they forget us, the more thou dost keep us in mind. The more they abandon us, the closer thou wilt bring us to thyself.

Pater, Ave, Gloria ...

Closing Prayer

God, who by the Precious Blood of thy only-begotten Son didst sanctify the standard of the Cross, grant, we beseech thee, that we who rejoice in the glory of the same Holy Cross may at all times and places rejoice in thy protection, through the same Christ, our Lord. Amen.

End with one Pater, Ave, *and* Gloria, *for the intention of the Sovereign Pontiff.*

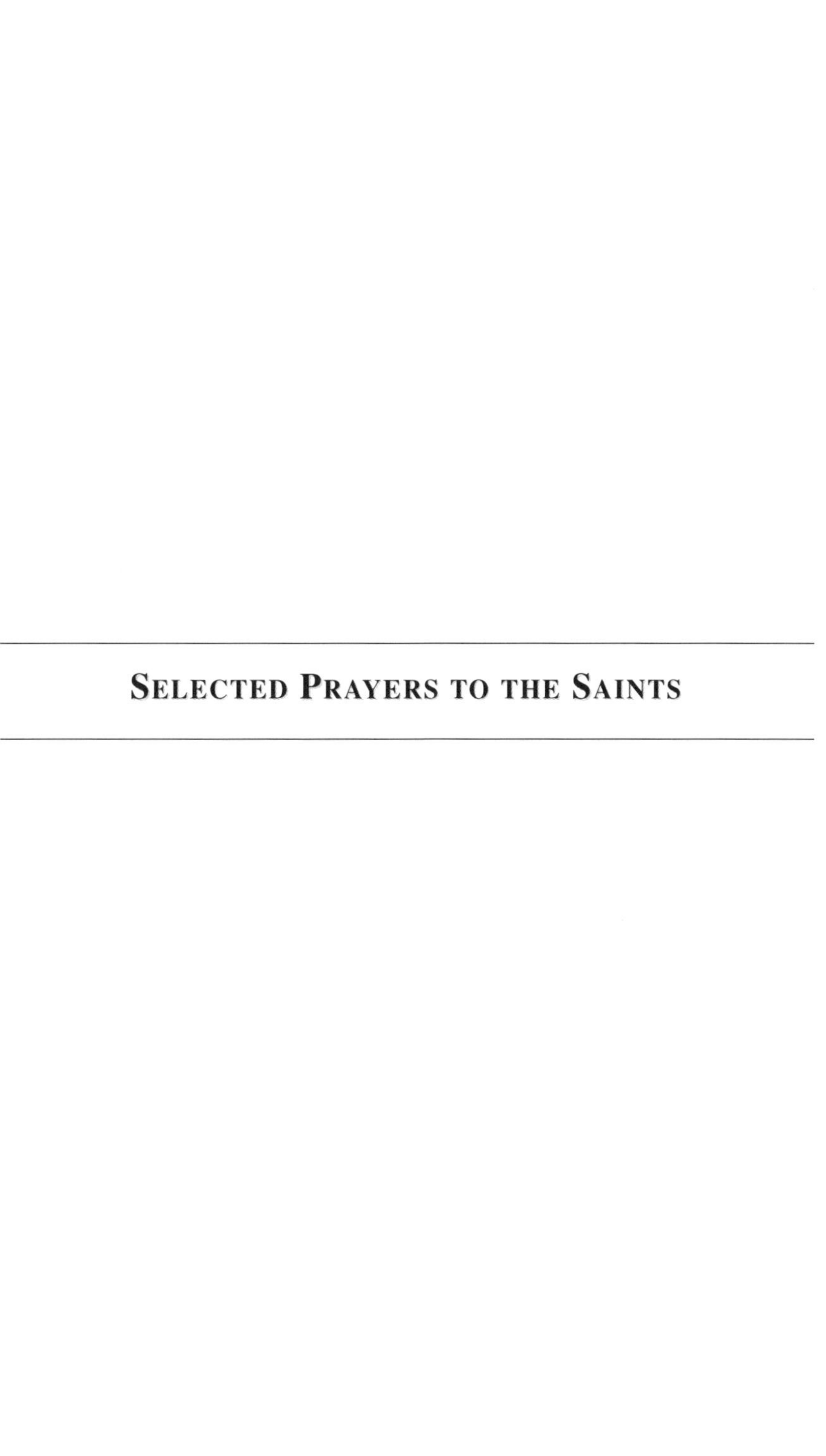

Selected Prayers to the Saints

Saint Agnes

I. O singular example of virtue, glorious Saint Agnes, by the living faith which animated thee from thy tenderest years, and rendered thee so pleasing to God that thou didst merit the martyr's crown: obtain for us the grace to keep our holy faith inviolate within us, and to profess ourselves Christians sincerely in word and work; may our open confession of Jesus before men cause Him to bear a favorable witness to us before His eternal Father.

Our Father, Hail Mary, Glory Be...

II. O invincible martyr, Saint Agnes most renowned, by thy confidence in God's help, when, being condemned by the impious Roman prefect to see the lily of thy purity stained and trampled in the mire, thou didst not despair, still trusting firmly in the God who giveth His angels charge over them that trust in Him: we beseech thee by thine intercession to obtain for us from Almighty God the forgiveness of all our sins and the sure confidence that He will bestow upon us life everlasting and the means necessary to merit.

Our Father, Hail Mary, Glory Be...

III. O courageous maiden, Saint Agnes most pure, by the burning love with which thy heart was on fire, and which preserved thee from harm in the midst of the flames of passion and of the stake, where the enemies of Jesus Christ sought to destroy thee: obtain for us from Almighty God that every unclean flame may be extinguished in us and only that fire, which Jesus Christ came to enkindle upon the earth, may burn within us; so that, after spending a blameless life in the practice of this fair virtue, we shall be worthy to have a share in the glory thou didst merit by the purity of thy heart and by thy martyrdom.

Our Father, Hail Mary, Glory Be...

* * *

Saint Aloysius Gonzaga

Saint Aloysius, adorned with angelic virtues, I, thy most unworthy client, commend to thee most earnestly the chastity of my mind and body. I beseech thee, for the sake of thine angelic purity, to commend me to the immaculate Lamb, Christ Jesus, and to His most holy Mother, the Virgin of virgins; and to protect me from every grievous sin. Permit me not to defile myself by any spot of impurity; nay, when thou seest me in temptation or in the danger of sin, banish far from my heart every unclean thought and desire. Awaken in me the thought of eternity and of Jesus crucified; imprint deeply in my heart a lively sense of the holy fear of God; set me on fire with the love of God; grant me the grace to imitate thee on earth that I may worthily enjoy the possession of God in heaven with thee. Amen.

Our Father, Hail Mary, Glory Be...

⁂

V. *Pray for us, Saint Aloysius,*
R. *That we may be made worthy of the promises of Christ.*

Let us pray.

O God, the Giver of all heavenly gifts, who in the angelic youth Aloysius didst join wondrous innocence with equal penance: be entreated by his merits and his prayers, and grant unto us who have not followed him in his innocence the grace to imitate him in his penance. Through Christ our Lord. Amen.

* * *

Saint Alphonsus Liguori

O my glorious and well-beloved patron, Saint Alphonsus, thou who didst toil and suffer so abundantly to assure to men the fruits of the Redemption, behold the miseries of my poor soul and have pity on me. By thy powerful intercession with Jesus and Mary, obtain for me true repentance for my sins together with their pardon and remission, a deep hatred of sin and strength ever more to resist all temptations. Share with me, I pray, at least a spark of that fire of love wherewith thy heart did ever burn; and grant that, following thy example, I may make the will of God the only rule of my life. Obtain for me likewise a fervent and lasting love of Jesus, and a tender and childlike devotion to Mary, together with the grace to pray without ceasing and persevere in the service of God even to the end of my life, that so I may finally be united with thee in praising God and most holy Mary through all eternity. Amen.

* * *

Saint Anne

Glorious Saint Anne, I desire to honor you with a special devotion. I choose you, after the Blessed Virgin, as my spiritual mother and protectress. To you I entrust my soul and my body, all my spiritual and temporal interests, as well as those of my family. To you I consecrate my mind, that in all things it may be enlightened by faith; my heart, that you may keep it pure and fill it with love for Jesus, Mary, Joseph, and yourself; my will, that like yours, it may always be one with the will of God.

Good Saint Anne, filled with love for those who invoke you with compassion for those who suffer, I confidently place before you my earnest petition: (Mention your request.) I beg you to recommend my petition to your daughter, the Blessed Virgin Mary, that both Mary and you may present it to Jesus. Through your earnest prayers may my request be granted. But if what I asked should not be according to the will of God, obtain for me that which will be for the greater benefit of my soul. By the power and the grace with which God has blessed you, extend to me your helping hand.

Merciful Saint Anne, I beg you to help me to master my evil inclinations and temptations, and to avoid all occasions of sin. Obtain for me the grace of never offending God, of fulfilling faithfully all the duties of my state of life, and of practicing all those virtues that are needful for my salvation. Like you, may I belong to God in life and in death through perfect love. And after having loved and honored you on earth as a truly devoted child, may I, through your prayers, have the privilege of loving and honoring you in heaven with the angels and saints throughout eternity.

With my heart full of sincere veneration, I prostrate myself before thee, O glorious Saint Anne. Thou art that creature of privilege and predilection, who by thy extraordinary virtues and holiness didst merit from God the high favor of giving life to her who is the Treasury of all graces, blessed among women, the Mother of the Word Incarnate, the most holy Virgin Mary. By virtue of so lofty a privilege, do thou deign, O most compassionate saint, to receive me into the number of they true clients, for so I profess myself and so I desire to remain throughout my entire life.

Shield me with thine effectual patronage and obtain for me from God the power to imitate those virtues wherewith thou wast so plentifully adorned. Grant that I may know and weep over my sins in bitterness of heart. Obtain for me the grace of most active love for Jesus and Mary, and resolution to fulfill the duties of my state of life with faithfulness and constancy. Save me from every danger that confronts me in life, and help me at the hour of death, so that I may come in safety to paradise, there to sing with thee, O most happy mother, the praises of the Word of God made Man in the womb of thy most pure daughter, the Virgin Mary. Amen.

Our Father, Hail Mary, Glory Be...

Saint Anthony the Abbot

O glorious Saint Anthony, who upon hearing only one word of the gospel didst forsake the riches and the ease of thy family, thy native land and the world, in order to retire into the wilderness; who, in spite of the heavy burden of advanced age and the ravages of severe penance, didst not hesitate to leave thy solitude to rebuke openly the impiety of heretics and to restore wavering Christians to a firmer hold upon their faith with all the zeal of a confessor desirous of martyrdom; who through thy conquest of self and the excellence of thy virtues wast endowed by our Lord with miraculous power over animate and inanimate nature; do thou obtain for us the grace to be ever zealous in the cause of Christ and His Church and to persevere even unto death in our imitation of thee, in our belief in revealed truth, and in our keeping of the commandments and the counsels of the Gospel; to the end that, having faithfully followed in thy footsteps here on earth, we may be enabled to become sharers in thy heavenly glory through all the ages of eternity. Amen.

Our Father, Hail Mary, Glory Be...

⁂

Let thy Church, O God, be gladdened by the solemn commemoration of blessed Anthony thy confessor: that she may evermore be defended by thy spiritual assistance, and merit to possess everlasting joy. Through Christ our Lord. Amen.

* * *

Saint Anthony of Padua

Saint Anthony, glorious for the fame of your miracles, obtain for me from God's mercy this favor that I desire: (Mention your request). Since you were so gracious to poor sinners, do not regard my lack of virtue but consider the glory of God which will be exalted once more through you by the granting of the petition that I now earnestly present to you.

⁂

Glorious wonderworker, Saint Anthony, father of the poor and comforter of the afflicted, I ask for your help. You have come to my aid with such loving care and have comforted me so generously. I offer you my heartfelt thanks. Accept this offering of my devotion and love and with it my earnest promise which I now renew, to live always in the love of God and my neighbor. Continue to shield me graciously with your protection, and obtain for me the grace of being able one day to enter the Kingdom of Heaven, there to praise with you the everlasting mercies of God. Amen.

⁂

O wondrous Saint Anthony, glorious by reason of the fame of thy miracles, who hadst the happiness of receiving within thine arms our blessed Lord under the guise of a little child, obtain for me of His bounty this favor that I desire from the bottom of my heart. Thou who wast so gracious unto poor sinners, regard not the lack of merit on the part of him who calls upon thee, but consider the glory of God, which will be exalted once more through thee, to the salvation of my soul and the granting of the petition that I now make with such ardent yearning.

As a pledge of my gratitude, I beg thee to accept my promise to live henceforth more agreeably to the teachings of the Gospel, and to be devoted to the service of the poor whom thou didst ever love and still dost love so greatly; bless this my resolution and obtain for me the grace to be faithful thereto even until death. Amen.

* * *

Saint Benedict Joseph Labre

O wondrous pattern of Christian perfection, Saint Benedict Joseph, from thy earliest use of reason even to thy dying day, thou didst keep unspotted the white robe of innocence, and, forsaking all things and becoming a pilgrim on the earth, thou didst gain naught therefrom save only suffering, privations, and reproaches. Miserable sinner that I am, I kneel at thy feet, and return thanks to the infinite goodness of the Most High God who hath willed to imprint on thee the living likeness of His crucified Son. At the same time, I am filled with confusion when I consider how different is my life from thine. Do thou, beloved saint, have pity on me! Offer they merits before the throne of the Eternal, and obtain for me the grace to follow thine example and to direct my actions according to the precepts and teachings of our divine Master: thus let me learn to love His sufferings and His humiliations, and to despise the pleasures and honors of earth: so that neither the fear of the former, nor the desire of the latter may ever induce me to transgress His holy law. May I merit in this manner to be acknowledged by Him and numbered amongst the blessed of His Father. Amen.

Our Father, Hail Mary, Glory Be...

V. *Pray for us, O holy Benedict Joseph,*
R. *That we may be made worthy of the promises of Christ.*

Let us pray.

O God, who didst cause thy holy confessor, Benedict Joseph, to cleave unto thee alone by his zeal for humility and his love for poverty: grant unto us, by the help of his merits, to despise all things earthly and to seek evermore the things that are heavenly. Through Christ our Lord. Amen.

* * *

Saint Blaise

O glorious Saint Blase, who by thy martyrdom didst leave to the Church a precious witness to the faith, obtain for us the grace to preserve within ourselves this divine gift, and to defend, without human respect, both by word and example, the truth of that same faith, which is so wickedly attacked and slandered in these, our times. Thou who didst miraculously restore a little child when it was at the point of death by reason of an affliction of the throat, grant us thy mighty protection in like misfortunes; and, above all, obtain for us the grace of Christian mortification together with a faithful observance of the precepts of the Church, which may keep us from offending Almighty God. Amen.

* * *

Saint Catherine of Siena

O Saint Catherine, thou lily of virginity and rose of charity who didst adorn the garden of Saint Dominic, heroine of Christian zeal who wast chosen like Saint Francis to be the special patron of Italy, to thee we have recourse with confidence, invoking thy mighty protection upon ourselves and upon the whole Church of Christ, thy Beloved, in whose Heart thou didst drink of the inexhaustible fountain of all grace and all peace for thee and for the world. From that divine Heart thou didst draw the living water of virtue and concord in families, of upright conduct in young people, of union among the discordant nations, of renewal of public morality and of brotherly love, which is compassionate and benevolent towards the unfortunate and suffering, and didst teach us by thy example how to unite the love of Christ with the love of country.

If thou lovest the land of Italy and its people entrusted to thee, if pity for us moves thee, if that tomb is dear to thee in which Rome venerates and honors thy virginal remains, oh! graciously turn thine eyes and thy favor upon our pain and upon our prayer, and fulfill our desires.

Defend, assist, and comfort thy fatherland and the world. Under thy protection and thy guidance be the sons and daughters of Italy, our hearts and our minds, our labors and our hopes, our faith and our love; that faith and that love which formed thy very life and made thee the living image of Christ crucified in thy intrepid zeal for His spouse, Holy Church.

O heroic and holy messenger of union and peace for the Church of Christ, thou who didst restore the successor of Peter to the apostolic Roman See in the splendor of its authority and teaching office, protect and console him in his paternal and universal solicitude, in his anxious cares and in his counsels for the salvation and the tranquility of the peoples of the earth; revive, preserve, and increase in us and in all faithful Christians, O heavenly patroness, the affection and the filial submission which thou didst cherish for him and for the fold of Christ in a world at peace. Amen.

⁂

O admirable Saint Catherine, thou who didst merit to make of thy whole life the noblest holocaust, constantly inspiring thyself to a most ardent love for Jesus, the Lamb without blemish, and of His beloved spouse the Church, whose right thou didst strenuously affirm and support in troubled times, obtain, likewise, for us the grace not only to pass unscathed through the corruption of this world, but also to remain unshakably faithful to the church, in word, in deed, in example, to see always, and to make others see, in the Vicar of Christ our anchor, as it were, in the storms of life, the beacon light that points the way to the harbor of safety in the dark night of our times and of men's souls.

* * *

Saint Dominic

I. O glorious Saint Dominic, thou who wast a model of mortification and purity, by punishing thy innocent body with scourges, with fastings, and with watchings, and by keeping inviolate the lily of thy virginity, obtain for us the grace to practice penance with a generous heart and to keep unspotted the purity of our bodies and our hearts.

Our Father, Hail Mary, Glory Be...

II. O great Saint, who, inflamed with divine love, didst find thy delight in prayer and intimate union with God; obtain for us to be faithful in our daily prayers, to love our Lord ardently, and to observe His commandments with ever-increasing fidelity.

Our Father, Hail Mary, Glory Be...

III. O glorious Saint Dominic, who, being filled with zeal for the salvation of souls, didst preach the Gospel in season and out of season, didst establish the Order of Friars Preachers to labor for the conversion of heretics and poor sinners, pray thou to God for us, that He may grant us to love all our brethren sincerely and to cooperate always, by our prayers and good works, in their sanctification and eternal salvation.

Our Father, Hail Mary, Glory Be...

✳

V. *Pray for us, Saint Dominic,*
R. *That we may be made worthy of the promises of Christ.*

Let us pray.

Grant, we beseech thee, Almighty God, that we who are weighed down by the burden of our sins may be raised up by the patronage of blessed Dominic, thy confessor. Through Christ our Lord. Amen.

* * *

Saint Fidelis of Sigmaringen

O God, who hast vouchsafed to glorify blessed Fidelis, inflamed with seraphic ardor of spirit, with the palm of martyrdom and the fame of miracles in the propagation of the truth faith: by his merits and intercession, we beseech thee so to strengthen us by thy grace in faith and charity, that we may deserve to be found faithful in thy service unto death. Through Christ our Lord. Amen.

* * *

Saint Frances of Rome

Bright jewel of the Order of Saint Benedict, illustrious Saint Frances of Rome, thou who wast led by divine providence through various stations in life, that thou mightest be a pattern of every virtue, to maidens, to matrons and to widows, pray for us to our divine Savior that we may be detached from the vanities of the world and may be able, under the guiding hand of our guardian angel, to grow daily in the love of God, of His Church, and of our neighbor, and finally to be made partakers in heaven of thy felicity. Amen.

* * *

Saint Francis of Assisi

O glorious Saint Francis, who, even in thy youth, with a generous heart didst renounce the comfort and ease of thy father's house in order to follow Jesus more closely in His humility and poverty, in His mortification and passionate love of the Cross, and didst thereby merit to behold the miraculous stigmata impressed upon thy flesh and to bear them about with thee, obtain for us also, we pray, the grace of passing through our life here below, as thou insensible to the ephemeral splendor of all earthly possessions, with our hearts constantly beating with love of Jesus Crucified even in the darkest and saddest hours of life and with our eyes ever serenely raised toward heaven, as though already enjoying a foretaste of the eternal possession of the infinite Good with His divine and everlasting joys.

Lord Jesus Christ, who, when the world was growing cold, didst renew in the flesh of blessed Francis the sacred marks of thy Passion in order to inflame our hearts with the fire of thy love; mercifully grant that, by his merits and prayers, we may always carry the cross and bring forth fruits worthy of repentance: Who livest and reignest forever and ever. Amen.

* * *

Saint Francis Xavier

Saint Francis Xavier, well beloved and full of charity, in union with thee, I reverently adore the Majesty of God; and since I rejoice with exceeding joy in the singular gifts of grace bestowed upon thee during thy life, and thy gifts of glory after death, I give Him hearty thanks for them; I beseech thee with all my heart's devotion to be pleased to obtain for me, by thy effectual intercession, above all things, the grace of a holy life and a happy death. Moreover, I beg of thee to obtain for me . . . (here mention the spiritual or temporal favor to be prayed for). But if what I ask of thee so earnestly doth not tend to the glory of God and the greater good of my soul, do thou, I pray, obtain for me what is more profitable to both these ends. Amen.

Our Father, Hail Mary, Glory Be...

* * *

Saint Gregory the Great

O invincible defender of Holy Church's freedom, Saint Gregory of great renown, by that firmness thou didst show in maintaining the Church's rights against all her enemies, stretch forth from heaven thy mighty arm, we beseech thee, to comfort her and defend her in the fearful battle she must ever wage with the powers of darkness. Do thou, in an especial manner, give strength in this dread conflict to the venerable Pontiff who has fallen heir not only to thy throne, but likewise to the fearlessness of thy mighty heart; obtain for him the joy of beholding his holy endeavors crowned by the triumph of the Church and the return of the lost sheep into the right path. Grant, finally, that all may understand how vain it is to strive against that faith which has always conquered and is destined always to conquer: "this is the victory which overcometh the world, our faith." This is the prayer that we raise to thee with one accord; and we are confident, that, after thou hast heard our prayers on earth, thou wilt one day call us to stand with thee in heaven, before the eternal High Priest, who with the Father and the Holy Spirit liveth and reigneth, world without end.

* * *

Saint Ignatius of Loyola

O glorious patriarch Saint Ignatius, we humbly beseech thee to obtain for us from Almighty God, above all things else, deliverance from sin, which is the greatest of evils, and next, from those scourges wherewith the Lord chastises the sins of His people. May thine example enkindle in our hearts an effectual desire to employ ourselves continually in laboring for the great glory of God and the good of our fellow men; obtain for us, likewise, from the loving Heart of Jesus our Lord, that grace which is the crown of all graces, that is to say, the grace of final perseverance and everlasting happiness. Amen.

* * *

Saint James the Greater

O glorious apostle Saint James, who by reason of thy fervent and generous heart wast chosen by Jesus to be a witness of His glory on Mount Tabor, and of His agony in Gethsemane; thou, whose very name is a symbol of warfare and victory: obtain for us strength and consolation in the unending warfare of this life, that, having constantly and generously followed Jesus, we may be victors in the strife and deserve to receive the victor's crown in heaven. Amen.

* * *

Saint Joachim

O Joachim, husband of holy Anne, father of the merciful Virgin, hither bring thy servants help for their salvation.

O great and glorious patriarch, Saint Joachim, what joy is mine when I consider that thou was chosen among all God's holy ones to assist in the fulfillment of the mysteries of God, and to enrich our earth with the great Mother of God, Mary most Holy! By this singular privilege, thou hast become most powerful with both the Mother and her Son, so as to be able to obtain for us the graces that are needful to us; with great confidence I have recourse to thy mighty protection and I commend to thee all my needs and those of my family, both spiritual and temporal; and especially do I entrust to thy keeping the particular favor that I desire and look for from thy fatherly intercession. And since thou wast a perfect pattern of the interior life, obtain for me the grace of interior recollection and a spirit of detachment from the transitory goods of this life, together with a lively and enduring love for Jesus and Mary. Obtain for me in like manner a sincere devotion and obedience to Holy Church and the Sovereign Pontiff: to the end that I may live and die in faith and hope and perfect charity, ever invoking the holy names of Jesus and Mary, and may I thus be saved. Amen.

Our Father, Hail Mary, Glory Be...

⁎

O great patriarch Saint Joachim, deserving by thy singular virtue to be chosen of old by divine providence to give to the world that immaculate Queen, in whom all nations were to be blessed, and who, in her virginal bosom, was to bear the Savior of the human race: we who are thy devout clients rejoice with thee in this thy great privilege, and implore thee to extend thy special protection to ourselves and our families. Permit us not to live unmindful of eternity, for which we have been created. Obtain for us from God a firm and unshaken faith.

Do thou, who art powerful by reason of that love which thy holy daughter Mary bears toward thee, assist the cause of the Church, gain for her the victory for which she sighs, scatter the powers of darkness, destroy their pride and grant that the light of the true faith may shine resplendent in all minds. Grant us, above all, a tender and filial devotion to thy beloved daughter and our Mother, Mary most holy, so that we, honoring her daily with our devout homage, may be made worthy to be numbered by her amongst her children; and after the miseries of this exile may be brought to praise and bless the mercy of God forever in heaven. Amen.

Our Father, Hail Mary, Glory Be...

* * *

Saint John

O glorious apostle Saint John, who for thy virginal purity wast so beloved by Jesus as to merit to rest thy head upon His divine bosom, and to be left, in His stead, as a son to His most holy Mother, I implore thee to set me on fire with a burning love for Jesus and Mary. Obtain for me, I pray, this grace from our Lord, that, even now, with my heart set free from earthly affections, I may be made worthy to be ever united to Jesus as His faithful disciple and to Mary as her devoted child both here on earth and then forever in heaven. Amen.

Saint John the Baptist

I. O glorious Saint John the Baptist, greatest prophet among those born of woman, although thou wast sanctified in they mother's womb and didst lead a most innocent life, nevertheless it was thy will to retire into the wilderness, there to devote thyself to the practice of austerity and penance; obtain for us of thy Lord the grace to be wholly detached, at least in our hearts, from earthly goods, and to practice Christian mortification with interior recollection and with the spirit of holy prayer.

Our Father, Hail Mary, Glory Be...

II. O most zealous apostle, who, without working any miracle on others, but solely by the example of thy life of penance and the power of they word, didst draw after thee the multitudes, in order to dispose them to receive the Messiah worthily and to listen to His heavenly doctrine; grant that it may be given unto us, by means of the example of a holy life and the exercise of every good work, to bring many souls to God, but above all those souls that are enveloped in the darkness of error and ignorance and are led astray by vice.

Our Father, Hail Mary, Glory Be...

III. O martyr invincible, who, for the honor of God and the salvation of souls, didst with firmness and constancy withstand the impiety of Herod even at the cost of thine own life, and didst rebuke him openly for his wicked and dissolute life; by thy prayers obtain for us a heart brave and generous, in order that we may overcome all human respect and openly profess our faith in loyal obedience to the teachings of Jesus Christ, our divine Master.

Our Father, Hail Mary, Glory Be...

V. *Pray for us, Saint John the Baptist,*
R. *That we may be made worthy of the promises of Christ.*

Let us pray.

O God, who hast made this day to be honorable in our eyes by the Nativity (or commemoration) of blessed John, grant unto thy people the grace of spiritual joy, and direct the minds of all thy faithful into the way of everlasting salvation. Through Christ our Lord. Amen.

Saint John Baptist de la Salle

O glorious John Baptist de la Salle, apostle of children and young folk, be thou, from the heights of heaven, our guide and our patron. Offer thy prayers and help us, that we may be kept free from every stain of error and corruption, and remain ever faithful to Jesus Christ and to the infallible head of His Church. Grant that we, practicing the virtues of which thou hast been so wondrous an example, may be made partakers of thy glory in heaven, our true country. Amen.

* * *

Saint John Berchmans

Saint John, angelic youth, sweet-scented flower of innocence, stalwart soldier of the Company of Jesus, ardent defender of the Immaculate Conception of the Blessed Virgin, whom the all-wise Providence of God hath set forth as a light and pattern, in order that He might reveal in thee the treasures of that holiness which consisteth in the devoted and holy fulfillment of the common duties of life, I earnestly beseech thee to make me ever constant and faithful in observing the duties of my state of life, pure in heart, fearless and strong against the enemies of my eternal salvation, and cheerfully obedient to the promptings of God's holy will. By thy singular devotion to the loving Mother of Jesus Christ, who looked upon thee also as her son, obtain for me the grace of a fervent love for Jesus and Mary, together with the power of drawing many others to love them in like manner. Wherefore, dear Saint John, I choose thee as my special patron, humbly beseeching thee to make me zealous in the things that pertain to the praise of God, and to assist me by thy mighty help, to lead a life filled with good works. Finally, when the hour of death cometh, do thou, of thy loving-kindness, cherish in me those motions of humble confidence, which, at the moment of thy departure from this world to thy mansion in the skies, as thou didst lovingly clasp to thy breast the image of Jesus Crucified, together with Mary's rosary and thy book of rules, impelled thee to utter these sweet words: "These three things are my dearest possessions; with these I am content to die."

V. *Pray for us, Saint John,*
R. *That we may be made worthy of the promises of Christ.*

Let us pray.

Grant, we beseech thee, O Lord God, unto thy faithful servants, to copy the pattern of innocence and faithfulness in thy service, wherewith the angelic youth, John, did consecrate to thee the very flower of his years. Through Christ our Lord. Amen.

* * *

Saint John Bosco

O glorious Saint John Bosco, who in order to lead young people to the feet of the divine Master and to form them in the light of faith and Christian morality didst heroically sacrifice thyself to the very end of thy life and didst found a proper religious institute destined to endure and to bring to the farthest boundaries of the earth thy glorious work, obtain also for us from our Lord a holy love for young people who are exposed to so many seductions in order that we may generously spend ourselves in supporting them against the snares of the devil, in keeping them safe from the dangers of the world, and in guiding them, pure and holy, in the path that leads to God.

* * *

Saint John of the Cross

O glorious Saint John of the Cross, great Doctor of the Church, who, from very longing to be configured to Jesus crucified, didst desire nothing more ardently, even to the last moment of thy holy life, than to suffer and to be despised and rejected of all men; and so great was thy thirst for suffering, that thy generous heart was filled with joy in the midst of most painful torments and afflictions. I beseech thee, dear saint, by the glory thou didst merit by thy manifold sufferings, intercede for me with Almighty God and obtain for me love of suffering, together with grace and strength to endure all tribulations and adversities with dauntless courage; for these are the sure means of coming into the possession of that crown of glory which is prepared for me in heaven. Ah yes, dear saint, from that high and glorious throne where thou sittest triumphant, hear, I beseech thee, my earnest entreaties, that, following thee, I may become a lover of the Cross and of suffering and thus may merit to be thy companion in glory. Amen.

* * *

Saint John of Matha

Glorious Saint John of Matha, thou wast inflamed with an ardent love of God and a tender compassion toward thy neighbor, and therefore wast chosen by God Himself to found the famous Order of the Most Holy Trinity, wherein thou didst spend thy days in glorifying this venerable mystery and in rescuing unhappy Christians from bondage; do thou obtain for us the grace to pass our days in like manner, glorifying the Most Holy Trinity and doing good to our neighbor with the deeds of Christian charity, that so we may hereafter obtain the happy lot of rejoicing in heaven in the beatific vision of the Father, and of the Son, and of the Holy Ghost. Amen.

* * *

Saint John Vianney

Dear Saint John Vianney, your childhood dream was to be a priest, to win souls for God. You endured years of toil and humiliation to attain the priesthood. You became a priest truly after God's own heart, outstanding in humility and poverty, prayer and mortification, totally devoted to the service of God's people. The Church has exalted you as model and patron saint of all parish priests, trusting that your example and prayers will help them to live up to the high dignity of their vocation to be faithful servants of God's people, to be perfect imitators of Christ the Savior Who came not to be served but to serve, to give His Life in ransom for many.

Pray that God may give to His Church today many more priests after His own heart. Pray for all the priests under your patronage, that they may be worthy representatives of Christ the Good Shepherd. May they wholeheartedly devote themselves to prayer and penance; be examples of humility and poverty; shining models of holiness; tireless and powerful preachers of the Word of God; zealous dispensers of God's Grace in the sacraments. May their loving devotion to Jesus in the Eucharist and to Mary His Mother be the Twin Fountains of fruitfulness for their ministry. Amen.

* * *

Saint Jude

Glorious Saint Jude Thaddeus, by those sublime privileges with which you were adorned in your lifetime, namely, your relationship with our Lord Jesus Christ according to the flesh, and your vocation to be an apostle, and by that glory which now is yours in heaven as the reward of your apostolic labors and your martyrdom, obtain for me from the Giver of every good and perfect gift all the graces of which I stand in need: (Mention your request).

Saint Jude, apostle of Christ and glorious martyr, I desire to honor you with a special devotion. I choose you as my patron and protector. To you I entrust my soul and my body, all my spiritual and temporal interests, as well as those of my family. To you I consecrate my mind, so that in all things it may be enlightened in faith; my heart, so that you may keep it pure and fill it with love for Jesus and Mary; my will, so that, like yours, it may always be one with the will of God.

I beg you to help me to master my evil inclinations and temptations and to avoid all occasions of sin. Obtain for me the grace of never offending God, of fulfilling faithfully all the duties of my state of life, and of practicing all those virtues that are needful for my salvation.

Pray for me, my holy patron and helper, so that, being inspired by your example and assisted by your prayers, I may live a holy life, die a happy death, and attain to the glory of heaven, there to love and thank God forever. Amen.

O God, you made your name known to us through the apostles. By the intercession of Saint Jude, let your Church continue to grow with an increased number of believers. Grant this through Christ our Lord. Amen.

* * *

Saint Juliana Falconieri

O faithful bride of Jesus and humble servant of Mary, Saint Juliana, thou who by practicing the most heroic virtues, especially the virtue of penance and the love of Jesus in His sacrament didst arrive at the highest peak of Christian perfection and didst merit to be fed miraculously with the bread of angels in thy last agony; obtain for me the grace to live a holy life in the exercise of every Christian duty and to be able to receive at the moment of death the comfort of the holy sacraments in order to come with thee to the blessed happiness of heaven. Amen.

* * *

Saint Lawrence

O glorious Saint Lawrence, martyr and deacon, who, being subjected to the most bitter torments, didst not lose thy faith nor thy constancy in confessing Jesus Christ, obtain in like manner for us such an active and solid faith, that we shall never be ashamed to be true followers of Jesus Christ, and fervent Christians in word and in deed.

Our Father, Hail Mary, Glory Be...

V. *Pray for us, O holy Lawrence,*
R. *That we may be made worthy of the promises of Christ.*

Let us pray.

Grant, we beseech thee, Almighty God, the grace to quench the flames of our vices, thou who didst enable blessed Lawrence to overcome his fiery torments. Through Christ our Lord. Amen.

* * *

Saint Louis

To thee do we have recourse in prayer, Saint Louis, lily of virginity, bright and shining star, and vessel of holiness. Through thine intercession pour forth the blessings of heaven upon the Catholic nations to which thou art allied, and over which thou hast been set by God as their protector. Do thou entreat Almighty God and the Immaculate Virgin, that the Christian peoples may once again be quickened by the faith of their fathers, that charity may burn fervently amongst them, and that their way of life may be made conformable to the law of God. Obtain true peace and concord for both rulers and people, the victory of our Holy Mother the Church over her enemies, perfect freedom for the Vicar of Christ in his sacred government of souls, and eternal happiness in heaven for all of us who implore thy mighty assistance. Amen.

* * *

Saint Lucy

I. By that admirable faith, which thou hadst, O glorious Saint Lucy, when thou didst declare to the tyrant that no one would have been able to take from thee the Holy Spirit, who dwelt in thy heart as in His temple, obtain for me from Our Lord that I may be so blessed as to live always in a holy and salutary fear of losing His grace, and to flee from everything that might be the occasion of my suffering so grievous a loss.

Our Father, Hail Mary, Glory Be...

II. By that singular predilection, O glorious Saint Lucy, which thy immaculate spouse, Jesus Christ, had for thee, when by an unheard of miracle He rendered thee immovable in spite of all the attempts of thy enemies to drag thee into a place of sin and infamy, obtain for me the grace never to yield to the temptations of the world, the flesh, and the devil, and to fight constantly against their assaults by the continual mortification of all my sense.

Our Father, Hail Mary, Glory Be...

III. By that glowing love which thou hadst of Jesus, O glorious Saint Lucy, when, after being consecrated to Him by an irrevocable vow, thou didst refuse the most eligible suitors and, after distributing all thy goods to feed the poor, thou didst also sacrifice thy life by the sword that passed through thy neck, obtain for me the grace to burn constantly with a holy love, by means of which I may be ready to renounce all earthly goods and to endure all evils rather than to become, even in the slightest degree, unfaithful to Jesus.

Our Father, Hail Mary, Glory Be...

V. *Pray for us, O blessed Lucy,*
R. *That we may be made worthy of the promises of Christ.*

Let us pray.

Mercifully hear us, O God of our salvation, that even as we rejoice in the constant faith of blessed Lucy, thy virgin and martyr, so we may be instructed in sentiments of loving devotion. Through Christ our Lord. Amen.

⁕

Dear Saint Lucy, whose name doth signify the light, we come to thee filled with confidence: do thou obtain for us a holy light that shall make us careful not to walk in the ways of sin, nor to remain enshrouded in the darkness of error. We ask also, through thy intercession, for the preservation of the light of our bodily eyes and for abundant grace to use the same, according to the good pleasure of God without any hurt to our souls. Grant, O Lucy, that, after venerating thee and giving thee thanks for thy powerful protection here on earth, we may come at length to share thy joy in paradise in the everlasting light of the Lamb of God thy beloved Bridegroom, even Jesus. Amen.

* * *

Saint Margaret Mary Alacoque

Saint Margaret Mary, thou who wast made a partaker of the divine treasures of the Sacred Heart of Jesus, obtain for us, we beseech thee, from this adorable Heart, the graces we need so sorely. We ask these favors of thee with unbounded confidence. May the divine Heart of Jesus be pleased to bestow them upon us through thy intercession, so that once again He may be loved and glorified through thee. Amen.

V. *Pray for us, O blessed Margaret.*
R. *That we may be made worthy of the promises of Christ.*

Let us pray.

O Lord Jesus Christ, who didst wondrously open the unsearchable riches of thy Heart to blessed Margaret Mary, the virgin: grant unto us, by her merits and our imitation of her, that we may love thee in all things and above all things, and may be worthy to have our everlasting dwelling in the same thy Sacred Heart: Who livest and reignest world without end. Amen.

* * *

Saint Michael the Archangel

O glorious Saint Michael, seraph inflamed with the most ardent love of Jesus in the Blessed Sacrament, who didst spend thy nights and days in His real presence and didst find there thy dearest joys, so that thou didst swoon away for very love: vouchsafe, I pray thee, to obtain for me a lively faith, a firm hope, and an ardent love toward this inestimable treasure, this precious pledge of glory everlasting; in order that I may be able to be a fervent worshiper of Jesus in the Blessed Sacrament, and thereby rejoice with thee to behold Him face to face in an eternity of bliss. Amen.

Our Father, Hail Mary, Glory Be...

* * *

Saint Nicholas

Glorious Saint Nicholas, my special patron, from thy throne in glory where thou dost enjoy the presence of God, turn thine eyes in pity upon me and obtain for me from our Lord the graces and helps that I need in my spiritual and temporal necessities (and especially this favor...provided that it be profitable to my salvation). Be mindful, likewise, O glorious and saintly bishop, of our sovereign pontiff, of the Holy Church, and of all Christian people. Bring back to the right way of salvation all those who are living steeped in sin and blinded by the darkness of ignorance, error, and heresy. Comfort the afflicted, provide for the needy, strengthen the fearful, defend the oppressed, give health to the infirm; cause all men to experience the effects of thy powerful intercession with the supreme Giver of every good and perfect gift. Amen.

Our Father, Hail Mary, Glory Be...

V. *Pray for us, O blessed Nicholas,*
R. *That we may be made worthy of the promises of Christ.*

Let us pray.

O God, who hast glorified blessed Nicholas, thine illustrious confessor and bishop, by means of countless signs and wonders, and who dost not cease daily so to glorify him; grant, we beseech thee, that we, being assisted by his merits and prayers, may be delivered from the fires of hell and from all dangers. Through Christ our Lord. Amen.

* * *

Saint Paschal Baylon

O God, who hast glorified blessed Paschal thy confessor by a wonderful love for the sacred mysteries of thy Body and Blood: mercifully grant that we also, like him, may deserve to taste the spiritual sweetness of this divine Supper: Who livest and reignest world without end. Amen.

* * *

Saint Paul of the Cross

O glorious Saint Paul of the Cross, on earth thou was a mirror of innocence and a model of penance! O hero of saintliness, chosen by God to meditate day and night on the bitter Passion of His only begotten Son, and to spread devotion thereto by word and deed as well as by means of thy religious family! O apostle, mighty in word and work, thou didst spend thy life in bringing back to the foot of the Cross the erring souls of countless unfortunate sinners! Do thou mercifully look down once more from heaven upon my poor soul and hear my petitions. Obtain for me so great a love of Jesus' suffering, that by constant meditation on His Passion I may make His sufferings mine. Let me realize in the deep wounds of my Savior the wickedness of my transgressions, and obtain from them, as from the fountain of salvation, the grace of bitter tears and an effectual resolution to imitate thee in thy penance, if I have not followed thine example of innocence. Obtain for me, also, Saint Paul, the favor that I now especially ask of thee, as I humbly kneel before thee: (mention your request). Obtain, moreover, for our Holy Mother the Church, victory over Her foes; for sinners, the gift of conversion; for heretics, the grace of returning to the unity of the Catholic faith. Finally, intercede for me that I may, by the grace of God, die a holy death, and come at last to enjoy with thee His blessed presence in heaven for all eternity. Amen.

Our Father, Hail Mary, Glory Be...

❋

O glorious Saint Paul of the Cross, who, by meditating on the Passion of Jesus Christ, didst attain to so high a degree of holiness on earth and of happiness in heaven, and, by preaching the same Passion, didst offer anew to the world the most certain cure of all its ills, obtain for us the grace to keep it ever deeply engraved in our hearts, that so we may be able to reap the same fruits both in time and in eternity. Amen.

Our Father, Hail Mary, Glory Be...

* * *

Saint Peregrine

O glorious wonder-worker, Saint Peregrine, thou who didst answer the divine call with a ready spirit, forsaking all the comforts of a life of ease and all the empty honors of the world, to dedicate thyself to God in the order of His most holy Mother; thou who didst labor manfully for the salvation of souls, meriting the title of "Apostle of Emilia"; thou who, in union with Jesus crucified, didst endure the most painful sufferings with such patience as to deserve to be healed miraculously by Him with a touch of His divine hand from an incurable wound in thy leg: obtain for us, we pray, the grace to answer every call from God; enkindle in our hearts a consuming zeal for the salvation of souls; deliver us from the infirmities that so often afflict our wretched bodies; and obtain for us the grace of perfect resignation to the sufferings which it shall please Him to send us; so may we, imitating thy virtues and tenderly loving our crucified Lord and His sorrowful Mother, be enabled to merit glory everlasting in paradise. Amen.

Our Father, Hail Mary, Glory Be...

* * *

Saints Peter and Paul

Defend, O Lord, thy people: and as they put their trust in the patronage of thy holy apostles, Peter and Paul, keep them ever by thy protection. Through Christ our Lord. Amen.

✳

O holy apostles, Peter and Paul, I choose you this day and for ever to be my special patrons and advocates; thee, Saint Peter, prince of the apostles, because thou art the rock, upon which Almighty God hath built His Church; thee, Saint Paul, because thou wast forechosen by God as the vessel of election and the preacher of truth in the whole world. Obtain for me, I pray you, lively faith, firm hope, and burning love; complete detachment from myself, contempt of the world, patience in adversity, humility in prosperity, attention in prayer, purity of heart, a right intention in all my works, diligence in fulfilling the duties of my state of life, constancy in my resolutions, resignation to the will of God even unto death; that so, by means of your intercession and your glorious merits, I may be able to overcome the temptations of the world, the flesh and the devil, and may be made worthy to appear before the chief and eternal Shepherd of souls, Jesus Christ, who with the Father and the Holy Ghost liveth and reigneth for endless ages, to enjoy His presence and love Him forever. Amen.

Our Father, Hail Mary, Glory Be...

V. *Thou shalt make them princes over all the earth,*
R. *They shall be mindful of thy name, O Lord.*

Let us pray.

O God, whose right hand raised up blessed Peter, when he walked upon the water and began to sink, and thrice delivered his fellow apostle Paul from the depths of the sea, when he suffered shipwreck: graciously hear us and grant, by the merits of them both, that we also may attain unto everlasting glory: Who livest and reignest world without end. Amen.

⁂

Thou art the shepherd of the sheep, the prince of the apostles, unto thee were given the keys of the kingdom of heaven.

V. *Thou art Peter;*
R. *And upon this rock I will build my Church.*

Let us pray.

Raise us up, we beseech thee, O Lord, by the apostolic assistance of blessed Peter, thine apostle: so that the weaker we are, the more mightily we may be helped by the power of his intercession: and that being perpetually defended by the same holy apostle, we may neither yield to any iniquity, nor be overcome by any adversity. Through Christ our Lord. Amen.

⁂

O glorious Saint Peter, who, in return for thy lively and generous faith, thy profound and sincere humility, and thy burning love, wast honored by Jesus Christ with singular privileges, and, in particular, with the leadership of the other apostles and the primacy of the whole Church, of which thou wast made the foundation stone, do thou obtain for us the grace of a lively faith, that shall not fear to profess itself openly, in its entirety and in all of its manifestations, even to the shedding of blood, if occasion should demand it, and to the sacrifice of life itself in preference to surrender. Obtain for us likewise, a sincere loyalty to our holy mother, the Church; grant that we may ever remain most closely and sincerely united to the Roman Pontiff, who is the heir of thy faith and of thy authority, the one, true, visible head of the Catholic Church, that mystic ark of our salvation. Grant, moreover, that we may follow, in all humility and meekness, her teaching and her counsels, and may be obedient to all her precepts, in order to be able here on earth to enjoy peace that is sure and undisturbed, and to attain one day in heaven to everlasting happiness. Amen.

V. *Pray for us, Saint Peter the apostle,*
R. *That we may be made worthy of the promises of Christ.*

Let us pray.

O God, who hast given unto thy blessed apostle Peter the keys of the kingdom of heaven, and the power to bind and loose: grant that we may be delivered, through the help of his intercession, from the bonds of all our sins: Who livest and reignest world without end. Amen.

⁜

Thou art the vessel of election, Saint Paul the apostle, the preacher of truth in the whole world.

V. *Pray for us, Saint Paul the apostle,*
R. *That we may be made worthy of the promises of Christ.*

Let us pray.

Almighty and everlasting God who, of thy divine mercy, didst instruct thy blessed apostle Paul what he should do that he might be filled with the Holy Ghost; by his admonitions directing us and his merits interceding for us, grant that we may serve thee in fear and trembling and so be filled with the comfort of thy heavenly gifts. Through Christ our Lord. Amen.

O glorious Saint Paul, who, from being a persecutor of the Christian name, didst become its most zealous apostle, and who, to carry the knowledge of Jesus, our divine Savior, to the ends of the earth, didst joyfully suffer prison, scourgings, stonings, shipwreck, and all manner of persecutions, and who didst finish thy course by shedding the last drop of thy blood: obtain for us the grace to accept, as favors bestowed by the mercy of God the infirmities, sufferings, and misfortunes of this life, that we may not grow slack in our service of God by reason of these vicissitudes of our exile, but that we may the rather show ourselves ever more devoted. Amen.

V. *Pray for us, Saint Paul the apostle,*
R. *That we may be made worthy of the promises of Christ.*

Let us pray.

O God, who hast taught the multitude of the Gentiles by the preaching of blessed Paul the apostle: grant unto us, we beseech thee, that we who keep his memory sacred, may feel the might of his intercession before thee. Through Christ our Lord. Amen.

* * *

Saint Philip Neri

Lowly Saint Philip, make intercession to the immaculate Virgin Mother of God for me.

SUNDAY
O my glorious patron Saint Philip, thou who wast so humble as to consider thyself a useless servant and unworthy of human praise but deserving the contempt of all, to such a degree as to renounce by every means the honors offered thee on numerous occasions by the supreme pontiffs themselves, thou seest what an exaggerated esteem I have for myself, how readily I judge and think ill of others, how ambitious I am even in well-doing, and how much I allow myself to be disturbed and influenced by the good or bad opinion which others entertain of me. Dear saint, obtain for me a truly humble heart, so that I may rejoice at being despised, may feel no resentment at being overlooked, nor be unduly elated by praise, but rather let me seek to be great in the eyes of God alone.

Our Father, Hail Mary, Glory Be...

MONDAY
My holy advocate Saint Philip, thou whose heart was so serene in the midst of adversity, whose spirit was so devoted to suffering, thou who when thou wast persecuted by the envious, or calumniated by the wicked who sought to discredit thee, or sorely tried by our Lord with many persistent and

painful maladies, didst endure it all with an admirable tranquility of heart and mind; obtain for me also the spirit of fortitude in all the tribulations of this life. Thou seest how perturbed and indignant I become at every light affliction, how angry and resentful at every insignificant contradiction, and how unable I am to remember that the cross is the only way to paradise. Obtain for me perfect patience and readiness like thine in carrying the crosses which our Lord daily gives me to carry, so that I may be made worthy to rejoice with thee in our eternal reward in heaven.

Our Father, Hail Mary, Glory Be...

TUESDAY
O glorious Saint Philip, thou who didst ever preserve intact the lily of chastity to such a degree that the splendor of this fair virtue shone forth in thy eyes, and so transformed thy whole body that it gave forth a delightful fragrance that consoled and inspired to devotion everyone who came into thy presence, obtain for me from the Holy Spirit that grace which thou didst obtain for so many of thy spiritual children, the grace of defending, preserving, and increasing within me that virtue which is so great, so fair, so necessary.

Our Father, Hail Mary, Glory Be...

WEDNESDAY
Saint Philip, I am filled with admiration at the great miracle wrought in thee by the Holy Spirit, when He poured forth His charity so abundantly into thy heart that it was dilated, even physically, to such an extent that two of thy ribs were broken. I marvel, too, at the pure and glowing love of God, which fired thy soul to such warmth that thy countenance was illumined with heavenly light and thou wast caught up into an ecstasy so as to be desirous of shedding thy blood to make Him known and loved by the heathen nations. What shame I feel when I observe the coldness of my heart towards God, whom nevertheless I know to be the supreme and infinite Good. I love the world, which attracts me but cannot make me happy; I love the flesh, which tempts me but cannot satisfy my heart; I love riches, which I cannot enjoy, save for a few, fleeting moments. When shall I learn from thee to love nothing else except God, the only and incomprehensible Good? Make me, O holy patron, through thy intercession, begin to love God from this day forth at least, with all my mind, with all my strength, even until that happy hour when I shall love Him in a blessed eternity.

Our Father, Hail Mary, Glory Be...

THURSDAY
O glorious saint, who didst employ thyself wholly in favor of thy neighbor, esteeming, sympathizing with, and assisting everyone; who in the whole of thy lifetime didst make everyone's salvation thy special care, never refusing the labor involved nor reserving for thyself either time or convenience, in order to win all to God, obtain for me, I pray thee, a like charity towards my neighbor, even such as thou didst entertain for thy many devoted clients, in order that I too may love everyone with a charity that is pure and disinterested, giving a helping hand to everyone, sympathizing with everyone, and treating everyone, even my enemies, with that sweetness of manner, and that eager desire for their good, with which thou wast able to overcome and convert thy very persecutors.

Our Father, Hail Mary, Glory Be...

FRIDAY
Great saint, thou who didst prefer a life of poverty and obscurity to one of ease and comfort which was thine by inheritance, obtain for me the grace of never attaching my heart to the fleeting goods of this life. Do thou, who didst desire to become so poor as to be reduced to beggary and not to find anyone willing to give thee even the barest means of livelihood, obtain for me also a love of poverty, so that I may turn all my thoughts to the things that are eternal. Thou who didst wish to live in a lowly station rather than to be advanced to the highest dignities of the Church, intercede for me that I may never seek after honors, but may be content with that station in life in which it has pleased Our Lord to place me. My heart is too much preoccupied with the vain and passing things of earth; but do thou, who didst ever inculcate this great maxim: "And then?," which brought about so many wonderful conversions, obtain for me that this saying may ever remain so firmly fixed in my mind that I may despise the nothingness of this world, and may make God the only object of my affections and my thoughts.

Our Father, Hail Mary, Glory Be...

SATURDAY
O my holy patron, Philip, thou who didst always persevere in well-doing, who didst preach the need of perseverance, and didst admonish us to pray for perseverance continually from Almighty God through the intercession of the Blessed Virgin; thou who didst desire that thy spiritual children should not overload themselves with devotional practices, but rather that they should persevere in those which they had already undertaken, thou seest

how easily I grow weary of the good works I have begun and forget my good resolutions so often repeated. I have recourse to thee, in order that thou mayest obtain for me the great grace of never forsaking my God again, of never again losing His grace, of being faithful to my religious exercises, and of dying in the embrace of my Lord, fortified with the holy sacraments and rich in merits for eternal life.

Our Father, Hail Mary, Glory Be...

* * *

Saint Rita

O God, who didst vouchsafe to communicate so great a grace to Saint Rita that she imitated thine example in the love of enemies and bore in her heart and on her countenance the sacred marks of thy love and passion: grant, we beseech thee, by her merits and intercession, that we may love our enemies and ever contemplate with deep contrition the sorrows of thy Passion: who livest and reignest world without end. Amen.

O glorious Saint Rita, thou who didst share in a marvelous manner the sorrowful Passion of our Lord Jesus Christ, obtain for me the grace to suffer in patience the miseries of this life, and by my refuge in all my necessities.

* * *

Saint Stephen

Almighty and everlasting God, who didst consecrate the first-fruits of thy martyrs in the blood of blessed Stephen the deacon; grant, we beseech thee, that he may pray for us, even as he also prayed for his persecutors, to our Lord Jesus Christ thy Son, who liveth and reigneth, world without end. Amen.

* * *

Saint Tarcisius

O unvanquished martyr of the faith, Saint Tarcisius, who wast inflamed with the most intense affection for the Holy Eucharist and didst enjoy the happiness of dying united to Jesus in the Eucharistic species, we beseech thee to obtain for us from our Lord that our hearts also may be filled with a like love in receiving Him frequently into our breast and above all in the final moments of our lives, and so united with Him we may enter into a blessed eternity. Amen.

V. *Pray for us, O blessed Tarcisius,*
R. *That we may be made worthy of the promises of Christ.*

Let us pray.

Grant, we beseech thee, Almighty God, that even as we praise thy mighty works in the passion of Saint Tarcisius, so we may obtain thy forgiveness through his loving entreaties. Through Christ our Lord. Amen.

* * *

Saint Teresa of Avila

O Saint Teresa, seraphic virgin, beloved spouse of thy crucified Lord, thou who on earth didst burn with a love so intense toward thy God and my God, and now dost glow with a brighter and purer flame in paradise: obtain for me also, I beseech thee, a spark of that same holy fire which shall cause me to forget the world, all things created, and even myself; for thou didst ever greatly desire to see Him loved by all men. Grant that my every thought and desire and affection may be continually employed in doing the will of God, the supreme Good, whether I am in joy or in pain, for He is worthy to be loved and obeyed everlastingly. Obtain for me this grace, thou who art so powerful with God; may I be all on fire, like thee, with the holy love of God. Amen.

* * *

Saint Therese of the Child Jesus

O Saint Therese of the Child Jesus, Patroness of the Missions, pray for us.

O marvelous Saint Therese of the Child Jesus, who, in thy brief mortal career, didst become a mirror of angelic purity, of daring love, and of whole-hearted surrender to Almighty God, now that thou art enjoying the recompense of thy virtues, turn thine eyes of mercy upon us who trust in thee. Obtain for us the grace to keep our hearts and minds pure and clean like unto thine, and to abhor in all sincerity whatever might tarnish ever so slightly the luster of a virtue so sublime, a virtue that endears us to thy heavenly Bridegroom. Ah, dear saint, grant us to feel in every need the power of thy intercession; give us comfort in all the bitterness of this life and especially at its latter end, that we may be worthy to share eternal happiness with thee in paradise. Amen.

V. *Pray for us, O blessed Therese,*
R. *That we may be made worthy of the promises of Christ.*

Let us pray.

O Lord, who hast said: "Unless you become as little children, you shall not enter into the kingdom of heaven"; grant us, we beseech thee, so to walk in the footsteps of thy blessed Virgin Therese with a humble and single heart, that we may attain to everlasting rewards: who livest and reignest world without end. Amen.

O God, who didst inflame with thy spirit of love the soul of Saint Therese of the Child Jesus, grant that we too may love thee and make thee loved exceedingly. Amen.

* * *

Saint Thomas Aquinas

Angelic Doctor, Saint Thomas, prince of theologians and model of philosophers, bright ornament of the Christian world, light of the Church and patron of all Catholic schools, who didst learn wisdom without guile and dost communicate it without envy, pray for us to the Son of God who is Wisdom itself, that, by the coming of the Spirit of Wisdom upon us, we may clearly understand that which thou didst teach, and, by imitating thee, may bring to completion that which thou didst do; that we may be made partakers both of thy doctrine and thy holiness, whereby thou didst shine on earth even as the sun; and finally that we may enjoy with thee in heaven for evermore the most delectable fruits of the same, praising together with thee divine Wisdom through endless ages. Amen.

* * *

Saint Vincent Ferrer

O glorious apostle and wonder-worker, Saint Vincent Ferrer, our loving patron, receive our humble prayer, and send down upon us a plentiful shower of divine favors. By the fire of love in thy heart, obtain for us from the Father of mercies the pardon and remission of all our sins, steadfastness in faith, and perseverance in good works, that so we may live as good and fervent Christians and become worthy of thy powerful patronage. Extend thy protection to our bodies also, and deliver us from sickness. Keep our fields from hurtful tempests and storms of hail, and banish all misfortunes far from us. Blessed by thy favors both in body and soul, we shall ever be thy devoted clients, and one day we shall come to heaven to join with thee in praising God through all eternity. Amen.

⁜

O Saint Vincent, glorious worker of miracles, who in thy lifetime didst convert many sinners by preaching the last judgment, grant that we too, by meditating on the four last things, may be enabled to obtain from Almighty God through thine intercession the healing of all our spiritual maladies. Let thy heart be tender toward us, O mighty saint: stretch forth thy hand over us, and obtain for us those graces for the welfare of both soul and body, which we so earnestly ask of thee. Amen.

* * *

Saint Vincent de Paul

O glorious Saint Vincent, heavenly patron of all charitable associations and father of all who are in misery, whilst thou wast on earth thou didst never cast out any who came to thee; ah, consider by what evils we are oppressed and come to our assistance! Obtain from thy Lord help for the poor, relief for the infirm, consolation for the afflicted, protection for the abandoned, a spirit of generosity for the rich, the grace of conversion for sinners, zeal for priests, peace for the Church, tranquility and order for all nations, and salvation for them all. Yea, let all men prove the effects of thy merciful intercession so that, being helped by thee in the miseries of this life, we may be united to thee in the life to come, where there shall be no more grief, nor weeping, nor sorry, but joy and gladness and everlasting happiness. Amen.

* * *

Patron Saint

O heavenly patron, in whose name I glory, pray ever to God for me: strengthen me in my faith; establish me in virtue; guard me in the conflict; that I may vanquish the foe and attain to glory everlasting. Amen.

* * *

Seven Holy Founders of the Servite Order

O glorious patriarchs, the seven holy founders of the Order of the Servants of Mary, you who by reason of your sublime holiness were worthy to be called by the Blessed Virgin to found in the Church a new religious order dedicated to fostering and spreading devotion towards her and the honoring of her sorrows; you who were separated from the world in the solitude of Monte Senario and were given to the most severe penances, nourishing your hearts with meditation on the eternal truths and the infinite love of God towards us; you who were constrained by the bonds of charity, and with your mission of peace gave to the world a noble example of brotherly love; obtain for us a tender devotion to Jesus Crucified and to the Queen of Martyrs, an ardent longing for an interior life, for mortification and penance, and for a burning charity towards our neighbor, which may increase our zeal in every good work. Amen.